For Gabriel—

Dior

AND HIS

DECORATORS

In celebration of
the eternal chic of
Dior—
        with best wishes.
                Maureen Footer

Dior

AND HIS

DECORATORS

Victor Grandpierre,

Georges Geffroy,

and the New Look

MAUREEN FOOTER

Foreword by

HAMISH BOWLES

VENDOME

NEW YORK · LONDON

CONTENTS

FOREWORD

By Hamish Bowles

When Christian Dior created his first collection, in the frigid winter of 1946, his vision was escapist. In a Paris assaulted and traumatized by the years of war and the Occupation, Dior imagined a bouquet of flower women, of full *corolle* skirts and melting shoulders, hand-span waists and plumply buttressed bosoms—the silhouettes of his Edwardian infancy, before the vicissitudes of that conflict transformed the world order for the affluent classes.

Dior's vision for décor ran along similar lines, for although he came of age as a purveyor of avant-garde art, by the time he reached his forties, he thought not of a brave postwar modernism, but of Les Rhumbs, his family's pretty pink house nestled in rose gardens on the cliffs of Normandy, symbol of the affluent bourgeois life that the Diors had led before the crash of 1929.

To realize a vision in décor that would match his concept of fashion, Dior turned to the talents of his two friends Victor Grandpierre and Georges Geffroy. As an unusually fashion-obsessed little boy, I found a copy of *Dior by Dior*, the designer's elegantly written autobiography, in a jumble sale and devoured its riveting contents. I therefore knew of Dior's diplomacy in distributing the decorating of his opulent townhouse in Passy between Grandpierre and Geffroy, two men as steeped in fashion as their friend and client. Grandpierre had been a fashion photographer, and Geffroy a designer for Jean Patou, a forward-thinking rival to Gabrielle Chanel in the 1920s.

In a world that was looking to reinvent a postwar aesthetic in architectural, furniture, automotive, and fashion design through innovation that focused on practicality, speed, and labor-free invention, this triumvirate created a parallel modernism. Their brave new world of fashion and interior design was steeped in the past—the world of Sem and the Comtesse Greffulhe (who came to witness Dior's debut collection looking as though she had stepped from a Lartigue photograph in a Merry Widow picture hat and lavish fur stole).

Just as Dior's ateliers found themselves reviving Victorian dressmaking techniques to bring his elaborately constructed clothes to life, the interior design artisans drew on techniques honed over generations to provide their perfect setting. Chez Dior, the well-heeled denizens of café society, the stars of screen, stage, and the cultural firmament who came in droves to admire the couturier's creations were enveloped in melting dove gray and perched on the sort of Louis Quinze revival sofas and Louis Seize oval-backed chaises on which the sitters of Boldini and Helleu had posed half a century earlier.

When Dior's young protégé Yves Saint Laurent inaugurated his eponymous haute couture house in 1962, the dauphin created a tabula rasa—a spare white décor that suggested the promise of the Youthquake era and provided a neutral foil to the mannish pantsuits and hippie de luxe evening extravaganzas that redefined the way women wanted to look.

By the time I made my own debut in the perfumed world of haute couture in the early 1980s, however, Saint Laurent's mood was elegiac rather than revolutionary. He had moved his haute couture establishment to a grandiose Haussmannian townhouse on avenue Marceau, where, nostalgic for the spirit of his master Christian Dior, he had summoned that designer's accomplice in décor, Victor Grandpierre, to create an environment that evoked both Dior's couture salons and private residence.

Underfoot, carpet swirled in whorls of moss and bottle green like the shimmering pools of a bolt of watered silk; the high-back sofas were tufted in crimson damask and shaded by potted palms. The *cabine* mannequins, dressed in stockings and heels and their uniform starched white wrappers as they waited to be fitted by the master, looked like Toulouse-Lautrec houris in a *maison de passe*—although admittedly an establishment with royal and imperial patrons.

It was the perfect backdrop to the Saint Laurent clothes of the era—clothes of impeccable construction executed in a breathtaking gamut of colors. It was haute couture for the home and it seemed to me then and now to represent the giddiest height of high style. At home on the rue Babylone, meanwhile, Saint Laurent and Pierre Bergé worked with Jacques Grange—inheritor of the spirit of Geffroy and Grandpierre—to create a wonderland of eclectically arranged treasures. The dining room, however, like the avenue Marceau salons, was a direct quote from Dior, Grandpierre, and Geffroy. The rock crystal droplets that hung from the chandelier, the eighteenth-century tapestries on the pale walls, and the fall of emerald damask at the windows evoked the defiantly mid-century look of Dior and his co-conspirators in design, nostalgia on nostalgia, a look that swept the world, then and now.

PREFACE

Parisian elegance first drew me to Christian Dior's decorators, Georges Geffroy and Victor Grandpierre. They were highly elusive—no books on either existed, and all that remained of their design of Dior's townhouse were a few photographs from *Vogue*. A little research, however, showed that their connections with Dior went beyond mere decorating, or even friendship. Geffroy had engineered Dior's entrée into the world of haute couture, while Grandpierre devised the palette and vocabulary that signifies, to this day, the Christian Dior brand. Glamour added yet another layer to their mystique: countesses, couturiers, divas, and doyennes, style setters Daisy Fellowes and Gloria Guinness, and those ultimate sophisticates, Yves Saint Laurent and Pierre Bergé, flocked to Geffroy or Grandpierre (they worked separately) for designs that captured the moment and, often, predicted the future. Naturally, too, Dior, Geffroy, and Grandpierre ended up in Venice at Charles de Beistegui's legendary ball.

Most striking about Dior, Geffroy, and Grandpierre was that their artistry intermingled. Not only did their lives and careers overlap, but their haute couture creations and high-style interiors spoke, through different media, the same language. The writings of Christian Dior—who sketched his world as deftly as its fashions—illuminate the postwar mood and explain how the New Look, like *le Jazz Cool*, captivated postwar sensibility. Together, the formation, lives, and work of these three men express both an era and the mysterious bond of fashion and design.

Today, whenever tastemakers reach for gray and white, leopard and houndstooth, satin skirts and sunburst mirrors, they pay homage to the New Look chic of Dior, Geffroy, and Grandpierre. These men knew how to draw upon heritage—modified, preserved, but never embalmed—to enhance the everyday. Silhouettes, techniques, ideas, and palettes of the past inspire relevant, new visions. Craftsmanship honed over centuries invests daily life with tactile pleasures. Knowledge makes for abundant, and more apt, choices. Waving their ormolu wands—while refitting "Bar" jackets and re-covering bergères—Dior, Geffroy, and Grandpierre show us how to live more richly in our present.

PROLOGUE

Paris in the Spring, 1947

No one had seen clothes like this before, dresses that captured a civilization in a flounce. Even those legendary paragons of chic, Étienne de Beaumont and the Comtesse Greffulhe, leaned forward in their gilt-wood chairs to take in the wonders of silhouette and technique unfurling before them. One sighed with pleasure at the perfection of it all: poised clothes, a hint of perfume, soigné rooms with no shabby reminders of the recent Occupation. Though peace had been declared two years earlier, France still struggled to find its economic, social, and political footing. In Paris, the mood was depressed. Rationing, strikes, record cold, and spotty electricity still dimmed its brilliance. With one swish of silk skirt, Christian Dior's New Look promised anew romance, civility, and sophistication. Spring had returned to Paris.

The unveiling of the New Look on February 12, 1947, was a *succès fou*. Overnight, the swagged hobble skirt, worn by smart debutantes at Club Forty-Five, became outmoded. In the dressing rooms at Maison Dior, well-bred Parisians morphed into lionesses as they vied to order the new, opulently skirted dresses. A few blocks away, at the Jockey Club, where fashion chat once centered on racing silks, members now spoke of nothing but Dior. And in an era increasingly interconnected by new modes of travel and media, what began as a Paris fashion became a worldwide vogue. Soon, in New York, Tokyo, and Caracas, the name Dior had as much recognition as that of de Gaulle.

Dior waved off his triumph, demurring that he simply reflected the era. Certainly, the trajectory of his life—a gilded youth spent at the avant-garde cabaret Le Boeuf sur le toit, a father ruined by the Crash, a promising art gallery that failed, a career interrupted by war—followed the arc of the time. As the century lurched on its erratic course, the memory of the Belle Époque, with its confidence and elegance, acquired mythical status for Dior. Indeed, for him and many others, it became a collective anchor. A wistful mirage of *dîners en ville*, musicales, and race enclosures at Longchamp prompted Dior's creation of feminine clothes that women craved at the very moment they were resigned to the utilitarian skirts and boxy jackets that war shortages had made

PRECEDING PAGES

Resonating with its time, Christian Dior's "Bar" suit summarized romance and tradition. Fashion to Dior was not merely "a sort of Vanity Fair" but the outward sign of an ancient and great civilization that must survive.

LEFT

The Crillon boudoir at the Metropolitan Museum reveals the aesthetic and techniques of Louis XVI style. Like Dior, Victor Grandpierre and Georges Geffroy translated— for a modern era—traditions developed at Versailles and perfected over generations.

necessary. His flirty dresses revived the neglected art of pleasing. And though Dior's interpretation was unique, the appeal of the past was pervasive. In the very month that Dior's Merry Widow silhouette first dazzled, a posh nightclub, À la belle époque, opened to the sound of champagne corks in the same arrondissement.

Romantic, exquisitely crafted, and idyllic, the New Look was, however, more than a nostalgic silhouette: it was a reaction. In much the same way that the Renaissance reached back past the Dark Ages to the grandeurs of classical civilization for renewal, French artists now referred to light-filled chapters of their own history—particularly the Enlightenment and its derivative, the Belle Époque, for inspiration. Prompted by patrimony, Dior's sweeping vision contained not only flower-like dresses but old-fashioned good manners, workmanship, refined tables, and—notably for this story—houses.

On the same wave of tradition, technique, and fantasy arrived a new current in interior design. Two decorators associated with Dior, Victor Grandpierre and Georges Geffroy, also drew inspiration from the Enlightenment and Belle Époque, as well as another grand chapter in French history, the Empire, to create worldly interiors of trompe l'oeil, tiger velvet, and saturated color. Like the New Look dresses, the breadth of references, craftsmanship, and offhand grandeur of their rooms were real-time summations of the era by modern sophisticates conversant with tradition. And as these French interiors filled with fauteuils, ormolu, and Christian Bérard drawings epitomized chic—every bit as much as the duchesse-satin perfection of a Dior gown—to an emerging international elite, their rooms and their renown crested into a global phenomenon. Villas in Palm Beach and houses in Buenos Aires acquired parquet de Versailles floors, boiserie, a smattering of smart modern lacquer, deep sofas, and signed Louis XVI chairs.

Even newlyweds on Third Avenue emulated the new glamour with applied moldings, animal-print accents, and gilt-wood mirrors.

Just as houses reflect both their owners and the moment, Dior's own interiors chart the evolution of his vision. While each reveals a new layer of his aesthetic, two of his interiors mark turning points in twentieth-century design. The launch of the postwar decorating meteor occurred at Maison Christian Dior itself, where restrained eighteenth-century taste met Belle Époque sensuality and cool sophistication. Here, designer Victor Grandpierre, son of a fashionable architect, refreshed the somewhat dusty Louis XVI-and-bamboo aesthetic of the Belle Époque into a couture house as clear, linear, and rational as a theorem by Descartes. Though referencing the architecture, furniture, and very esprit that had made France the undisputed style leader of the world for centuries seemed right again, Grandpierre did not settle for sentimental pastiche. Instead, he infused classical vocabulary into the context of the modernism that had prevailed before the war. In spare gray-and-white salons, classic fauteuils and gilt sconces acquired glamour from the sexy addition of Second Empire ballroom chairs and shirred Austrian shades. Not only did these interiors ignite trends for gray, portières, and streamlined neoclassicism (and determine the decoration of many a couture house), but they so captured the spirit of Dior that they still characterize the interiors of Dior boutiques.

Though the 1947 interiors carried a whiff of historicism, they delivered an avant-garde punch: they shaped a brand long before *brand* became a verb. While creating an environment that encapsulated the polish, luxury, good manners, and joie de vivre that Dior and his designs represented, Grandpierre concurrently established the template for Dior communications. Typeface, logo, signage, packaging (including the design of the bottle and box of Dior's first perfume, Miss Dior), advertising, future boutiques, hotel suites, and even Dior's own house in Paris—all would follow the cues of Grandpierre's stylistic direction.

Just as Dior defined New Look fashion, his Paris residence epitomized New Look decoration. Like Gaul, Dior's townhouse was divided into three parts, the distribution of roles determined by the personalities of three decorators: Georges Geffroy, social butterfly and connoisseur par excellence, decorated the reception rooms; reserved Victor Grandpierre, mastermind of the Maison Christian Dior interiors at 30, avenue Montaigne, designed the private rooms, study, and winter garden; and Pierre Delbée of Jansen was in charge of continuity in upholstery, curtains, and woodwork. The finished project, including a winter garden draped in Chinese silk, a drawing room with velvet walls, a bath with gold swan fittings, all accessorized with Aubussons, Louis XVI bergères, and kentia palms, sparkled with references to the Belle Époque and the eighteenth century. The final touch of *je ne sais quoi*, a handsome Spanish butler, spoke to the era's penchant for luxury and internationalism.

Of course, heritage decoration floated in the postwar *air du temps*. The taste for classicism had been nurtured before the war by architects such as Jean-Charles Moreux and André Arbus. Now, just as Jacques Fath and Pierre Balmain designed extravagant skirts and tiny bodices concurrently with Christian Dior (or, as sticklers may point out, slightly before), other decorators, from the amateur Charles de Beistegui to professionals like Emilio Terry and Fred de Cabrol, also filled houses with sumptuous fabric, brilliant color, and antiques. Georges Geffroy and Victor Grandpierre, however, stand apart.

OPPOSITE

Picking up where the eighteenth-century room left off (see pages 12–13), New Look rooms in Paris became warm and personal. Colors intensified; ceremony yielded to comfort; ritual ceded to amusement. Always, however, design was refined and beautiful.

While their mid-century work introduced ideas of reductive and eclectic comfort that are now obligatory in contemporary design, their professional and personal associations with Christian Dior wove them into the creative heart of postwar Paris. In their aesthetic formation, the sweep of twentieth-century history comes alive.

Christian Dior, Georges Geffroy, and Victor Grandpierre came of age in Paris in the 1920s, steeped in the vibrant world of the arts. Two influences, the stage and fashion, were particularly critical to shaping their aesthetic. Each had collaborated on productions for the theater or ballet, the most dynamic art forms of the time, which mixed musicians (Francis Poulenc, Henri Sauguet), writers (Jean Cocteau, Max Jacob), artists (Pablo Picasso, Christian Bérard, Eugène Berman), and choreographers (George Balanchine, Serge Lifar) in a fantastic cocktail that would in turn produce the theatricality of the clothes and interiors of the New Look. Thanks to the theater, Geffroy and Grandpierre knew just how to transform mere rooms into glamorous stages, and Dior conjured dresses that commanded standing ovations. (In homage to the theater, he named looks of his Spring–Summer 1952 collection after Oscar Wilde, Marcel Aymé, and playwrights-of-the-moment Jean-Pierre Gredy and Pierre Barillet.)

Fashion, the canvas of Christian Dior, had also shaped the eye of Geffroy and Grandpierre. Geffroy, a designer at Patou in the 1930s, and Grandpierre, an erstwhile fashion photographer, worked for the creators of fashion as well as the fashionable. Their background and connections in haute couture exerted a kind of gravitational force on their work, investing it with sensuality, splendor, and innovation, as well as bespoke designs and execution. And just as a good couturier understands that a beautiful gown comes alive only when worn, both designers knew that the success of a room depends on the human activity that unfolds within its walls. In all their passementerie and peau de soie splendor, their rooms neatly avoided the grim fate of static set pieces. Given their clientele of couturiers and fashionables, as well as their approach, their respective bodies of work (they worked independently, and, in fact, cared little for each other), represent the intersection of fashion and interior design.

Mixed into this potent brew of theater, fashion, design, and romance were societal shifts that further impacted French aesthetics. Glamorous internationals flocked to Paris, the indisputable cultural and social capital of the world, after the war. Many of Geffroy and Grandpierre's clients, such as Daisy Fellowes, Gloria Guinness, Arturo and Patricia López-Willshaw—or at least their money—came from places like the Americas, where vast fortunes were insulated from (or possibly enhanced by) the war. Others hailed from Eastern Europe. Some of the newer arrivals needed the accoutrements essential for entrée into the social life of Paris—gowns, jewels, houses, even a little tutoring in French ways—on which Grandpierre and, particularly, Geffroy willingly advised. While both men were investing the richness of their experience and culture into the dazzling drawing rooms of their clients, another key exchange took place: the well-heeled internationals' fast cash, fresh energy, and foreign ideas of comfort and luxury injected postwar decoration with café society dash. French couture and decorating entered its golden age.

Nothing rivaled Paris workmanship. Anyone who could afford it wanted it. At Dior, the standards were so exacting that dresses were largely stitched by hand and, therefore, a single sewing machine sufficed for seventeen seamstresses. Dior's ribbons, flowers, embroidery, buttons, buckles, and lace came from suppliers who had perfected

their craft over generations of court patronage. Victor Grandpierre dressed walls with Corinthian pilasters, pink silk, and gilt baguettes with the ease of knotting his ascot. Georges Geffroy meticulously dismantled Louis XV corner cabinets of Japanese lacquer and foliate ormolu by the eighteenth-century *ébeniste* Bernard van Risenburgh (aka BVRB) to re-create new cabinets in dimensions more appropriate to a project. The results were superbly balanced, exquisite cabinets that were in perfect accord with the overall composition. Conceivably, only in France could craftsmen, still cognizant of eighteenth-century techniques, pull off such a coup.

Beauty, whether expressed as a ball gown or a bergère, raises the sightlines and the soul. This was, of course, the point of such laborious technique. Legacy, however, explains the existence of such standards of perfection. Three hundred years earlier, Louis XIV defused his mutinous nobles and placed them in the gilded cage of Versailles, thereby providing his court with endless idle time to obsess over every nuance of elegance. Further abetted by the Sun King's objective to dazzle the world with manifestations of his power (and by Minister of Finance Colbert's economic policy of fostering luxury trades), art, architecture, decorative arts, couture, and its auxiliary crafts, thrived and were continuously refined as technique was handed down, often within one family, from generation to generation. These trades live-streamed into the

mid-twentieth century in the guise of operations such as the embroidery house Rébé, beadwork atelier Ginesty, silk weaver Prelle, the furniture craftsmen of the faubourg Saint-Antoine, and antiques dealers like Aveline on the rue du Faubourg Saint-Honoré who continued the traditions of the great *marchands-merciers*, the eighteenth-century purveyors of luxury. Patronage now segued from royalty and aristocrats to the new stars of café society, decorators and couturiers.

Whether decorative or fine, art eloquently illuminates a specific moment in time. In that regard, the composed elegance expressed by Dior's iconic "Bar" suit and couture headquarters, Geffroy's silk velvet drawing room for the Vicomtesse de Bonchamps, and Grandpierre's tented smoking room for the Prince and Princesse de Brancovan are extraordinary because they occurred not in a moment of supreme confidence but in one of uncertainty. Although the years after the war are poetically referred to as *Les Trente Glorieuses* (like the phoenix, France reclaimed her industrial base and achieved an enviable standard of living between 1945 and 1975), their underside was riddled with continuously toppling governments, deepening class antagonism, and crippling strikes, boycotts, and riots. For many, the advances of the Marshall Plan, Communism, and mass production—threats to the French way of life—seemed an ominous code for the future. Dior and his decorators, producing hand-sewn dresses and specifying gilt-bronze cornices, custom damask, and yards and yards of leopard silk velvet, were protectors of meticulously bred technique.

Politicians of the Fourth Republic spoke abstractly about reviving the glory of France—couturiers and decorators knew its palpable history still lingered in every fold of silk, white kid glove, and sliver of marquetry. As much as Voltaire, the Napoleonic Code, and Brillat-Savarin's meditations on gastronomy, signed furniture, porcelain, and lavish gowns were tangible links to a grand civilization. The New Look spoke at once of time-honed refinement, a history of influence, and a lingua franca of international diplomacy. Whispering with self-confidence and full of implication, the worldliness of the self-assured day suits and grand-entrance gowns, as well as the glittering salons and velvet-lined libraries, affirmed and revalidated French savoir vivre. Despite the recent seismic shifts in geopolitics and economics, and the breakneck speed of changes in society, Dior, Grandpierre, and Geffroy demonstrated that France's cultural authority remained unassailable.

Relevant style looks forward, even while glancing backward. Embedded in the rooms of Dior, Grandpierre, and Geffroy are keys to how decoration can be streamlined, tailored, and personalized to modern specifications. Looking outward, Geffroy reached for inspiration in stainless steel and far-flung objects. Grandpierre's client-centric designs brought comfort and function to a heretofore unknown level that anticipated two important themes of modern design: curated eclecticism and sprawling comfort. It is fascinating to think what Dior, with his finger on the contemporary pulse of the visual arts and music, might have conceived for future couture collections if he hadn't died at the age of fifty-two in 1957, at the height of the French style wave. Certainly, in his own manner of living, and interiors, he planted new ideas about understatement and familiarity. And of course, in his anointed heir, Yves Saint Laurent, the world acquired street chic. In matters of taste, it was as if the Sun King still reigned. In fact, Christian Dior, Victor Grandpierre, and Georges Geffroy were his emissaries to the future.

OPPOSITE

Whatever the whim, the rage, the dernier cri, French tradition anchored the New Look aesthetic. Fashionably bare and meticulously hand-pleated, Dior's "Mozart" gown of 1950 would be perfectly at ease in the Hall of Mirrors at Versailles.

ABOVE

Left and right: Silk velvet walls and tiger pillows, banquettes and Empire tenting were smartly updated—and emblematic of postwar chic.

OPPOSITE

The Duff Cooper library at the British Embassy in Paris was the first decorating tour de force after the liberation of Paris. Worldliness, charm, architectural elements, and trompe l'oeil countered grim reality with style—and meet acclaim to this day.

22   ■   DIOR AND HIS DECORATORS

PART ONE

Cultivating the Vision

THE ELEMENTS OF STYLE

Christian Dior, 1905~1946

Before he dreamed of dresses, Christian Dior envisioned houses. In another life—the one in which his cautious parents *did* allow him to study architecture at the École des Beaux-Arts—the couturier might have designed buildings that rose ethereally above solid foundations rather than dresses that floated over structured underpinnings. In the end, however, the medium hardly mattered; Christian Dior, the most consistent of men, would have accomplished the same feat and answered the same muse—elegance that revitalized long-standing French tradition. • Houses first exercised their hold on the young Dior in 1906, when his family acquired Les Rhumbs, a twin-gabled Anglo-Norman villa in the seaside town of Granville. With its high ceilings and many rooms, its reassuring rituals and rhythms, the house conveyed the gentility of the Belle Époque. Though in later years the adult couturier would decry its late nineteenth-century architecture. Les Rhumbs, as well as the dreamy childhood it fostered, decisively influenced Dior's aesthetic, inspiring broad-brimmed hats, swaying waistlines, palm-filled interiors, and a reverence for French institutions. Like the spell of Combray on Proust's narrator, Les Rhumbs would define the man Christian Dior would become—and transform how women all over the world would dress.

Sound enterprise fueled the bourgeois comforts at Les Rhumbs. Like the fabulously rich Chilean Arturo López-Willshaw, whose neglected wife would count among Dior's most elegant clients, Louis-Jean Dior, the couturier's great-grandfather, made his (substantially smaller) fortune from transforming guano into fertilizer. "L'engrais Dior, c'est de l'or!" (Dior fertilizer is gold!) punned, oh so presciently, the company's publicity. In an era when landed aristocracy gave way to clever industrialists, many of whom harnessed new technology to commercial interests—other branches of this industrious family successfully produced detergents, bleach, beer, a minister of commerce, and even a trailblazing woman doctor—the story of the Dior family was emblematic, if unusually expansive. This background provided the young Christian with the access, education, and refinement that would infuse his sensibilities.

Dior's penchant for domesticity began in this house. In the linen room, housemaids taught the boy to sing and, fortuitously, the rudiments of sewing. At a young age, he was introduced to *les arts de la table* (a favorite childhood task was setting the table for guest dinners) and the pleasures of gastronomy. He learned of interior design from his mother, Madeleine, who added a fashionable conservatory with a compass-rose tiled floor to the front façade; he was, in fact, so taken with its ambience that a winter garden would later be a criterion for his own house in Paris. In future bedrooms, he would install canopied beds or sleeping alcoves to re-create the security he had known at Les Rhumbs. Helping his mother fuss over the three-acre garden overlooking the Channel, Dior discovered lily of the valley, the talisman flower that, according to legend, was sewn into the hems of his dresses for good luck, learned color theory firsthand, and drew inspiration for dresses that often mimicked the structure of a flower. Anticipating the international celebrity who opted for quiet dinners at home followed by a round of canasta rather than galas, the child Dior so loved the comfort of home that he reluctantly left this refuge to attend children's parties at the casino. (Prophetically, too, once at his destination, he was endlessly amused by anything elaborate, flowery, frivolous, or sparkling.)

In its theatrical proportions and solid connection to its lot, and in the contrast of sober house and exuberant garden, the architecture of Les Rhumbs echoed the combination of dignity and desire that was at the heart of Dior's appeal. The civilized patterns of life at Les Rhumbs in the early twentieth century fostered an enduring idealized view of life (and the appropriate clothes in which to lead it) that effloresced in Dior's undulating silhouettes and impeccable accessories. The soft pink and gray of its façade influenced the palette of Dior, who would forever associate pink with happiness and gray with elegance. From the very beginning, these colors ribboned through his collections. The 1947 unveiling of the New Look included the pale gray "Parc Monceau" skirt of Gibson Girl effect, and "Bonbon," the perfect pink dress for a garden party at the Élysée Palace. The following season, the theme continued most spectacularly in the delicate "Eugénie" ball gown.

While Dior would translate elements of the house's façade—as well as his stylish mother and glamorous Angevin grandmother—into the ladylike look that typified a Dior creation, the eclectic interiors of Les Rhumbs enlivened his own classically inspired houses with eccentricity. The nineteenth-century discovery of Japanese printmakers Utamaro and Hokusai did more than flatten the canvases of Mary Cassatt and Edgar Degas into stylized tableaux; Japanese style vocabulary entered the homes of the bourgeoisie, becoming a kind of Morse code for middle-class artistic leanings. (Proust's Odette de Crécy, for example, grew Japanese chrysanthemums, which the sophisticated Charles Swann disparaged.) Characteristic of her class and time, though a few years later (Granville was not Paris, after all), Madame Dior interpreted Japonisme with pagoda-shaped overdoors of bamboo and straw in her reception rooms. And with the same blithe disregard for harmony that characterized her architectural additions to Les Rhumbs, she paid scant heed to coherence in her interiors. Instead, she followed the prevailing convention of attributing certain styles to specific rooms: a Louis XV-style drawing room filled with indifferent figurines, Venetian glass, satin flowers, and feathers in tall vases adjoined a yellow Second Empire sitting room; the Henri II dining room was next to Maurice Dior's Renaissance-inspired study, which also housed a novelty—the telephone.

Though antiques dealers and decorators talk to his day about Dior's unerring instincts for quality—a practiced eye and a partiality for neoclassicism are infallible assets—Dior found character in the cluttered eclecticism of Les Rhumbs and would rail against overly poised, soulless rooms. A too-perfect room, to Dior, was the equivalent of a pretty woman without charm. When a journalist for *Time* found the couturier in his velvet-walled library surrounded by fine paintings, ancient Greek amphorae, and Roman busts, he was surprised by the incongruous presence of plastic dolls and plaster statuettes. The prevailing king of fashion responded, naturally, with a wardrobe analogy: a house that doesn't reflect personal taste is like wearing someone else's clothes.

Neoclassicism and Feather Boas

When Maurice Dior relocated his business and family to Paris in 1911, the world opened up for six-year-old Christian. Though the romanticism of Granville would always pervade Dior's work, neoclassicism emerged as a powerful new influence. Strictly speaking, it was not the eighteenth-century neoclassicism of Ange-Jacques Gabriel and Robert Adam that captivated Dior, but Parisian neoclassicism circa 1910. An urbane fusion of linear paneling and potted palms, parquet floors and pale walls—a style that Dior would refer to as "Louis XVI-Passy,"—became his unwavering design compass, prevailing over couture salons, corporate identity, and homes, while the gentle cadences of Granville would inform his manners and rituals.

Prince Jean-Louis de Faucigny-Lucinge recounts that at the time the Dior family settled in the 16th arrondissement, the quarter was in its heyday. Even long-entrenched natives of the faubourg Saint-Germain were migrating to the 16th, lured, perhaps, by its proximity to the bridle paths, menagerie, and ongoing parade of finery, steeds, and conquests along the Allée des Acacias in the Bois de Boulogne. It was here, on the rue Richard-Wagner, that the Dior family took up residence. Besides being the locus of the new classicism, it had an added bonus—the ample opportunity that afternoon walks provided to observe feather boas, tilts of hats, and up-to-the-minute allure that would imprint themselves on Dior's developing sensibilities.

By Parisian standards, the airy 16th arrondissement was quite modern. Slightly outside historic Paris, nestled between the Seine and the Bois de Boulogne, it was largely the creation of Napoleon III and his prefect Baron Haussmann. By annexing villages, raising dark medieval streets (including the one where the baron himself was born), and creating the broad avenues that now so distinguish Paris, Haussmann established an urban plan that transformed Paris into a clean, light, efficient, and defensible city while unleashing a building boom. The 16th arrondissement was formed by linking the suburbs of Auteuil and Passy to central Paris.

Though the controversial Haussmann found himself out of a job in 1870, work on his project continued through the late 1920s. Presciently, the efficient baron had imposed a building code consistent with his vision for the City of Light. All over the city, uniform façades of massive cut-stone blocks were erected. To assure that Paris was bathed in light, the building height was determined by a fixed ratio to street width (with six stories as the strict cutoff). The interiors of these new apartment buildings were correspondingly sunny and spacious, characterized by high ceilings, multiple reception rooms, parquet floors, double doors, tall windows, beveled glass, ornate moldings, and the latest modern conveniences. None of this was lost on the visually acute young Dior, whose particular appreciation of the quality of light in the new family apartment on rue Richard-Wagner—so luminous, warm, and welcoming—might have particularly gratified Baron Haussmann. Thanks also to the baron's restrictions on building height, the child who loved nature, flowers, and gardens was able to glimpse trees in the park of La Muette from his fifth-floor bedroom window.

The new Haussmannian buildings—neither aristocratic palaces nor Balzacian garrets—dictated a new decorating style. No one, for the moment, wanted pagoda-shaped overdoors or vases of peacock feathers. Eschewing the dense world-bazaar aesthetic of Les Rhumbs, Madeleine Dior ditched her Japonisme for the eighteenth-century-inspired modernity that was all the rage. The interiors of her new apartment glowed with white enamel paint, pastel damask or pretty cretonne in the insets of paneled walls, and, for the times she and Christian couldn't visit their florist, Orève, to select fresh blossoms, rococo enameled flowers. Though these flowers reflected more the ambience of Vuillard than that of Vigée-Lebrun, they were at the time considered "very Louis XVI" and, therefore, the height of chic.

In fact, precious little in these interiors, save their debonair spirit, evoked Marie-Antoinette and her posh getaway, the Petit Trianon. Austerity of style had not yet wrought its havoc on exuberance; instead, the so-called Louis XVI rooms of Passy blithely exuded an ease and a sense of worldly pleasure completely of their time. Responding to the radiance of the new architecture, taste made a hard right from piano shawls and paisley to white-painted wood and a light cluttering of furniture, some from the epoch of Louis XV and Louis XVI, the rest unapologetic reproductions. The detailed canons of eighteenth-century design were reduced to a few impressionistic brushstrokes.

No one produced these brushstrokes better than society painter Paul-César Helleu. Whether capturing the Duchess of Marlborough, the Comtesse Greffulhe, or his biographer, world-class dandy Robert de Montesquiou, in chalk, pastel, or oil, Helleu preserved this feather-light world awash in pale color and movement. Through his sketch-quick renditions of nudes on Louis XV canapés, his refined wife at her Louis XVI-style secretary, a pensive adolescent portrayed in umpteen inflections of white, and Marcel Proust on his deathbed, Helleu was the court reporter pro tem of the aesthetic that Christian Dior would come to esteem above all others for decoration and fashion design. And like Dior, the worldly Helleu had an uncanny ability to steer his vision into contemporary relevance. It was Helleu who advised arch-modernist Coco Chanel to adopt beige—the color of the sand in the early morning at Biarritz—as a signature color, and who brought his refined talents to create the starry ceiling of that temple of American efficiency and entrepreneurship, Grand Central Terminal. Dior so identified with the pale, light-filled sensibility of Helleu that he later acquired his own Helleu drawing.

OPPOSITE

Left and right: From the tilt of a fashionable hat to a white-framed Louis XV-style settee, artist Paul-César Helleu captured in loose brushstrokes the world of Dior's Parisian youth. Dior so admired Helleu's aesthetic that he would acquire his work as a young professional. Helleu's worldly sophistication and lightness would permeate the interiors of Christian Dior Haute Couture as well as residential decoration in the New Look era.

Like any love affair, Dior's happy years amid the white Louis XVI-circa-1910 interiors were numbered. In 1919 the growing family moved to an apartment on the rue Louis-David, where a new décor replaced the airy ambience of the rue Richard-Wagner. Though also in the 16th arrondissement (and coincidentally quite close to the gracious avenue Georges-Mandel, where Victor Grandpierre's father had designed a palace for Princesse Winnaretta Singer-Polignac), the new street was oddly dark and, perhaps for this reason, the apartment lacked the sparkle of its predecessor. Time had moved on too. After Diaghilev, Bakst, and the Ballets Russes had unleashed color on the public consciousness, and in the wake of World War I's darkness, the once dernier-cri whites of the Ritz and the Belle Époque were now out of step.

A new neoclassicism, one that was considered very pure, now reigned in the conservative reaches of Paris. Gone were the white-lacquered wood panels and pastel tones of Louis XVI circa 1910, replaced by color, rich upholstery, and paneling picked out in contrasting shades believed to be much closer to the interiors of Versailles. (However, in 1919 "Versailles colors" were largely a matter of conjecture. The palace remained largely bedraggled until 1924, when John D. Rockefeller Jr. financed an early restoration.) In the same decade that Syrie Maugham designed her all-white library in Le Touquet, Madeleine Dior amassed reproduction furniture, densely patterned walls, and knickknacks according to the new, circa 1920, interpretation of the eighteenth century.

Though the apartment bore elements of the graceful Louis XVI style—fluting, rosettes, pilasters, and lattice—it sank under the weight of decoration. The chasm

between appropriating the vocabulary and understanding the essence of a style became textbook clear. Dark statuary and fringed tablecloths overburdened a gallery with glass lanterns and a latticed alcove, while a hefty (and anachronistic) dining table with Louis XVI motifs dwarfed a dining room filled with rich arabesques. Another room, packed with cabriole-legged chairs and paintings (some, apparently, by Boucher and Lépicié) resembled less a salon of the ancien régime than a stand at the Marché aux Puces, the bustling flea market and treasure trove north of Paris. Whereas Dior was profuse in his enthusiasm for the previous apartment, he tactfully limited his comments on the new residence in his memoirs.

Other muses exerted their powers on Dior and his developing aesthetic. While officially preparing to pass his baccalaureate, the adolescent Dior focused his energies on following artistic trends. The well-bred boy who avidly read the plant catalogues of the celebrated horticultural supplier Vilmorin-Andrieux, relaxed with the seamstress, and avoided parties had become a precocious Parisian who frequented art galleries on the rue de la Boétie, embraced the architecture of Le Corbusier, and reveled in German expressionist film. He often ended his nights at the bar of the Boeuf sur le toit, the nexus of his avant-garde, carefree world. After obtaining his baccalaureate in 1923, Dior dreamed of studying architecture at the École des Beaux-Arts, but his cautious parents, judging the path of an architect too iffy, steered their son into the blue-chip École Libre des Sciences Politiques (Sciences-Po), a classic training ground for gentlemen-diplomats.

Like many sent in the wrong direction by well-meaning parents, Dior outwardly acquiesced to parental demands but took full advantage of Sciences-Po's laissez-faire curriculum to pursue his own agenda. For an intellectually curious young man, the enticements of avant-garde Paris were endless: the nihilism of Dada, the seductions of Louise Brooks, parties given by the Comte de Beaumont, Cocteau's ballet *Les Mariés de la Tour Eiffel*, productions of Chekov's plays, Cubism, and primitive art overshadowed anything that could be taught in a lecture hall. Ultimately recognizing the absurdity of the situation, Monsieur and Madame Dior relented and allowed their son to study musical composition.

Music offered Dior the amplitude that economics lacked. He became a passionate champion of Erik Satie's School of Arcueil as well as Les Six, a consortium of avant-garde composers led by Jean Cocteau who strove to create a musical movement to parallel that of Cubism in the visual arts and Surrealism in literature. Naturally, Dior found fellowship in the pursuit of personal interests. A meeting with composer Henri Sauguet, who had already had his work performed at the Théâtre des Champs-Élysées, turned into friendship and led to camaraderie with historian Pierre Gaxotte, future actor Jean Ozenne, and artist Christian (Bébé) Bérard. Bérard and his drawings, which transformed the mundane into a world of passion and nostalgia, resonated immediately with Dior.

The 1920s was a decade of streamlined affluence. With its speed and ability to soar above worldly constraints, aviation captivated the collective imagination. Despite the 1925 Exposition Internationale des Arts Décoratifs et Industriels Modernes, which celebrated all that pointed to an industrially driven future, the decade's greatest—and most ironic—indulgence was the expression of luxury in simple lines and humble materials, executed with the finest handcraftsmanship. The unlined linen curtains of Eugenia Errázuriz and parchment walls of Jean-Michel Frank epitomized the chic of the minimal moment. Music and literature followed stripped-down suit, with Arnold Schoenberg's 12-tone music and André Breton's convention-liberated prose. In fashion, Coco Chanel devised sweaters in utilitarian jersey for the smart set.

Yet Modernism, like Shiva, arrived in many guises. Not everyone subscribed to full-on minimalism. Rather than break with the past, some modernists extended and explored long-held traditions. Composers like Henri Sauguet wrote lyrical music that defied categorization, including the score for the Diaghilev-commissioned ballet *La Chatte*, choreographed by a new young talent, George Balanchine, in 1927. Christian Bérard countered Cubism with haunting figurative paintings. Marrying poetry with

OPPOSITE

Though Dior absorbed important cultural traditions as he accompanied his mother to fittings, selected household flowers, and set the dining table for dinner parties, his family lacked the debonair flair that was at the heart of his aesthetic. Their apartment on the rue Louis-David in Paris, circa 1919, had a few fine paintings and a mix of reproduction furniture. Whereas the Diors accumulated brown bergères, young Christian favored white Louis XVI chairs.

OVERLEAF

Much of Dior's golden youth was spent in the legendary bar Le Boeuf sur la toit, where he encountered modernism in its many modes: Cubism, Surrealism, Dadaism, primitive art, cutting-edge music, and contemporary theater. With his antennae attuned to his time, he was poised to become an astute gallerist and, later, an insightful couturier.

LE BŒUF SUR LE TOIT

* * *

technology, the aviator Saint-Exupéry wrote *Courrier sud*, and Madeleine Vionnet innovated bias-cut dresses that fluttered in flight.

Though romance and neoclassicism were central to Dior's aesthetic, intellectual curiosity, broad cultural exposure, and interest in evolving art forms further sharpened his eye. He had, after all, seen firsthand the undiscerning appropriation of old decorative forms in his parents' apartment. Just as his closest friends were engaged in modern interpretations of their respective arts, Dior would reconsider and reinterpret old forms, toss the irrelevant, and embrace age-old techniques to create something new. His homes and his clothes would be inspired by the past, but, with one youthful exception, they would breathe with the spirit of their time.

A Room of One's Own

Ensconced in bourgeois comfort on the rue Louis-David, studying musical composition by day and steeping himself in the arts by night, hosting musicales at which guests sat in scandalous semidarkness on the floor of his mother's salon, and adorning his room with drawings by his new friend Christian Bérard, Dior continued his privileged youth. At some point, music as a career was lightly jettisoned. Instead, after compulsory military service in 1928, at the ripe age of twenty-three, Dior, in partnership with Jacques Bonjean, founded an art gallery on the rue de la Boétie. Dior's capital investment was put up by his parents, who stipulated, nevertheless, that the family name not be tainted by "trade" and, in particular, by appearing on an ignominious shop sign. (It is perhaps fortunate that neither lived to see their son's later marquee success.) Buoyed by a booming market and exhibitions of masters Matisse, Picasso, and Dufy, as well as emerging talents Salvador Dalí, Max Jacob, Christian Bérard, Pavel Tchelitchew, and Eugène and Leonid Berman, the momentum of the gallery reassured even his skeptical parents. In 1929 Dior demonstrated his interest in design with an exhibition devoted to the architect, interior decorator, and landscape designer Emilio Terry.

If life had continued, as all expected, on its upward trajectory, sustained by ever-greater advances in industry, the arts, and the stock market, Dior might well have become a famous mid-century gallerist. Without a doubt, he had the acumen. His immersion in the ballet, the fine arts, and the cinema, and even the hours spent in the bar at Le Boeuf sur le toit had bestowed him with an awareness of his time as well as discernment. The resulting sophistication, sprinkled with the fairy dust of prescient commercial instincts—qualities that would also benefit future undertakings—moved art and made news. One moment, Dior's fiscal conservatism ruffled the proud Tchelitchew (it rankled that Bérard commanded higher prices); the next, Dior penned courtly notes on gallery letterhead, inviting key contacts to pass by and see the current Picassos and Braques on display.

The role of art dealer suited his temperament too. Unassuming and modest, famously resembling a bland country curate made of marzipan, Dior was content facilitating the success of others and applauding talent from the sidelines. Many of the artists were personal friends, and he also acquired other new friends in those years— novelists, editors, set designers, and a fashionista named Georges Geffroy—often while participating in high jinks organized by Max Jacob, the ill-fated artist and writer who

was the de facto leader of the clique. Improvising costumes, ballet parodies, and musical spoofs, and occasionally undertaking more serious endeavors, such as an operetta by Henri Sauguet with libretto by Jacob and design by Christian Bérard, the group fostered bonhomie, collaboration, theatricality, and stylish presentation.

Foresighted when spotting artistic talent, in hindsight Dior regretted parting with his inventory, given that Dalí, the Bermans, and Bérard commanded millions of French francs after the war. Alas, in the early 1930s Dior did not have the luxury of choice. The decade began with personal tragedies—the chronic illness of a brother and the death of his mother—and descended into financial ruin and Dior's physical breakdown. After Dior et fils went public in 1923, Maurice Dior flipped the proceeds into prudent, if untimely, real estate in staid Neuilly, and was forced into bankruptcy when Crash-panicked investors called for liquidity in 1931. Under duress, the Diors sold off the Bouchers and bergères in the rue Louis-David apartment at distressed prices. Simultaneously, the art market stagnated.

Thus began the vagabond years for a now homeless and penniless Christian Dior. Young and idealistic, he made a quixotic trip to the Soviet Union with a group of architects in search of alternatives to capitalism but returned with disillusionment and to the news

that his gallery partner, Jacques Bonjean, was also ruined. Too cash-strapped to stay in a hotel, Dior serially bunked with friends, attempting to be as unobtrusive as possible, and carefully hid the fact that he often went without supper. Mercifully, kind nightclub and hotel owners supplied an occasional meal; the clever Louis Moysés at Le Boeuf sur le toit sometimes footed the bill for his old regulars, realizing that his paying clientele came precisely for the cachet of dining among the artistic set. Meanwhile, Dior collaborated with poet-turned-art dealer Pierre Colle on mounting exhibitions of surrealist and abstract art that merely drove away any remaining, and now cautious, collectors. They were forced to sell off inventory cheaply. Under such dismal market conditions, any sale that did not entail a staggering loss was considered successful.

Two leaky garret rooms above Le Boeuf sur le toit shared with Nicholas Bongard—nephew of Paul Poiret and later business partner of café society jeweler Jean Schlumberger—and Bongard's mistress temporarily ended Dior's wandering and provided a bit of bohemian stability. But dripping ceilings, cramped quarters, sketchy meals, late nights, and relentless anxiety ground down Dior's defenses and resulted, in 1934, in a severe case of tuberculosis. While recuperating in Ibiza, Dior discovered needlepoint, which rekindled his interest in needlework and led to a new ambition: creating something with his own hands.

When Dior returned to Paris in 1935, Jean Ozenne, Christian Bérard's cousin and, ultimately, a well-known actor, stepped in to offer both shelter in his apartment, which had captivating views of the Seine, and coaching in his own métier of freelance sketcher-designer for couturiers, milliners, and fashion exporters. Dior, enthralled by this new undertaking, which combined art, handcraftsmanship, and vision, applied himself as he had never done at Sciences-Po. Ozenne's partner, Max Kenna, pitched in with advice on mixing and applying color. Michel de Brunhoff, editor in chief of *Vogue* (and brother of Jean de Brunhoff, creator of Babar the elephant), and Georges Geffroy, at the time hovering under the wing of Brunhoff, offered additional critiques. When Ozenne sold six of Dior's designs, Dior's new career was launched.

Years of admiring the expressive lines of Cocteau, Bérard, and Matisse now produced fashion drawings alive with suggestion and movement. Most couture and millinery houses at the time purchased designs from freelance artists, and Dior's careful recording of his sales to Alix Barton (Madame Grès), Jean Dessès, Nicole Groult, Heim, Jenny, Patou, Schiaparelli, Ricci, Rochas, Worth, Madeleine de Rauch, Molyneux, Paquin, and even Balenciaga, as well as milliners Suzy, Agnès, Rose Valois, and Blanche et Simone, and glover Alexandrine demonstrate the breadth of recognition for the newcomer's talent. Calls for editorial work from *Le Figaro* and *Harper's Bazaar* rounded out his portfolio.

Brisk sales of his fashion designs meant that Dior's peripatetic house guesting came to an end. With cash in hand for the first time in years, he moved into the Hôtel de Bourgogne near the place du Palais-Bourbon. The 7th arrondissement was as smart then as it is now, but at the time, living in hotels provided a tax loophole, which conceivably explains why Christian Bérard, Boris Kochno, Jean-Paul Sartre, Simone de Beauvoir, and others opted to reside in hotels during the 1930s. The attractive mix of provincial aristocracy visiting relatives in the faubourg Saint-Germain, pre-Existentialists, and fashion types who inhabited the Hôtel de Bourgogne lent the place a charm that would

OPPOSITE

It was Georges Geffroy who brought Dior (standing) to the attention of haute couturier Robert Piguet (seated). Piguet, who had once championed dresses in batik and later trained with the flamboyant Paul Poiret, honed his reductive style of skimming silhouettes and draped skirts at the distinguished Redfern. While working for Piguet, Dior learned the first great lesson of chic: one must omit to attain elegance.

have appealed to the intellectually avant-garde but socially conservative Dior. Nevertheless, a furnished room is not quite a home, particularly for one enamored of domesticity.

Georges Geffroy, also in residence at the Hôtel de Bourgogne, introduced Dior to Robert Piguet, then a rising star in Paris fashion. Piguet, an elegant minimalist, purchased a few of Dior's sketches and then hired him in 1938 as a *modéliste*, responsible for overseeing the translation of sketches into actual dresses. Hubert de Givenchy, another Piguet alum, allowed that Piguet's designs were highly wearable but found them too discreet ("all navy with white linen") for his own adventurous taste. Dior, in contrast, quietly observed and refined his skills during his three seasons with Piguet, from whom he learned to omit, recognizing that there can be no elegance without simplicity.

At Piguet, too, Dior first realized the power of his own vision. Referencing the illustrations of the beloved children's books by the Comtesse de Ségur, he designed high-waisted dresses with eyelet skirts and starched round collars, daring dresses that his savvy Norman instincts told him spelled success. One of these dresses, "Café Anglais," was, indeed, Dior's first hit. Based on its notoriety, Christian Bérard introduced Dior to saloniste and *Harper's Bazaar* representative Marie-Louise Bousquet, who in turn flagged him to the all-powerful Carmel Snow, the fashion doyenne who later christened Dior's first collection the "New Look."

Having risen through the ranks at Piguet from promising apprentice to seasoned journeyman, Dior was now in possession of a steady income and in reach of his dream, a home of his own. After years of uncertainty and shelter in sanitariums, transient hotels, and friends' homes, Dior's paramount objective was to create a home filled with art and objects of personal meaning, reminiscent of his serene, sheltered youth. The very location of the apartment he found—five rooms in a walk-up at 10, rue Royale, gracefully situated between the place de la Madeleine and place de la Concorde in the 8th arrondissement—was laden with souvenirs of the Belle Époque: it was across the street from Maxim's and his late mother's couturière, Rosine Perrault, where he had accompanied her as a child-consultant. It was also on the same street as the couturier Dior most admired, Edward Molyneux. As with the daringly distinctive "Café Anglais," Dior sought his decorating muse in the past. Not for Dior the soigné curves of an ocean liner or the inlaid palisander of Jules Leleu; recovering his old bed and scouring the Marché aux Puces with Bébé Bérard was what he wanted. Assembling Napoleon III tables, palms on velvet pedestals, deep chairs with antimacassars, Venetian tazzas, and treasured paintings, Dior attained his desired apartment.

Still a young man—despite all his experience, he was but thirty-three—Dior had not yet acquired the taste that would distinguish his couture house and future homes, from the rustic mill near Fontainebleau and urbane house in Passy to the dignified manor in the Var. Though his ear for music, his instinct for art, and his eye for fashion were well

Bonne Année

MENU

du

2 janvier 1940

Menu dessiné par le sapeur Christian Dior de la 47e Cie du génie

belles Huîtres de la Rochelle

Pâté de tête Charles VII

...mon de la Loire
en coquilles

Bouchées Lyonnaises

...in de Beauvoir
à la St Hubert

...bois du pays
...pur du périgord

Salade de Saison

Savarin Mehunois

cultivated, his antenna for interior design had not yet benefited from tutelage by the equivalent of a Sauguet, Ozenne, or Piguet, or even from his own methodical research. Lessons learned in one medium are ultimately, but not immediately, translated into another. Hence, while Dior was learning to edit and omit at Piguet, romantic reverie had a free hand as he re-created the atmosphere of Les Rhumbs on the rue Royale. Chintz curtains and damask wallpaper, delicate Napoleon III faux-bamboo and stolid brown furniture, haunting Bérards and bizarre lamps formed a phalanx of security. With time, his reverence for quality and French tradition, along with his innate aesthetic barometer, would counterbalance his emotion. Later, too, he would have Victor Grandpierre to smooth his romantic tendencies into a polished and sophisticated personal style and Georges Geffroy to steer him toward a more purist vision. But for the moment, the lightly barbed verdict on the rue Royale apartment—from *Vogue*—was that it looked provincial.

This is not to say that Dior considered interior design a lesser pursuit. He noted how fashion related to design, pointing to Chanel, whom he admired for her ability to imagine exquisite dresses with no link to the past that nevertheless blended perfectly with the Venetian-inspired backgrounds and gilt baroque so popular at the time. He noticed, too, in those prewar years, that Schiaparelli—with her flash and fuss and lobsters on evening dresses—stood for an elegance that accorded well with the décors of a Jean-Michel Frank and the extravagances of Surrealism. Even though Dior championed surrealists like Pavel Tchelitchew, Eugène Berman, and Salvador Dalí in his gallery, he was in essence a rational spirit with tastes moderated by education, logic, and inherited traditions, and could never conceivably design a hat that looked like a high-heeled shoe. Much more to his liking was Molyneux, whose sober and clean lines, softened by a subtle Parisian femininity, represented the poised perfection he sought to master.

Dior reveled in his rue Royale apartment, assembling and entertaining friends about him. American *Vogue*'s Paris editor at the time, Bettina Ballard, recalls the intimacy of his parlor, which was evocative of *Madame Bovary*, stuffed with potted palms, wicker chairs, Victorian knickknacks, and as Dior adored food, the glorious odors of tantalizing meals prepared by Denise, his turbaned Martiniquan cook. Henri Sauguet, Christian Bérard, and Marie-Louise Bousquet could always be counted on for clever and wicked repartee, invariably at someone's expense, while the Camille-like Countess Nicole de Montesquiou and Mitzah Bricard contributed the feminine elegance that Dior had adored since childhood.

Suited to his new career and appreciative of stable employment, Dior was content executing beautifully crafted clothes and harbored little ambition. Enjoying his newfound domesticity, entertaining friends, eating well, and pursuing the arts, he settled into a pleasant routine at Piguet. He undertook the occasional costume project, which provided a laboratory to develop new ideas for couture clothes (the 1938 play *Captain Smith*, for which he created beribboned and crinolined costumes, was described by *Ce Soir* as looking like a fashion plate of the past). He designed his last collection for Piguet in 1939, the year he was recalled into the army. Throughout the war, Dior held on to his treasured apartment, which his sister Catherine, a member of the Resistance, would occasionally use when in Paris.

OPPOSITE

Dior was both artistic and domestic—and particularly appreciated good food. Even in wartime, he upheld the traditions of the table. To celebrate the New Year of 1940, he planned and illustrated a menu for his comrades in the 47th Company of Army Engineers.

ABOVE

Haute couturier Lucien Lelong viewed his role as president of the Chambre Syndicale de la Haute Couture as the protector of sacred traditions and techniques. It was a view that Dior, as a couturier, would also embrace. While working for Lelong, Dior learned respect for the specialized crafts that supported haute couture production.

OPPOSITE

Dior's dashing hat designs for Lelong often referenced the Belle Époque.

In June 1940, when the armistice with Germany was signed, the French army disbanded. At loose ends, Dior moved to the Free Zone in the south and lived with his father and sister near Grasse, eking out a livelihood with a kitchen garden. He sold his produce in the market in Cannes, met Victor Grandpierre, provided sketches for Paul Caldaquès, fashion editor at *Le Figaro*, and resisted Piguet's entreaties to return to Paris. When he finally returned in 1941, Piguet had filled his old position. (He had dithered for so long that Piguet had resorted to hiring a young fellow from Chanel, Antonio Castillo.) Paul Caldaquès, pitying the young designer adrift in Paris, introduced him to Lucien Lelong, who hired him to co-design his collection alongside Pierre Balmain.

As president of the Chambre Syndicale de la Haute Couture at the time, Lelong shrewdly negotiated with the Germans, who wished to relocate the world fashion center to Germany or Austria. To his enormous credit, Lelong kept haute couture in Paris. As haute couture depended as much on highly skilled artisans in tiny ateliers scattered throughout the city as on the couturiers and their substantial staff, he insisted that it was impossible to move the industry. Further, he argued, as the techniques of these suppliers, as well as those of the seamstresses in the ateliers, had been painstakingly perfected through generations of refinement, they simply could not be taught elsewhere overnight.

Lelong himself did not design; rather, he produced clothes designed by others, while keeping his eye on the cohesion of his collections. His style had ranged from sporty

LUCIEN LELONG

COUTURIER À PARIS

16, RUE MATIGNON
(ROND POINT DES CHANPS ÉLYSÉES)

ÉLYSÉES 13 - 13

TÉLÉPHONE :

PARIS 8e LE

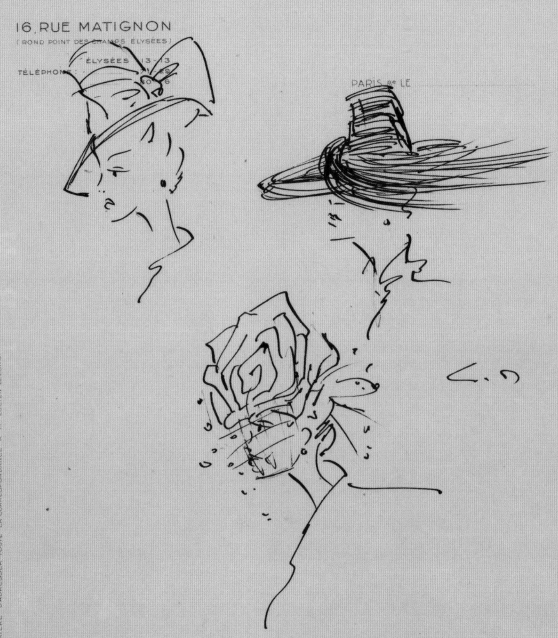

R.C Seine 68.693

in the 1920s to flowing and full of movement in the 1930s, when his wife at the time, Princess Nathalie Paley, was his muse. In the 1940s, with Dior and Balmain designing his collections, Lelong's style changed once again, often marked by fuller skirts and fitted waistlines. Fashion editors who had dismissed Lelong as not particularly interesting suddenly noticed sparks emanating from the house.

After the Liberation of Paris in August 1944, some nine months before the end of the war in Europe, haute couture began to collect itself. Bleak times, shortages of materials, and the dampening of elegant social life had eroded couture's fortune and influence during the war. Aggravating the situation, Americans had been cut off from French couture for more than four years, during which time Seventh Avenue had emerged as a significant source for clothes, developing its own style and diluting the primacy of Paris. New York designers looked to street fashion and pioneered separates; maverick Claire McCardell even designed a cotton "Kitchen Dinner Dress" that had—horrors—a matching apron.

To sell itself again overseas, French fashion required a new dose of ingenuity from the Chambre Syndicale de la Haute Couture and its president, Lucien Lelong. Their brainchild was the traveling exhibition *Le Théâtre de la mode*, the ostensible purpose of which was to raise money for Parisian charities (a charge it fulfilled very successfully), but its real aim was to revive the visibility of French haute couture. Mounted shortly after the Liberation, *Le Théâtre de la mode* was a serious mission masquerading as a genteel diversion.

Shortages of materials, and the impossibility of sending models overseas when transportation was inundated with demobilized soldiers returning to their homes,

BELOW

A Georges Geffroy-designed set for *Le Théâtre de la mode,* the traveling fashion exhibition that revived the visibility of Parisian couture after the war. The challenge of finding miniaturists to work to Geffroy's famously exacting standards may explain the spare furnishings.

OPPOSITE

Dior assumed the guise of a lion, King of the Jungle, for Étienne de Beaumont's 1949 Kings and Queens-themed ball. Pierre Cardin, whom Dior had first encountered in the theater, and who, as the first director of tailoring at Christian Dior, had made the "Bar" suit, provided the costume.

precluded promoting Parisian style the usual way—traveling fashion shows with live models. Instead, inspired by the commercial French fashion dolls that had been sent all over Europe in the eighteenth century, Paul Caldaquès suggested an exhibition of dolls dressed by the couture houses, with the added cachet of high-style sets. The idea took wing. Christian Bérard, appointed art director, orchestrated the talents of his friends, among them Boris Kochno, Jean Cocteau, veteran set designer Jean-Denis Malclès, newcomer André Beaurepaire, and Georges Geffroy. Sets representing a miniature opera house, an enchanted grotto, the Champs-Élysées, and the Palais Royal were conceived to display 27-inch mannequins in theater clothes, evening gowns, city suits, and daywear.

Staff at every couture house worked in secrecy, vying to outdo one another. Everything, down to buttonholes, embroidery, silk underwear, belts, jewelry (by Cartier, Van Cleef & Arpels, Chaumet, and Boucheron), and hats were hand-crafted on a miniature scale. Lack of heat forced seamstresses to wear bulky mittens while executing the minuscule designs. Unavailable necessities, like sewing needles from Germany, had to be improvised. Sewing machines were moved about Paris several times a day, depending on where electricity could be found. Amid these hardships, everyone focused on glamour, which would be the draw of the show. Christian Dior, Lucien Lelong's designer (Balmain had left in early 1945 to establish his own house), created a dance dress with a full black silk surah skirt and a candy-pink crepe top held in place with a rose. Perhaps even more prophetically, he designed a full-skirted turquoise garden-party dress with a white organdy collar and a ribbon-trimmed picture hat. Adieu, pedestrian kitchen dresses.

With the triumvirate of style influencers Louise de Vilmorin, Marie-Blanche de Polignac (daughter of Jeanne Lanvin), and Marie-Laure de Noailles in attendance, *Le Théâtre de la mode* opened on March 27, 1945, at the Pavillon de Marsan at the Musée des Arts Décoratifs. Paris, so long deprived of displays of beauty and elegance, was rapt; the engagement had to be extended to accommodate demand. Afterward, the exhibition traveled to London, New York, San Francisco, Vienna, Barcelona, Copenhagen, and Stockholm, to universal acclaim. Reasserting the vitality and talent of Paris couture, the *Théâtre de la mode* exhibition was, in effect, the warm-up act for the New Look.

Life-size theater further groomed Dior's vision after the war. As with *Captain Smith* in 1938, costume design was a vehicle for Dior and his contemporaries to work collaboratively and forge a new aesthetic—part nostalgia, part theatrical sketch. While working for Lelong, he designed diaphanous negligées and bustle skirts for the film *Le Lit à colonnes*, based on Louise de Vilmorin's novel. And it was in the theater that Dior met the young Pierre Cardin, fresh from his stint at Schiaparelli and assisting with costumes at the Comédie-Française. He would become the tailor who brilliantly

OVERLEAF

Left: Ballet and theater provided a laboratory for Dior and his contemporaries to test dramatic ideas and collaborate with other artists. The experience influenced their work in fashion and decoration. As Leslie Caron looks on, Christian Dior adjusts a costume for Roland Petit's *Treize Danses*. Right: In 1942 Dior designed Belle Époque silhouettes for a film adaptation of Louise de Vilmorin's *Le Lit à colonnes*.

executed Dior's famous "Bar" suit and would recall years later how Dior had insisted on such a tiny waistline that when the model breathed, buttons inevitably popped.

After much internal debate, Dior reluctantly left the diplomatic Lelong in 1946, when textile magnate Marcel Boussac offered him his own couture house. The forty-one-year-old now had the sharpened sensibilities and confidence to design as dictated only by his own muse. Though his vision of draping women in romance, riches, and refined technique was unique, its appeal was universal. The house of Christian Dior would define the look of its era.

A QUEST FOR GRANDEUR

Georges Geffroy, 1905~1946

Though Georges Geffroy was born into the twentieth-century bourgeoisie, he had the qualities of an eighteenth-century courtier. Advising princes of industry, aristocrats, connoisseurs, and bon vivants, and presiding over a salon, his life was, for all intents and purposes, courtly. He also was enamored of grandeur. Throughout his life, Geffroy alluded to grand maternal ancestry without providing the particulars, murmuring that even the mention of the exalted name would be preposterous. Of course, these cryptic allusions suggested, as probably intended, visions of ancestors taking their first halting steps in the Schönbrunn or, perhaps, splashing in the fountains of Sans Souci. In life, as in decorating, Geffroy was a master of invention. • Certainly taste, erudition, and style, if not birth, linked Georges Geffroy to the grand tradition. Whether

entertaining a bejeweled Duchess of Windsor in his elegant walk-up apartment or making the rounds of antiques dealers in his liveried Morris-Wolseley with red leather interiors, Geffroy exuded élan disproportionate to his respectable, Protestant background. In fact, his grandfather and father were sober lawyers who served on the Superior Court of Paris. Perhaps it was via his Latvian-born grandmother that Geffroy acquired his taste for the exceptional as well as his slightly exotic eyes.

After growing up in a bourgeois apartment on the rue de Grenelle, the decorator's father, Paul Louis Geffroy, married Jeanne Berthe Marie Rose Voelker, the daughter of a doctor, in 1894. Setting up house in the faubourg Saint-Germain, the couple produced in quick succession, between 1895 and 1899, three daughters with the flowery Belle Époque names Andrée Wilhelmina Rose, Berthe Louise Antoinette Pauline, and Marguerite Louise Jeanne. Perhaps prompted by the needs of a growing family, they moved across the Seine to a new apartment at 59, rue de Richelieu, just down the street from Madame's family, in the 2nd arrondissement. It was here, swaddled in history, romance, and intrigue in the heart of Paris, that Georges Geffroy was born on January 8, 1905.

Though far removed from royal grandeur, the street, with its dark urbanity and whiff of connoisseurship, was an appropriate launch for Geffroy—socialite, aesthete, and man of contradictions. The Geffroys' Haussmannian apartment building stood on the site of a townhouse where the Maréchal Duc de Richelieu had once enjoyed racy escapades with a married actress. Across the street was the seventeenth-century palace of Cardinal Mazarin, now the Bibliothèque Nationale. The enchanting Jeanne-Antoinette Poisson, later Madame de Pompadour, had grown up at 50, rue de Richelieu.

Geffroy's childhood garden was the nearby square Louvois, a small jewel of greenery on the densely built street. Its fountain, depicting the four great rivers of France, is considered one of the most beautiful in Paris. Before Baron Haussmann redefined Paris with grand boulevards, the narrow rue de Richelieu, housing luxury jewelers, hosiers, clockmakers, perfumers, and artificial flower makers, was considered the Bond Street of Paris. Proximity to the auction rooms of Hôtel Drouot had attracted dealers in coins, prints, silver, furniture, and paintings to the upper reaches of the neighborhood—a boon for Paul Geffroy, who dabbled in collecting. In collector's instinct, as well as looks, young Geffroy took after his father; both had oval faces with high foreheads, chestnut hair and eyes, rounded chins, and strong noses.

Despite these historical and treasure-laden surroundings, Georges Geffroy's childhood was prosaic. His family was practical and close-knit, decidedly not dreamy. Two sensible dental surgeons signed his birth certificate. One of those two witnesses, Geffroy's uncle Alexandre Berlioz, lived just steps away on the rue de Louvois. Sixty-six years later Berlioz's son, Dr. Charles Berlioz, along with Geffroy's sisters, would announce his decorator cousin's death in *Le Monde*, neatly wrapping Georges Geffroy's life in matter-of-fact family ties. By and large, Geffroy's sisters also adhered to a dutiful path. One married a government clerk and *polytechnicien*, a graduate of France's most prestigious school for administrators; another married a doctor. Georges, on the other hand, was inclined to fancy; he was born, one said, with *goût qui chante* (taste that sings).

A connoisseur rather than a scholar, Geffroy was seemingly indifferent to the educational subsidies that the government provided him following the death of his father in 1917—*mort pour la France*, the official designation of one who died serving his country. His close friend the Duchesse d'Harcourt recalled the passion and erudition with which he could monopolize a dinner party, extolling, with his slight stammer, the curve of a chair leg, but could little imagine him in the confines of a school. There is no record of a baccalaureate or university degree. In fact, owing to an inconveniently timed bout with tuberculosis at age sixteen, it is quite possible that Geffroy did not sit for his baccalaureate exam. Nevertheless, knowledgeable observers such as the Duchesse d'Harcourt and interior architect Alain Demachy consider Geffroy to have been highly cultivated, if not conventionally educated. Others suggest that supremely confident taste was the true foundation of his talent. But, whatever his training, no one ever doubted that he had style.

Fashionable Experiments

Like Dior, Geffroy wandered circuitously toward professional accomplishment, picking up useful elements along the way. At twenty, he co-designed the sets for *Les Aventures de Robert Macaire*, a silent movie directed by the rising young filmmaker and theorist Jean Epstein. One of the first to legitimize film as an art form, Epstein was also among the earliest to exploit film's potential for atmosphere and emotion. Though *Robert Macaire* contains its share of silent-film clichés—the male star wore heavy eye makeup and lip rouge; gestures were grossly theatrical—Geffroy, along with Jean-Adrien Mercier and Lazare Meerson, devised sets that supported Epstein's premise, conveying oppressive summers, ominous intrigue, and dusty dereliction in the provinces. Shortly thereafter, while Epstein directed an acclaimed film adaptation of Edgar Allan Poe's *Fall of the House of Usher*, Geffroy provided illustrations for two issues of Lucien Vogel's fashion journal, *Le Jardin des modes*. One featured a sleek, turquoise Louis XV-inspired commode. He then headed off for mandatory military service.

Military service did not suit Geffroy's fragile constitution. With his sclerotic lungs, his record reads more like a medical file than a military dossier. In June 1928, hardly a month after arriving for infantry duty, the twenty-two-year-old was sent home for bed rest at 5, rue Hippolyte-Lebas, the apartment on the outskirts of the Nouvelle Athènes district in the 9th arrondissement, where his family had lived since World War I. He was frail, as he would be for the rest of his life, but that never much impacted his social life. After he was demobilized in 1929, Geffroy worked for the couturier Rolande and continued to frolic with the Max Jacob clique at the Hôtel Nollet, where he met the gallerist Christian Dior.

Though Geffroy also worked briefly for Poiret and Redfern, there are no documents pointing to details or accomplishments. In fact, like many in an industry particularly hard hit by the Crash, he seems to have been unemployed in the mid-1930s. By 1935, Michel de Brunhoff, the *Vogue* editor famous for nurturing fledgling talents (most memorably Christian Dior and Yves Saint Laurent), was doing his best to help the foundering Geffroy. Unlike the drawings turned out by Carl Erickson and Christian Bérard with effortless charm, Geffroy's sketches were stilted and uncompelling. Painfully aware of his inadequacy, Geffroy would apologize profusely in his famous idiosyncratic patois, which Bettina Ballard described as "complicated Proustian phrases," Pierre Le-Tan as "affected Antilles," and Edmonde Charles-Roux as "drawn-out alembic phrases." Perceptively, Ballard also noted that Geffroy was given to chronic suffering, most often over friendships.

A position at Jean Patou in the summer of 1936 ended Geffroy's moping in the *Vogue* offices. Working at Patou, the great rival to Chanel, had been exciting until March 1936, when Jean Patou died, mysteriously, in a suite at the Hôtel George V. Like Coco Chanel, Patou produced clothes of pared-down luxury that allowed for unfettered movement but had an elegance uniquely his own. Having concluded that the flapper silhouette had run its unbecoming course, Patou raised waistlines and dropped hemlines to define the graceful line of the 1930s. Committed to modern life (he created the first suntan oil), modern clothes (he pioneered the tennis skirt, knitted swimwear, and the cardigan as a fashion item), and modern women (he dressed Josephine Baker and Louise Brooks, when they wore clothes), Patou was as renowned for exquisite craft, particularly embroidery and stitching, as for daring backless dresses.

The Crash had not been kind to Patou, withering his important American client base and weakening sales in France. His superb standard of craftsmanship—he went so far as to dye his own yarn to attain perfect, saturated colors for his clothes—made his prices prohibitive for the newly prudent buyer. Nearly a year before Geffroy's arrival, the company was in liquidation, though under the direction of Patou's sister and muse it preserved the aesthetic spirit of its founder.

OPPOSITE

Jean Patou, along with Chanel, pioneered the flapper silhouette, but dropped hemlines and raised waistlines in 1929 to usher in the profile of the 1930s. His luxury was a modern one. He favored rich fabrics, precise, if subtle, detailing, and showmanship. At his cocktail openings, he handed out lipsticks in Cartier cases as favors.

OVERLEAF

Left: Modeling Patou in Charles de Beistegui's penthouse. Beistegui filled the modern space, designed by Le Corbusier, with baroque furniture and concluded, "He who thinks 'modern' is already outdated." Right: The height of fashion, circa 1933: Reboux hats, Paquin and Patou dresses. Both Patou and Beistegui influenced Geffroy's aesthetic.

Reboux – Paquin

Even one step removed from the glamorous Patou, Geffroy assimilated the couturier's panache. An instinctive showman given to grand pronouncements ("To be truly soigné a man must have eighty suits" was but one throwaway comment), Patou was famous for luxurious silks and satins and his particular affection for ladies of the aristocracy and international society. Fond of lofty assertions and of natty attire, Geffroy, too, relished sumptuous fabrics, exacting details, and confidences with fashionable women. Madame Renate de Grandsaignes of his loyal workroom, Decour, recalls that as a decorator Geffroy would order custom silk from Lyon, rejecting dye lot after dye lot, demanding spot-on rather than good-enough results, and would start a project all over again to obtain the envisioned result, regardless of cost and deadline. Most relevantly, he would adopt Patou's aesthetic of luxurious simplicity for his classical interiors.

Geffroy thrived in the environment of fashion and the fashionable, so different from his own stolid background. Newfound confidence now tempered the insecurity and anxiety that had plagued him in the *Vogue* offices. Living in the haute bohemian Hôtel de Bourgogne, where the fashion journeyman Christian Dior would eventually join him, he dressed in tawny suits, beautiful ties, and shirts the color of aged ivory, and appeared in the pages of *Vogue*, dapper in a tail coat, poised and chatting with Bébé Bérard and Coco Chanel at opening nights. Self-assurance also engendered generosity of spirit—Geffroy notably coached Dior in his early forays into fashion and introduced him to Robert Piguet (with whom he had probably overlapped at Redfern) in 1937.

Perhaps owing to Patou's teetering uncertainty, Geffroy's pendulum swung back toward a variation on set design when his path crossed in the 1930s with Duc François-Charles d'Harcourt, a friend of Coco Chanel and Misia Sert. The meeting led to Harcourt's hiring of Geffroy for the decoration of his eighteenth-century *hôtel particulier* on the rue de Verneuil and, more importantly, to Geffroy's discovery of his true métier.

A respected connoisseur and descendant of three maréchals de France, the Duc d'Harcourt actively directed the decoration of his house, filling it with family Fragonards and Savonneries, while relying on Geffroy to help scout antiques. Geffroy's talent for visualizing the possibilities in the dustiest objects in the deepest recesses of a store impressed Harcourt, who quickly learned he could count on Geffroy's subtle eye and originality. Their collaboration, in addition to providing Geffroy with a connoisseur's tutelage and a first-rate entrée into the world of design, fostered a lifelong friendship.

Certainly, Geffroy, with his profound attachment to his own antiques, would bond with a man who reputedly responded to a doctor's orders to change beds with the question "Of which epoch?" Over the years, Geffroy informally advised Harcourt on the restoration and decoration of his château, Champ de Bataille, in Normandy. And when the duc remarried, Geffroy, the only outsider at an intimate family wedding, exhibited his unconventional taste in his choice of wedding present: a steel-gray meteorite, unassuming yet exquisite in its natural perfection. Over fifty years later, it still graces the collection of semiprecious stone eggs resting on a skirted table in the duchesse's salon.

Geffroy was emerging as a significant talent. Piguet hired Geffroy to design the private salon above his couture house at 3, rond-point des Champs-Élysées. Though not yet authoritative, the room, with its crimson screen in sharp contrast to spare white walls, tiger skin splayed on the emerald sofa, marble bust, and bronze Louis XIV gilt-wood bracket, was, nevertheless, distinctive and, via publication in *Images de France*,

OPPOSITE

Robert Piguet, who had run Redfern Paris until 1931, probably first met Geffroy when he, too, worked at the couture house. One of the first to recognize Geffroy's nascent talent as an interior designer, Piguet tapped Geffroy to design the private salon of his couture house. Elements of Geffroy's mature style—grand curtain treatments, references to antiquity, and tiger—are already apparent.

brought him into the public eye. In 1940 Geffroy designed the sets for a production of Richard Sheridan's *School for Scandal*, and Dior, then working at Piguet, designed the costumes. Several newspapers, and even *Vogue*, noted the visual production, citing the input of two relative unknowns, Dior and Geffroy. But the momentum that was gathering about Dior and Geffroy in their respective fields was soon interrupted—both men were summoned by the mobilizing army.

Unlike Geffroy's cushy first stint in the army, which consisted largely of home rest and hobnobbing with Max Jacob, his second experience was difficult, for his character was even less suited than his constitution to army life. Though the old lung issues remained at bay, and he was deemed technically fit for service, recurrent psychotic episodes required isolation. Demobilized after the Armistice of 1940, he was soon living in occupied Paris.

248, rue de Rivoli

Geffroy's acquisition of a mansard apartment at 248, rue de Rivoli was a positive note in a period of turmoil. The rue de Rivoli, a triumph of Napoleonic urban planning, features a uniform arcaded façade that runs from the place de la Concorde to the Louvre. Though the architectural elegance undoubtedly appealed to his aesthetics, the deciding factor for Geffroy was, by his own account, the view. The writer Robert de Saint-Jean, who acquired the apartment after Geffroy's death, describes the extraordinary calm of the apartment at night, with its panoramic view of the Louvre, the Seine, the spires of Sainte-Clotilde, the Tuileries, and the "willow giraffe" (Saint-Jean's poetic description of the Eiffel Tower). For the rest of his ambitious and hectic life, the small apartment was Geffroy's private oasis, as well as his personal stage set.

Though the architecture of the low-ceilinged mansard was less compelling than the view, Geffroy turned architectural defects into virtues. He knocked out walls to create a reception-size living room, replaced doors with portières to improve spatial flow, and further lowered the ceiling in the vestibule to make the salon and dining room ceilings seem higher in contrast. Wisely, he largely respected the inherent character of the apartment, retaining its plain moldings, hardwood floors, and the humble hexagonal terra-cotta tiles (*tomettes*) in the vestibule, saving extravagances of paneling and parquet de Versailles for the more noble spaces of his clients. The dining room, which had a number of awkwardly placed doors, posed a particular problem. Geffroy resolved it by lining the room in continuous glazed doors, adding faux doors where necessary. He backed each glazed panel with grenadine silk faille, creating a jewel-box effect that glittered at night with reflected candlelight. Even the many flights of stairs to the attic apartment served a useful purpose: they handily sorted out the fit from the laggards among Geffroy's potential beaux. The result was the mix of elegance, measure, and surprise that characterizes Geffroy's best work.

The traits of the Geffroy style coalesced in these early rooms. Despite the restrictive scale, he did not shy away from large statements. His furniture was Louis XVI with a swagger—not timid, late-reign furniture but confident Louis XVI pieces with gleaming mahogany veneers and emphatic ormolu mounts, which he deftly mixed with the architectural lines of Empire and Directoire pieces. Unexpected rugs, perhaps selected at the rue du Faubourg Saint-Honoré gallery of Geffroy's friend Sami Tarica, whose eye for modern art was as sharp as his nose for unusual rugs, added interest over the years. In decoration, Geffroy's emphasis was typically on public space. His own apartment was no exception; he lavished the reception rooms with antique furnishings and objects by Riesener, Pluvinet, Weisweiler, and Gouthière, collector's curios, tiger silk velvet, and exotic rugs. In contrast, the nominally decorated bedroom, with its exposed sink, narrow bed, and ungainly closets, seemed a monastic afterthought.

Though Geffroy's mansard apartment was modest, architectural sleight of hand transformed it into a showcase. With real and faux glazed doors backed by grenadine silk faille, his dining room became a symmetrical jewel box, illuminated only by candlelight.

Strapwork walls and ceiling dramatically encased the small entrance hall. Handsome bronze urns with ormolu mounts, resting on trompe l'oeil porphyry columns, created the illusion of height, while an Indo-Portuguese blue-and-white flatweave rug broke from the conventions of eighteenth-century French decoration. The dining room, too, had a cool, studied allure. A stone floor, blue silk tablecloth that complemented the grenadine door panels, and an exotic Bessarabian rug provided an understated background, while the unelectrified chandelier cast a candlelit glow and rose Sèvres porcelain provided an unexpected note of prettiness. Geffroy's godson, Nicolas Petitjean, recalls the impressive presence of an enormous, varnished tortoise shell in later years.

The relatively plain study—featuring a tall clock with case by Riesener and works by Bourdier, and a seating alcove lined in red-and-white-printed Indian cotton that neatly disguised an errant beam—was but a teaser to the pièce de résistance, the dramatic salon. Walls upholstered in a dark green satin-and-silk stripe and floors covered in chestnut wall-to-wall carpeting set the stage. Four mahogany x-frame stools, attributed to Demay, a mahogany sofa table, hanging shelves for displaying the collector's objects, a grand Weisweiler mahogany table à crémaillère (a clever eighteenth-century mechanism for adjusting table height), and a piano said to have been owned by Maurice Ravel anchored the furniture plan. Two sofas, one modern, the other a Louis XVI canapé, were partially covered in tiger silk velvet, with leopard velvet throw pillows.

Geffroy's penchant for animal-motif velvets, hand woven by Le Manach in Tours, is a prime example of how he and Victor Grandpierre transformed decorative traditions into signature elements of postwar design. Used for practical purposes in the eighteenth century—as acoustic insulation in the opera at Versailles, for instance—tiger and leopard came into decorative vogue after the Napoleonic campaigns in Egypt and Asia, with leopard carpeting lining the empress's boudoir in the Grand Trianon, and the skins, or facsimiles, covering benches and secondary seating elsewhere. Geffroy understood that his use of tiger and leopard silk velvet on the rue de Rivoli dovetailed with the apartment's late eighteenth- and early nineteenth-century neoclassical aesthetic, but he also exploited these exotic prints for their graphic qualities, covering deep sofas and down pillows alike in them. To this day, tiger and leopard silk velvet, as well as their lesser cousins, connote luxury and sophistication.

Though rigorously neoclassical, the salon managed to be inviting and warm. Pale blue silk on benches with scrolled arms glowed in the monochrome green room, relieved by occasional accents of neutral brown and oyster. A 1926 Bérard painting stood on an

BELOW
A small vestibule became a gracious entrance, with the assist of plaster strapwork. Counterintuitively, Geffroy dropped the ceiling so the moderate heights of adjacent rooms appeared taller. Towering faux-porphyry columns topped with elegant mounted bronze urns added to the illusion and contributed panache.

An alcove lined in an Indian cotton print disguised an awkward beam in Geffroy's study. Though the cozy room appears at first glance unpretentious, a desk by Riesener stands in the foreground and a bronze of Mercury by Jean Boulogne surveys the scene.

easel in a corner. Superb gilt-bronze objects—sconces modeled by Gouthière, andirons, candlesticks, an inkwell that had belonged to Talleyrand—and the mechanical mantel clock, emitting music and animation, a gift to Marie-Antoinette by the City of Paris on the birth of the Dauphin, added glamour and opulence to the modestly scaled but majestically appointed room. Its beauty was not just in the objects but in Geffroy's eye for proportion and assembly.

The apartment defined Geffroy. As a sort of personal vitrine, it showcased his culture and public persona. Naturally, it evolved as Geffroy evolved; over the years, his collection grew, and colors and fabrics were tweaked. Though it took him the better part of a decade to complete the architectural changes and assemble the nucleus of the furnishings, by 1941 the apartment was sufficiently polished to receive the admiration of the young aesthete Philippe Jullian. Shortly thereafter, *Vogue* published an article featuring its sassy interim blend of tiger velvet, tiny rugs, and an exposed trap ladder, and by the late 1940s, the apartment assumed its mature guise. As prestigious magazines covered each change of palette and addition of an important antique, Europeans, South Americans, and Americans seeking au courant models of French decorative chic

soon knew of Georges Geffroy. One stylish New York decorator, Natalie Davenport of McMillen, closely followed everything Geffroy created—and with good reason. His sharp eye put him steps ahead of others.

Geffroy's cocktail parties brought him further renown. Given the size of his apartment, these soirées were intimate—typically five or six guests, rarely more than eight. Frequency, however, made up for size: Geffroy, who loved being both a host and the center of the attention, entertained nearly every night in his jewel box, ably seconded by a housekeeper who was said to be the daughter of Proust's maid. Chatting lightly about his projects, lunch dates, and Paris activities, Geffroy stood throughout these evenings, circulating constantly with a lit Gitane in hand, pausing only to top off his whiskey or casually rest a knee on an eighteenth-century chair. Occasionally, invitations printed by society stationer Cassegrain would be issued, florists would hang garlands, jewels would come out of safes, and everyone, including the Duchess of Windsor, would mount the six flights of stairs to dance under the eaves.

Perpetual entertaining kept Geffroy abreast of new faces, fashions, and ideas. Jean Cocteau, Henri Sauguet, Philippe Jullian, Michel de Brunhoff, the Harcourts, Robert

ABOVE

The living room, site of the famous Geffroy cocktail gatherings, was filled with rigorous neoclassical furniture and contemporary art. A 1926 painting by Christian Bérard was displayed near the acclaimed Weisweiler table.

A QUEST FOR GRANDEUR ▓ 67

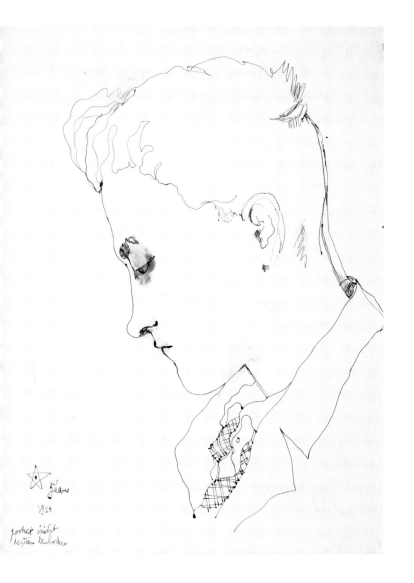

Ricci, Pierre Le-Tan, society photographer André Ostier, decorator-painter (and subject of Charles Aznavour's ballad "*Comme ils disent*") Androuchka Braunecker, and a mix of clients and *copains* turned up regularly with updates on *le tout Paris*, some of which would be of business interest to a decorator. When Geffroy met the newly arrived Jimmy Douglas, a friend of Barbara Hutton, he sniffed the makings of a good client and whisked him off immediately to see Baron de Redé's Hôtel Lambert. (And indeed, Geffroy landed the contract and designed a great apartment.) By the 1960s, friends recalled Geffroy's salon as essentially a men's club—although Iris Clert, the gallerist who exhibited Yves Klein, Jean Tinguely, and Robert Rauschenberg on the rue des Beaux-Arts, made occasional flamboyant appearances, and Geffroy's neighbor, Arlette Ricci, a granddaughter of Nina Ricci, would pop in from time to time.

Though fond of gossip, witty, and savvy, Geffroy was discreet, kindhearted, and even, perhaps, slightly sad. One young guest noticed that on the rare occasions when he stopped holding court, a fleeting expression of regret would register on his face. He also seemed loath to be alone. By the 1960s, as a party dwindled, Geffroy would invariably scoop up the last stragglers and invite them to dinner at a restaurant.

Conspicuously absent from this world of repartee and style was Geffroy's family. Even Marguerite, the one sister who had strayed off bourgeois course to marry Charles Soudant, a society sculptor who spent the 1920s casting custom Art Deco automobile hood ornaments (such was the affluence of the decade) and would later create the commemorative stele to Resistance fighters in the Luxembourg Gardens, was not in attendance. Nevertheless, family ties remained discreetly intact; though his mother continued to live on the rue Hippolyte-Lebas, she died in Geffroy's apartment during the war. Whether Geffroy had nursed his mother through a chronic illness or her death occurred unexpectedly in the course of a visit is not known.

Other enigmas crept in during the war. With headquarters for the German Occupation at the Hôtel Meurice just a few blocks away, stories—some, perhaps, apocryphal—circulated about shady visits from powerful Germans. After the Normandy landings in June 1944, the apartment sheltered Resistance leader Jean Desbordes, the sensual poet, playwright, and former lover of Jean Cocteau. War had transformed Desbordes into a disciplined organizer of intelligence along the coast of Normandy and in the airfields of Cherbourg that was critical to the success of the Allied landings. After D-Day, though now a marked man, Desbordes continued his intelligence work in Paris, while hiding in the rue de Rivoli apartment. In July, at age thirty-five, Desbordes was—depending on the narrator—arrested either in Geffroy's apartment or near the Madeleine, and tortured to death by French auxiliaries of the Gestapo. The details of his interrogation were gruesome, but Desbordes, heroically, never divulged a word or a name. Coincidentally, two other Resistance fighters, Dr. Charles Berlioz, Geffroy's cousin, and Dior's sister Catherine were arrested on the same day. The task fell to Berlioz, as a doctor, to certify the death. Though Geffroy's war record remains ambiguous, Desbordes's name is engraved in the Pantheon, resting place of heroes.

Beauties and Bookcases

The Liberation of Paris meant, happily, the reopening of embassies. When the new British ambassador, historian, author, roué, and statesman Duff Cooper arrived at his embassy, he was enchanted by the stately eighteenth-century Hôtel de Charost but noted it lacked a library. To address this shortcoming, he offered to donate 1,500 of his own books if the British Foreign Service's Office of Works would in turn foot the bill for converting his sitting room into a library. He reckoned that it would cost 1,000 pounds sterling. When the staff architect proposed a design of cost-effective, utilitarian bookcases and a boxy modern sofa, Duff and Lady Diana paused; they wanted the books housed in a beautiful setting that suited the gold-and-white splendor of the Hôtel de Charost. They turned to an old friend, Charles de Beistegui, owner of the Château de Groussay, for advice on how to achieve something a little more stylish. Beistegui—a master of ambience, brilliant at creating assemblages in which overall effect trumped individual objects, and designer of his own superb library—had a vigorous aesthetic that favored perfect proportions, bold profiles, large objects, and strong colors. He, the top tastemaker in Paris at the time, recommended an up-and-coming designer: Georges Geffroy. The loyal Lady Diana would acknowledge Geffroy's role in designing the library, but always considered her friend Beistegui, who lent a guiding eye to the project, its true creator.

The assertive architectural style of the library anticipated Geffroy's emerging chic. The similarities between Geffroy and Beistegui are also apparent. Both emphasized character and unity over mere loveliness, a sophisticated approach that endeared them to trendsetters like Diana Cooper, if not to the sentimental. In a time characterized by theatricality and invention, including a string of famous and fanciful costume balls, the library, like Beistegui's at Château de Groussay, has the air of a stage set. As in his own apartment, Geffroy dexterously manipulated scale, accentuating the library's ceiling height with bookcases that rise to the cornice. The contours of the slim colonettes, recalling those at Malmaison but in fact inspired by a room Beistegui greatly admired, the Grand Ducal bedroom at Tsarskoe Selo by architect Charles Cameron, counter the library's angularity.

After the Liberation, everyone was weary of gray dilapidation and thirsted for luxury—or at least the appearance of it. Although materials were scarce and hard to come by, Geffroy achieved grand effects using inexpensive materials and special-effects painting. Faux-bois panels and stucco colonettes simulating Cuban mahogany, highlighted with gilded bases, moldings, and stylized Ionic capitals, stand out against an ivory ground. The mirror over the mantel adds visual width to the room. Underscoring the theatricality of the room, the hollow colonettes make no pretense of supporting the weighty entablature, on the ledge of which papier-mâché urns and busts, imitating basalt, alternate rhythmically. False book spines camouflage a jib door. Their titles—

Jean Cocteau's poet protégé, the lovely young Jean Desbordes, was transformed by war into a Résistance hero whose service to his country is commemorated in the Pantheon. Though Geffroy hid him in his apartment, Geffroy's involvement with Desbordes— and the war—remains murky.

LEFT

For the acclaimed design
of the library at the British
Embassy in Paris, Georges
Geffroy implemented the
vision of Charles de Beistegui,
added some flair of his own,
and launched, with Grandpierre
at Dior, postwar decorating.
Christian Bérard advised
on the soft furnishings. The
project established Geffroy
as a talent to watch.

Experiments in Medicine by C. Borgia; *Fun and Frolic* by John Stuart Mill—are as clever as the concealed door itself and were probably the personal contribution of the ambassador. Above the two primary passage doors are bas-relief medallions of former owners of the Hôtel de Charost, Pauline Borghese and the Duke of Wellington. Contributing to the richness, gilt fringe edges the bookshelves; although the books are beautifully bound, none of them is turned showily outward, an ostentation that Beistegui despised.

Christian Bérard, who had turned the ambassadress's bathroom into a trompe l'oeil striped tent, selected the rug and the dark green velvet curtains with black banding, and arranged the green leather sofa, two chairs, and a desk believed to have belonged to the Duke of Wellington. The desk lamp and the clock were signed by Thomire. The gilded inscription commemorating Duff Cooper in Latin on the entablature, composed by Patrick Leigh Fermor and André de Staercke with Diana Cooper, was added in 1958. Beistegui selected the font for the lettering. A rug with the monogram of Elizabeth II at its center, needlepointed by Lady Gladwyn Jebb, Madame Pol Roger, and other friends of the Coopers, appeared in 1960 but is no longer in the room.

Geffroy, whose objective was uncompromised perfection, was indifferent to budgets. Even with the use of inexpensive materials, the final cost ran to more than twice the estimate. (No doubt the lavish gilding was the culprit.) Nobody seemed to care except the accountants. The smashing room, completed in early 1946, functioned exactly as Duff and Diana Cooper had intended, contributing to the embassy's place-to-be allure and attracting the likes of Gaston Palewski, Louise de Vilmorin, Noël Coward, Jean Cocteau, Georges Auric, and Cecil Beaton.

Acquiring ever-more-lustrous connections and associations with tastemakers such as the Duc d'Harcourt, Charles de Beistegui, and Christian Bérard, Geffroy further burnished his reputation when Marcel Rochas, the preeminent couturier of the 1940s, and his young wife, Hélène, commissioned him to design their home, an apartment with a garden that looked out on the dome of Les Invalides over a screen of trees on the rue Barbet-de-Jouy. An exquisite canvas for any decorator, in Geffroy's hands the apartment became a prism of light, charm, restraint, and exceptional furniture. Though hired in 1944, he seems to have worked slowly and deliberately, for the home was not featured in a magazine until 1948.

Space and a sense of calm pervaded the Rochas home. The rooms were neither overdecorated nor overloaded with furniture. The walls of the reception rooms were creamy white. In the salon, Geffroy placed two terra-cotta busts by Carpeaux on their original pedestals to either side of a divan upholstered in gold velvet with a ruched skirt. The divan was flanked symmetrically by gilded chairs that were covered in a green tone-on-tone striped fabric and separated by Empire-style gueridons. Slightly exotic, probably Russian, their finely detailed ormolu bandings were studded with porcelain cameos. Yellow curtains were drawn back simply to highlight views of the garden. The dining room was controlled and elegant, with English mahogany furniture and plain eighteenth-century silver.

With Geffroy, who was observed wearing makeup, appearances could be deceptive. Having succeeded in pulling off masterly sleight of hand in the design of Duff Cooper's library, he continued his flirtation with trompe l'oeil on the rue Barbet-de-Jouy. The

OPPOSITE

Geffroy's first high-visibility project after Duff Cooper's library was the home of Marcel and Hélène Rochas, where his strong style and use of antiques gained confidence. Rochas's handsome bedroom, with sober lines and rich, dark colors, reflected Geffroy's infatuation with trompe l'oeil. When describing the apartment and its designer, socialite playwright Jean-Pierre Gredy quipped that Geffroy invented the Louis XVII style.

walls of Marcel Rochas's bedroom, which appeared to be upholstered in a vibrant red, navy, and green imberline stripe, were actually laboriously hand painted. Towers of books flanking an inky fireplace supplied character; glints of gold on frames, andirons, and lamps added glamour. Furnishing the room with a red upholstered and tufted bed, a Bessarabian rug, an Empire chandelier, and a caned Louis XVI chair with a perfectly placed plaid throw over one arm, Geffroy provided the era's preeminent couturier with a moody, masculine retreat.

Geffroy further explored illusion in Hélène Rochas's bedroom. Inspired by the scenic wallpapers of Zuber, but not content with imagery that did not conform to the architecture of the room, Geffroy directed artisans to paint similar panels—in a shade of blue matching the eyes of *la belle Hélène*—that perfectly corresponded to the room's dimensions. With the exception of clean-lined mahogany pieces (bedside tables, bergères *en gondole*, a rolltop desk with handsome bronze ornamentation, a nineteenth-century cheval glass and Viennese occasional table), everything else in the room was pale white and gray, from the wainscoting and upholstery to the satin bed dressings on the *lit à la polonaise*. Of note was the similarity of the desk, once believed to be by Roentgen, to one at Beistegui's Château de Groussay.

Hélène Rochas's celestial bedroom. Exceptional in its calm, beauty, color, and originality, it represents Geffroy's first masterpiece. Rochas lived in this apartment to the end of her life, and though she redecorated it over the years, she kept much of the furniture that Geffroy had selected for it.

Subtly in some instances, less subtly in others, Geffroy decorated the Rochas apartment with virtuosity and originality. Hélène Rochas prized his selection of antiques and held on to most of them for the rest of her life; indeed, many appeared in the 2012 auction catalogue of her estate at Christie's. Expert assessment, however, called their significance into question. Pieces that had been identified in a 1948 *Plaisir de France* article as by Roentgen, Jacob, and Pluvinet were downgraded by Christie's to more obscure workshops, or, in the case of the Jacob chairs, merely attributed to the maker. Geffroy's misidentifications might be explained in part by the fact that his celebrated connoisseurship was still in formation when he decorated the Rochas apartment. Another possible explanation is that the avid demand for eighteenth-century furniture after the war resulted in a marketplace of antiques with dubious provenances and hasty attributions that were credulously snapped up by buyers—Rochas and Geffroy, apparently, among them. In any case, the beauty of the flat was in its embodiment of the Beistegui principle that overall composition takes precedence over any individual element.

After the war ended, Paris slowly drifted back to life, luring the Duchess of Windsor, Pamela Harriman, and other internationals. Bettina Ballard returned in 1946 from her post with the Red Cross, surprised to find Geffroy very different from the wan man Michel de Brunhoff had desperately tried to hold back from the precipice. No longer a forlorn observer, he had transformed into a prosperous decorator with social stature and a flat filled with signed eighteenth-century furniture. Now in the know, he introduced the new It Girl, Gloria Rubio (soon to be Princess Fahkry Bey and later Mrs. Loel Guinness), to Ballard, who quickly had her photographed for *Vogue*. When the decorator Elsie de Wolfe (Lady Mendl) invited Geffroy (and Grandpierre) to lunch at Le Grand Véfour to celebrate her return to Paris, Geffroy met Baron Alexis de Redé, a fellow aficionado of eighteenth-century fantasies, newly arrived from New York, in the entourage of Arturo and Patricia López-Willshaw.

For his new pal Redé, Geffroy created a princely suite at the Hôtel Meurice (see page 19). Upholstered walls, window curtains, and a pillowed divan, all in the same red damask velvet, provided a cohesive framework in the drawing room. Gilt fringe on the valance, Louis XV armchairs upholstered in gold gauffraged velvet, and a carved Louis XV console added splendor, while a low table with a metal base and witty trompe l'oeil surface of scattered playing cards lightened the grandeur. Behind the gilt-wood console Geffroy parted the damask curtains to reveal a framed mirror, a device he would use to dramatic effect several years later for Gloria Guinness. Like Geffroy, Redé must have appreciated the view overlooking the Tuileries, for a handsome telescope had pride of place on the table.

Though rarely associated with the literary world, Geffroy exploited his connections and talent to surprising effect to conceive and edit the privately printed *Calendrier des Dames pour 1947*. Underwritten by Marcel Rochas, the book was intended as both a Christmas gift for Rochas clients and a fundraiser for postwar charities. (Presumably the book was sold in the Rochas boutique.) Following, very loosely, the format of a daily prayer book, each month is introduced by a drawing of a prominent Parisian beauty accompanied by a profile penned by an illustrious writer. Geffroy drew lavishly on his acquaintances to assemble the book, whose subjects included the Baronne de Cabrol, the Duchesse d'Harcourt, Madame Jean Larivière, and Princesse Edmond de Polignac. Though it may not have been difficult to convince women to allow themselves to be

OPPOSITE

In 1946 Geffroy conceived and executed the book *Calendrier des Dames pour 1947* for Marcel Rochas. The project exemplifies Geffroy's versatility and culture, as well as the prevailing fluidity of exchange across the arts. One coup was the page dedicated to the Comtesse de Beaumont, which dazzled with text by Cocteau and illustration by Picasso.

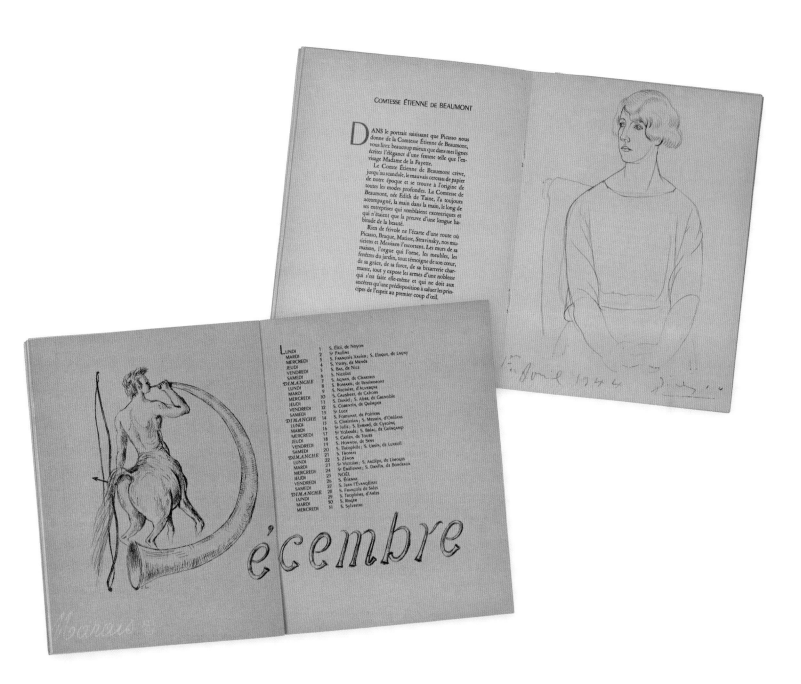

praised in print, getting artists and writers on board for the project, most likely on a pro bono basis, was more challenging. Nevertheless, Geffroy enlisted an impressive roster of contributing writers (including Jean Cocteau, Princesse Bibesco, Louise de Vilmorin, and Denise Bourdet) and artists (Christian Bérard, Pablo Picasso, André Derain, Étienne Drian, Leonor Fini, and Kees van Dongen, among others). Every bit as much as the showy names in the table of contents, the book design reflects Geffroy's finesse. Given the economic and material limitations of the time, the fine quality of the printing and heavy paper stock is impressive. Drawings for the title page and figured initial capital letters were by the Franco-Italian artist Stanislao Lepri. While the graphic design takes its cues from the sun-in-splendor motif—the manifestation of Louis XIV—the Bauhaus-influenced font by Cassandre and Peignot is assuredly modern. It was also prescient. Twenty years later Cassandre would design the logo for Yves Saint Laurent.

Henri grandpierre
avec Coluca   Aline   moi
adrien

AN AESTHETIC ODYSSEY

Victor Grandpierre, 1906~1946

While Dior was happily ensconced in the 16th arrondissement, Victor Grandpierre was growing up across the Champs-Élysées in somewhat more unusual circumstances. Though Victor bore a physical resemblance to his father, the architect and society darling Henri Grandpierre, he never knew him. Born in 1856 to a carpenter in Suippes, Henri Grandpierre moved to Paris and made his way in society through his charm and wit, not unlike Balzac's hero Rastignac. He first practiced an earnest form of architecture, traveling to England to study workers' lodgings, publishing tracts on housing reform, and building attractive, inexpensive houses in Auteuil that earned him the accolade "architect of the future." By 1890, Grandpierre Frères was a thriving architectural practice in Paris and, probably through a combination of talent, natural inclinations, and superb social contacts, Henri and his brother began receiving Beaux-Arts and neoclassical commissions in up-and-coming areas of Paris—particularly the 16th arrondissement and the area around the Parc Monceau—as well as farther afield in Berlin and Buenos Aires, where they no doubt contributed to the city's reputation as "the Paris of South America."

There were also projects for such artists as Caran d'Ache and Henri Gervex, for Henri Grandpierre, like his son, mixed easily in bohemian circles. In fact, it was his work for the singer Jean de Reszke and the painter Jean-Louis Forain that brought him to the attention of Winnaretta Singer (Princesse Edmond de Polignac, Singer sewing machine heiress, humanitarian, painter, and music patroness, as well as the aunt who would raise Daisy Fellowes) and led to his best-known commission, the Hôtel Singer-Polignac, designed specifically to host the princess's musical and artistic receptions. Its façade, featuring a series of Ionic pilasters, echoes the neoclassical configurations of Alexandre-Théodore Brongniart (1739-1813), the architect of the Paris Bourse and guiding light of Henri Grandpierre. The music room, with grisaille murals by José Maria Sert (painted after Grandpierre's death) and windows that could be covered with sliding mirrors as in the Queen's Boudoir in the Petit Trianon (see page 15), welcomed Stravinsky, Satie, Fauré, and Cole Porter. Completed in 1904, the house on the avenue Georges-Mandel represented one of the last grand aristocratic commissions in Paris and, for Victor Grandpierre, a treasured legacy from his father. Colleagues recalled that Grandpierre would point out the house whenever he passed its limestone façade.

In the Old World manner, Henri Grandpierre's architectural practice was located in his townhouse on the rue Offremont, just around the corner from Sarah Bernhardt's home and conveniently on the flat Plaine Monceau, which lent itself to the fashionable new sport, cycling. Grandpierre raced competitively with the aristocratic Cercle d'Omnium, known as the Jockey Club of the cycling set. As a dapper bachelor, his race results peppered the daily papers along with notices of his comings and goings in London, Cannes, Barcelona, and Paris, where he was spotted mingling with society painter Giovanni Boldini, the Duc de Montmorency, and the comtes de La Rochefoucauld at openings and receptions.

It was therefore hardly surprising that on Valentine's Day 1906, *Le Figaro* noted the wedding in Cannes of "the distinguished Parisian architect" Monsieur Henri Grandpierre, 49, to Mademoiselle Floarea (Florence) Suditu, aged 27, of Bucharest, daughter of Monsieur Jean Suditu, Romanian senator. Little is known about the much younger bride, how the couple met, or the Suditu family, except that they were part of the Romanian establishment, had social connections with the Bibesco clan, seemed to live off the income from their lands, and traveled en masse to Cannes that winter. When signing the wedding register, the bride's brother Victor Suditu casually described himself as without occupation. The bride's second witness was her brother-in-law, a member of the Romanian parliament. Henri's best man was Rêné Gilbert, portraitist of Paul Verlaine.

On April 17, 1906, barely unpacked from his honeymoon in Venice, Henri Grandpierre died at home. In contrast to his wedding, his death received perfunctory notices, for the concurrent San Francisco earthquake and death of Pierre Curie dominated the news. Florence Grandpierre quickly vacated the townhouse off the Parc

Victor Grandpierre, fresh faced and well dressed (center), in the country visiting Emilio Terry (right) at the Château de Rochecotte with Henri de Castellane (left), accompanied by the ever-faithful Coluca and Pline. Notably, Terry, the great neoclassicist of his generation, named his dog after Pliny the Younger.

OPPOSITE

Henri Grandpierre's neoclassical townhouse for Winnaretta Singer (Princesse Edmond de Polignac) was purpose-built for her musical salons. Over the years, Princesse de Polignac hosted performances by Igor Stravinsky, Francis Poulenc, Gabriel Fauré, and Reynoldo Hahn (trailed by his romantic interest, Marcel Proust). Her salons—both in Paris and in her palazzo in Venice—attracted an artistic elite that included Jean Cocteau, Claude Monet, Serge Diaghilev, and Colette.

Monceau but, pluckily resisting the comfort of Bucharest and family, elected to stay on, alone, in Paris. On November 24, 1906—a scant thirty-six weeks after the wedding—Henri Louis Jean Victor Grandpierre was born in a Haussmannian building with tall arched windows at 1, rue Lincoln, just south of the Champs-Élysées. Though officially named after his father, the child would be known throughout his life as Victor, the name of his mother's idle, and presumably favorite, brother. Perhaps for sentimental reasons, Victor, as an adult, used his father's initial, "H," as his sole middle initial.

Madame Grandpierre raised her son with propriety at 2, avenue de Friedland, a broad Haussmannian boulevard that begins at the Arc de Triomphe and ends at the rue du Faubourg Saint-Honoré. Close to the carousel and winding paths of the Parc Monceau, the apartment was well located for raising a family and also appropriately bourgeois—a stone's throw from the grand private home of Salomon de Rothschild—for a widow of personal means but standing on ambiguous social terrain. After all, Madame Grandpierre had been living in Paris for less than a year and widowed so quickly after her marriage that she could hardly have been introduced, let alone integrated, into her husband's circles. Further, the breakneck succession of marriage, death, and birth, traumatic in itself, veiled her in a cloud of mystery, if not doubt.

Proper breeding and a liberal education—which upper-class Romanians provided as a matter of course to their daughters as well as their sons—seems to have stood Florence Grandpierre in good stead as a mother. In 1929, her slender, blue-eyed son, age twenty-three, finished his studies and embarked on his compulsory military service at Saint-Cyr, where his tidy record in the meteorology unit included two promotions and a citation for good conduct, indications of conscientiousness and reliability. By the time he finished his service in 1932, the Grandpierres were living, perhaps rather grandly, at the foot of the Arc de Triomphe at 47, avenue de Friedland. Victor, putting his cosmopolitan background, language skills, and diligence to good use, worked as a hotelier.

Certainly, Victor Grandpierre, discreet, calm, and elegant, would have been perfectly cast as the manager of the Ritz. But he soon apparently had a change of heart and lifestyle. Like his father, he was drawn into the orbit of Singer sewing machine heiresses. By 1933, at the age of twenty-six, he was living in the faubourg Saint-Germain on the rue de Bellechasse with Daisy Fellowes's daughter Emmeline de Broglie (the one Daisy described as like her first husband, only more masculine) and her newlywed husband, the Comte de Castéja. What Grandpierre was doing there, exactly, or how long he lived on the rue de Bellechasse, is not very clear. Perhaps his natural diplomacy made him a buffer zone: the bride had been nearly an hour late for the wedding, and the groom looked less than overjoyed in the wedding photographs. Paris *Vogue* captured the Comtesse de Castéja, in a hat from the milliner Talbot, jauntily bicycling in tandem with Victor Grandpierre in the Bois de Boulogne. He, equally natty, sports a boutonnière.

I Am a Camera

The economically lethargic decade of the 1930s posed a challenge for young people like Christian Dior, Georges Geffroy, and Victor Grandpierre who had multiple interests but no preordained course to follow, and latent talents still to discover. Grandpierre resourcefully tried his hand as a freelance journalist and photographer, an undertaking

OPPOSITE
A bicycle built for two—or three. Somewhat ambiguously, Victor Grandpierre lived on the rue de Bellechasse with the recently married Comte and Comtesse de Castéja (she a daughter of Daisy Fellowes). In the Bois de Boulogne, the Comtesse waves a gloved hand while Grandpierre imperturbably smiles under his Panama hat.

Victor Grandpierre captured the sweep, splendor, and subtleties of a royal tiger hunt, outfitted with teak, tents, and dhurries for *Vogue*. In addition to manicured and braceleted huntresses and liveried attendants, Grandpierre's lens memorialized the dead tiger (images omitted here), capturing Princess Brinda, Tikarani of Kapurthala, with one triumphant foot on the carcass. Another image shows pith-helmeted hunters surrounding their fallen prey like vultures.

that leveraged his bourgeois good manners and acquaintance with *le tout Paris*. Handily, writing and photography also provided opportunities to observe grand rooms and the grand manner.

At age twenty-seven, Victor Grandpierre went off to India to interview Edwin Bourbon—a descendant of a branch of the House of Bourbon that had established itself in India in the sixteenth century and served as nawabs for Mughals and princes—for *Le Jour* and to document a last-gasp-of-the-Raj tiger hunt for *Vogue*. His photos, vividly capturing slain tigers, maharanis, manicured English huntresses, marquis tents with dhurrie rugs and neoclassical folding chairs (teak models that Georges Geffroy would have coveted), caparisoned elephants, and private railroad cars, were both a chronicle and an indictment. In his off hours, he ordered a bespoke Hindu jacket. Returning to Paris in 1935, Grandpierre donned his new jacket, adorned it with a necklace of roses, and attended a party given by Daisy Fellowes, where Bébé Bérard, Coco Chanel, Cecil Beaton, and Misia Sert smoked nargilehs and applauded cabaret entertainer Bricktop and her trademark cigars.

All the while, Madame Grandpierre, like Maurice and Madeleine Dior, must have been wringing her hands. But like Dior, Grandpierre was acquiring an important education. As he refined his eye and facets of his artistry, he intersected with the talents who would define postwar culture and the patrons who would shape his own career.

Granted, for a few years parties seemed to take precedence over professional pursuits. But he was not yet thirty, curious to experience the world, and frequently pressed into duty as an extra man at dinner parties given by the Prince and Princesse de Faucigny-Lucinge (for whom he would later decorate) and at the Sporting Club in Monte Carlo alongside Daisy Fellowes and the Princesse de Polignac (one wonders if she, his father's patroness, told him stories about his father).

Indeed, for several years after he returned from India, Victor Grandpierre was in constant motion, appearing in Monte Carlo, Cannes, Deauville, and Venice. The press mentioned him with Lady Mendl, Lady Cunard, Barbara Hutton, the Pol Rogers, Baron Nicolas "Niki" de Gunzburg, and Lord Cholmondeley. Attracted to the arts, like his father, he also rubbed shoulders, however gently, with Édouard Bourdet, playwright and director of the Comédie-Française, writer-diplomat Paul Morand, and art patron Charles de Noailles. He and surrealist poet René Crevel found themselves fellow houseguests of the Comte and Comtesse Jean de Polignac at the Château de Kerbastic in Brittany. Coupling social acumen with photographic skills, Grandpierre whipped off a series of portraits and profiles of socialites for Lucien Vogel's *Le Jardin des modes*, captured Daisy Fellowes on her boat, crisp in a simple shipmate's hat, and documented the season in Venice for *Vogue*. At the Lido, Grandpierre turned his lens from bored Americans to haute bohemians, recording Coco Chanel in poor-boy hat and iconic

LEFT

Dance to the music of his time: Bewigged and beribboned, Grandpierre (far right) attended Étienne de Beaumont's 1939 Racine Ball, in an entrée that included Madame Arturo López-Willshaw (center, with white flowered neckline). In the foreground are two professional dancers.

OVERLEAF

Left: Daisy Fellowes, described by Cecil Beaton as exuding an air of just coming off a yacht, was photographed by Grandpierre for *Vogue* aboard the smaller of her two boats. Right: For *Vogue* Grandpierre also photographed Chanel relaxing at the Lido on Roussy Sert's boat, dressed in what appears to be a dhoti, and showcasing her flair for wearing jewelry at any time of day.

earrings aboard Roussy Sert's yacht. The newspapers chronicling the parties attended by Grandpierre simultaneously blazoned headlines about the Spanish Civil War, Hitler's massing of an army, and Charles Lindbergh in self-exile.

As the decade progressed, Grandpierre's sensibility shifted. It must have been obvious to a young man of serious—albeit well-concealed—disposition that the days of frequenting posh watering holes were numbered. Now in his thirties, Grandpierre focused increasingly on work. Gossip-column mentions dwindled as his reputation as a photographer grew. His inclusion in a photography exhibit alongside Jacques-Henri Lartigue, Hubert de Segonzac, and André Ostier attests to his professional stature. He tested, too, the waters of fashion photography, where his interest in the visual environment remained as evident as in his photos of tiger hunts in India. In a 1939 photo of a Creed sports ensemble shot for *L'Officiel de la couture et de la mode*, Grandpierre's lens explored the contours of the park-like setting as closely as the lines of the featured skirt and coat, foreshadowing his future work.

Theatrics in the Free Zone

Though Grandpierre was in the army reserves, military records provide no details of service before the Armistice of 1940. During the Occupation, however, it is known that Grandpierre lived in Cannes, in the Free Zone. Actors were also swarming into Cannes, buoyed by hopes that the Parisian film industry would relocate there. With so many members of the acting community around him, Grandpierre became involved in theater, an art form that would further influence his eye—and provide a meeting with Christian Dior.

Teaming up with the actor, director, and impresario Marc Doelnitz, Grandpierre organized amateur theatricals for the displaced actors. Their de facto stage was the studio of exiled Parisian painter Édouard MacAvoy, a friend of Dior. As Dior habitually stopped by the painter's studio after a day of selling his produce in Cannes, Grandpierre and Dior's paths naturally crossed. In this climate of uncertainty and artistic bonhomie, the two men formed a long-term friendship, tacitly bound by a shared refinement, breeding (what Dior described as "the right tradition"), artistic sensibility, and nostalgia for the Belle Époque, which could only have looked more civilized and beautiful in the dark light of war. Auspiciously, Grandpierre mentioned his nascent interest in interior design to Dior.

Other forms of drama surfaced in 1941, when Grandpierre, now director of a conference series in Cannes, booked André Gide for a lecture on the drug-inspired surrealist Henri Michaux. Deeming Gide a degenerate freethinker, right-wing Vichyists lobbied to cancel the lecture. Left-leaning literary lions André Malraux and Roger Martin du Gard fired back, arguing for freedom of expression. *Le Figaro* picked up the story, triggering a *cause célèbre* that resulted in a packed conference room, pointed comments by Gide on a unified France, constant interruptions of applause, and—the ultimate triumph—the resignation in protest of 160 members of the reactionary Légion Française des Combattants.

By the spring of 1942, with the conference series behind him, Grandpierre entered the circle of Agnès Capri. A singer associated with Le Boeuf sur le toit in Paris, Capri was mounting a revue with the choreographer Michel Savitzky of the Ballets de Diaghilev [*sic*] and composers Henri Sauguet, Francis Poulenc, and Georges Auric that would appear in Monte Carlo, Nice, and Marseilles. She cast Grandpierre in a piece by Jean Anouilh and in his own cameo, "Victor Makes Postcards." Even more significantly, Grandpierre worked on sets. And whether sketching, painting drops, or sourcing props, he became initiated into the mysteries, magic, and nuts and bolts of translating visions into reality.

Despite the excitement of new ventures and literary controversies, the war demoralized Grandpierre. Like Dior, he connected with the neo-humanism in the paintings of Christian Bérard, and it was to Bérard, incidentally another half orphan and architect's son, that he confided his existential angst. Though Bérard radiated friendliness and was adored by all, he was swept up in a maelstrom of parties, theatrical design, fashion sketching, and bad habits that barely left time for his own painting, let alone tending to melancholy friends. Grandpierre's letters to Bérard, often addressed to Bérard's partner, Boris Kochno, as well, leave a rare record of his emotions. He wrote of paintings that had moved him. He regretted he could not show Bérard and Kochno his maquette for the Auric ballet he was designing for Agnès Capri. He forwarded his poems for their critique. Most of all, he longed for news of them, for contact, but Bérard, evidently, was not much of a letter writer.

In July 1942, a photographic assignment provided an occasion for Grandpierre to see Bérard and Kochno. In a stylish act of defiance against the approaching Third Reich, Comtesse Lily Pastré planned a one-night production of *A Midsummer Night's Dream*, followed by a ball the next evening at her Château de Montredon near Marseille. The evening has become legend: Kochno directed, Bérard designed, Jacques Ibert composed the music, and Stravinsky's niece made the costumes. Textiles being scarce in wartime, Lily Pastré stripped antique fabric from her walls to use for the costumes. By early summer, Kochno and Bérard were in residence at Montredon, engrossed in mounting the production. Grandpierre, who knew the countess, arrived with his camera to document the undertaking. His haunting portrait of Bérard, seated on the floor amid scattered designs; his stills of Titania and Oberon in the land of enchantment; and his photos of ingénue fairies, including the very young Edmonde Charles-Roux, at the post-performance ball bear witness to the extraordinary event.

As Lily Pastré had intuited, the Free Zone collapsed soon thereafter—in the fall of 1942. Cannes no longer a sanctuary, Grandpierre returned to Paris and photography, settling into an apartment at 70, rue Bonaparte. Romania, which had joined the Axis in

1940, was cut off from communication, and he was anxious for news about his extended family. Learning that Princesse Bibesco, a friend of his aunt whom he had met in the past at the Polignacs' salon, was in town, he contacted her in hopes of getting updates from Bucharest. The princesse's response has not survived.

Artistic *Tout Paris*

After the Liberation of Paris, Grandpierre could be found lunching at the British Embassy with Diana and Duff Cooper (and at least once with Cecil Beaton), as well as at the ambassador's country house in Chantilly, where it is likely that he met the writer and enchantress Louise de Vilmorin, whose family business produced the seed catalogues that had mesmerized the young Christian Dior. By 1945, Grandpierre and the writer were cozily collaborating on a project that combined her poetry with his photography. With his camera, Grandpierre transformed random, sometimes kitsch, objects into still lifes molded by half-lights and shadows. Louise, famous for her charm and originality, composed surreal poems about the inner life of the objects for each photograph. They published their collaboration in the form of two clamshell boxes with marbleized boards, each containing thirty gilt-edged Bristol boards. Each heavy-stock board featured a sculptural photograph and an accompanying poem. Individually numbered and privately distributed, 255 sets were printed. Three of the sets are held in libraries in Paris, London, and Los Angeles; the other 252 are either lost or still in private hands.

For the April 1946 issue of a worldly new magazine, *Art et Style*, Grandpierre demonstrated his skill as an illustrator, producing a stylish cover of coral and teal ornamentation surrounding a sculptural masque on a matte black background. Reflecting once again the intimacy of the Parisian artistic world, this issue included articles by the Princesse Bibesco and Louise de Vilmorin and listed Boris Kochno as art director. For the next issue, Grandpierre produced an eleven-page photo essay on the rue Jacob, including a photo of the Temple de l'Amitié, the Directoire temple appropriated by American ex-pat Natalie Barney for her twentieth-century salon. In taming light to sculpt bark, skim peeling columns, and record the inscription on the architrave, "L'Amitié," Grandpierre composed an elegy to time past in a postwar photo. The awareness of vulnerability and beauty that underlies the postwar moment, as well as the work of both Grandpierre and Dior, crystallizes in this image.

But Grandpierre, while moved by the past, was a full participant in the present. He was, after all, the son of the architect whose 1894 renovation of the theater La Cigale, famous as the stage of Maurice Chevalier, Mistinguett, and productions financed by Étienne de Beaumont, included a state-of-the-art hydraulic lift that allowed the orchestra pit to be raised and lowered. He turned to writing once again to analyze architecture, interiors, and the context of home and occupant. Soon after the photo essay on the rue Jacob, he wrote and photographed a story for *Vogue* on Nohant, the country house of George Sand. For the March–April 1947 issue of *Vogue*, he profiled the Saint-Tropez fisherman's house designed by Philippe Tallien, the architect who would solicit government funding to preserve the war-scarred village. (This funding, combined with the arrival of Brigitte Bardot, secured Saint-Tropez's status as an haute bohemian mecca.) It is clear from the text and photos, which frame the façade of Tallien's house as reverentially

Le domino domina autant d'hommes
Que l'écarté écarta d'économes.

Je suis une dame timide.
Ne me regardez pas ainsi.
J'ai perdu ma beauté limpide
Dans un séjour, non loin d'ici
Dont le climat est fort humide.

as that of the Temple de l'Amitié, that Grandpierre admired the unconventional mix of terra-cotta and plaster, canvas, and Victorian furniture amid the scent of tar. At about the same time that Grandpierre was compiling his story on Tallien, Christian Dior was negotiating the lease for the building that would house his *maison de couture*.

For more than a dozen years Grandpierre had observed, composed, photographed, and analyzed environments. At Dior's request, he would soon turn his knowledge and skills to interior design. By drawing on the vocabulary of pilasters and pastels, cascades of silk and hand-span waists, good manners and fine craftsmanship to underscore the accomplishments of civilization in the face of dawning technocratic efficiency, Dior and Grandpierre would complete each other. Of course, without Victor Grandpierre there would still have been a great couturier named Christian Dior, but the Dior phenomenon would have looked radically different without the gray-and-white palette, *tous-les-Louis* furniture, and Fontanges bows assembled by Grandpierre that still define the Dior brand.

Just as Henri Grandpierre's best work combined references to eighteenth-century architect Alexandre-Théodore Brongniart with innovation, Victor Grandpierre's work would narrow the gap between the eighteenth and twentieth centuries. Grandpierre would respect Dior's vision but remove the fuss of the rue Royale apartment. With an uncanny ability to polish the couturier's rosy romanticism into cool elegance, Grandpierre would prove the words attributed to the philosopher Alain: The art of interiors lies halfway between architecture and fashion.

PART TWO

The
New
Look

Hommage
a Christian
Dior

Bérard 47

A VISION
BECOMES A STYLE

30, Avenue Montaigne

From the moment Ferdinand opened the door, the establishment of Dior conveyed civility. Across a limestone hall, up the broad stair, and past silvery satin portières, the creamy salon awaited. Velvet carpet muted sound. Chypre and jasmine, the scent of Miss Dior, tinged the air. Delicate dresses and graceful suits, timeless in workmanship but visionary in design, awaited. Calm and dignity prevailed. One sensed, like Holly Golightly, that nothing bad could happen here. • Dior understood that he was living at the dawn of a new era, one that required its own style. He reached to the past for the look of the future. From ostrich-feathered hat to delicate tip of Goya pump, the New Look combined reassuring elegance with novelty. The interiors at 30, avenue Montaigne followed suit. Everything seemed familiar—the tasseled Austrian shades, the Louis XV-style seating,

the pale tints—yet somehow radiant, pared down, and thoughtfully reconsidered. Here, both frock and frame were in accord.

From the first exploratory conversation with Marcel Boussac, his backer, Dior had a precise idea of the establishment he wanted, as well as its location. His couture house would be quiet and refined, with clients from the highest echelons of society. His dresses would break rank with the ubiquitous square-shouldered silhouette and uphold centuries-old French techniques of beading, embroidery, fine textiles, floral arts, and savoir faire. Long ago, on a walk with Pierre Colle, he had passed a discreet townhouse on the chestnut-lined avenue Montaigne that struck him as the ideal location for a couture house. His conviction never changed.

Across from the Plaza Athénée, on a gracious street that ran from the Seine to the Champs-Élysées, the building was convenient for foreign and Parisian clients alike. Moreover, it was perfectly scaled for the exclusive business he envisioned. Distinguished but unostentatious, it had good architectural bones and a very good provenance, providing you were not a royalist—it had been built in 1865–68 for the widow of Alexandre Colonna-Walewski, the son of Napoleon and Marie Walewska. It also happened to be in the most stylish neighborhood of the late nineteenth century, the wellspring of Dior's vision. Still evocative of that time, it was the ideal showcase for Dior's aesthetic.

Despite the odds, but in keeping with Dior's current run of luck, a lease for this coveted house materialized. (Highly convenient, too, was the fact that as business activity soared, he was able to expand into adjacent properties.) There was, however, one inconvenience: the house was not available until December 16, 1946, less than two months before the scheduled unveiling of the first collection on February 12, 1947. While vacationing in Cannes, Victor Grandpierre received an urgent summons from Dior to help with the interiors. Given the high stakes, Grandpierre hastened back to Paris and set to work. He had a complex undertaking and a limited time frame; the last nail was hammered as the first fashion show attendee arrived.

Hiring Victor Grandpierre, a photographer, writer, and illustrator but not a recognized designer, was good marketing. It added to the buzz in Paris that Dior was breaking with the past, up to something daring and new. But Christian Dior, a careful businessman, was not angling for sensation or taking risks.

As the "Bar" suit so elegantly demonstrated, Dior was both a cultivated product of the haute bourgeoisie and an artistic adventurer with a roadmap. He needed a backdrop that reflected history but promised innovation—and a subtle talent to create it. Victor Grandpierre had the background to understand Dior's vision and the eye to convert it into interior design. With camera and pen, Grandpierre had analyzed architecture, room décor, and ambience. With artist's crayons, he had ordered form and color into stylish compositions. He had conceived theatrical sets and understood from his work as a fashion photographer how to frame clothes. Thus, though a neophyte at decoration, Grandpierre was an astute choice.

PRECEDING PAGES

To commemorate Dior's New Look success, Christian Bérard sketched 30, avenue Montaigne. Dior so loved the pastel that he reproduced it on everything from programs to holiday cards.

ABOVE

Dior (foreground right) and Grandpierre (foreground left) shared a common vision: a light, clean, architectural reinterpretation of neoclassicism. While paring down the past, they maintained the standards of traditional craftsmanship in clothes and interiors..

OPPOSITE

Christian Dior chose 30, avenue Montaigne for his headquarters because it exemplified the discreet, elegant taste he sought.

Because haute couture was an established luxury trade in France, there was a long tradition of couture houses to reference. Contemporary models—that is to say, the couture salons of the 1930s, as design had effectively ceased during the war—included the couture house of Lucien Lelong, Dior's last employer, with sleek interiors by Jean-Michel Frank. Elsa Schiaparelli's couture house was also designed by Frank and had catchy window displays by Salvador Dalí. Lanvin, who had partnered with Armand-Albert Rateau on a horizontal brand extension, Lanvin Décoration, naturally had Rateau conceive her interiors. Curiously, Robert Piguet, that master of sedate, understated clothes, had a dramatic double staircase trimmed with passementerie leading to salons with neo-baroque furniture by Jansen and a ceiling painted by Drian. Though each of these interiors was marvelous in its own way, after the war they looked not only a little worse for wear but dated.

Dior had something quite different in mind. He cast his eyes back to earlier precedents. Among these, he admired the airy salons of Chéruit on the place Vendôme, which had closed before the war, with their pale painted boiserie, large mirror panels reflecting light, caned Louis XV benches, and Persian rugs. It was in the tradition of the house of Worth circa 1910—that vintage year for design in Dior's eyes—whose regal showroom of white paneling trimmed with gold, fitted carpeting, and the occasional Louis XIII chair imparted distinction. In 1925 Edward Molyneux, the couturier Dior most admired, opened a salon on the rue Royale that featured Trianon gray woodwork, Louis XVI bergères, Directoire side chairs, and even a sales staff dressed in gray.

Chanting the mantra of French tradition and history made modern, Grandpierre built his case for tradition reexamined throughout 30, avenue Montaigne. In contrast to the charming interiors of Chéruit or an Helleu painting, Grandpierre took Dior's naturally romantic vision and made it elegant and architectural. He started with the entrance, stripping it to its essence and preserving nothing but the austerity of the classic Parisian vestibule. Walls of roughcast limestone blocks, ormolu-and-glass Louis XVI–style lanterns, and stone floors connoted quality and discretion. No whimsy or gewgaws entered the scheme; like Dior, who cast out any irrelevant dresses, regardless of how beautiful, to maintain unity in a collection, Grandpierre understood the visual power of discipline.

A ceremonial staircase, covered in a solid taupe runner secured by brass carpet rods, with an old-fashioned velvet rope for the interior handrail, led to the piano nobile, pausing at a mezzanine that opened onto fitting rooms and, eventually, a fur salon and the hat department of Mitzah Bricard, the heavily jeweled and veiled former assistant of Edward Molyneux.

Reminiscent of Maxim's, but minus the predictable velvet draperies, windows were treated with sheer white Austrian shades that filtered light into the stairwell. Additional light came from the occasional Louis XV–style sconce. Kentia palms in simple cachepots marked the landings. By punctuating the monochrome scheme with a slash of wrought-iron handrail, Grandpierre reflexively echoed Dior's theme of highlighting light with dark in a collection.

One passed from the ashlar masonry on the second-floor landing into a small hall, a realm of snowy paneling that led to the inner sanctum: the two salons where collections were shown. Grandpierre framed the doorway to the salons with gray satin portières edged in scalloped silk fringe, one of his few concessions to "decoration." The elements encountered in the progression from Ferdinand's courtly bow to admittance into the cool vestibule and ascent up the stately staircase—taupe carpet, ormolu sconces, Austrian shades weighted with silk tassels, silvery satin portières—reappeared in the salons. Tall French windows were dressed in gray satin curtains and Austrian shades, frequently pulled up to admit more light and leafy views. With the exception of a few architectural and decorative elements—shaded crystal chandelier, Louis XVI mantel of Rouge Royal marble, and ornamental plasterwork typical of a nineteenth-century house—and the requisite seating, there was virtually no embellishment.

In the manner of old French houses, in which generations of furniture coexisted, the seating, as at Versailles, was mixed and hierarchical. Grandees like Carmel Snow

In two different media, the taste of Grandpierre and Dior aligned. While Dior chose black for a stroke of drama on his "Liszt" ballgown (Spring-Summer 1950), Grandpierre used the black iron railing at the couture house as a chic contrast to the muted palette of Louis-Dior.

An exuberance of flowers, luxurious gray satin, Austrian shades, and a soupçon of eclecticism add life to the serene salons at Dior. Note the casual mix of Louis XV and Napoleon III seating. The tickets on the chairs indicate seating assignments for the showing of a new collection.

of *Harper's Bazaar* were allocated the Louis XV settees; armchairs and side chairs were reserved for the other high-ranking guests; gilt Napoleon III ballroom chairs were provided for the rest. Jean Cocteau, other good friends, and late arrivals might be squeezed onto the stairs. And in time-honored tradition, when not in service, the seating upholstered in gray duchesse satin was protected with muslin slipcovers, so meticulously tailored that they appeared to have been made in the ateliers upstairs. Ashtrays, now archaic but then a necessity, were metal bowls mounted on white fluted columns.

The color scheme throughout was, famously, gray and white. It was practical, setting off the line and color of the dresses to perfection. It was restrained yet fresh, signaling a new moment. It was also modern. In the eighteenth century, gray had played a supporting role in colorful interiors; now it took center stage, complemented by lavish amounts of white. This minimalist interpretation of eighteenth-century interiors, with its discernment and elegance, was Grandpierre's masterstroke—and the perfect expression of Dior. Gray and white have endured as the brand's signature palette ever since.

When empty, the salons were sparse but not vacuous. As Dior noted, it is not the hat itself, but the proportion of the ensemble that matters—and Grandpierre had indeed struck a delicate balance. Of course, the rooms were rarely seen vacant. For major occasions, the house florist, Lachaume (later this role was taken over by Madame Paule Dedeban), filled the rooms with flowers, swagging mirrors in dense garlands that would have been the envy of that other great lover of blossoms, Louis XIV. The one caprice that Grandpierre permitted—in contrast to the restraint of the whole—was an Italianate trompe l'oeil of urn and flowers.

Grandpierre's interiors achieved the Helleu-esque salons of Dior's dreams, white and pearl gray, Parisian and polished. Dior appreciated the fact that the space was decorated but not gratuitously ornamented. It went without saying that sentimentality had no place in this environment. There was not a trace of the nostalgia that permeated Dior's rue Royale apartment—with one exception. In addition to his command center in the atelier, Dior had a small private office in a connected, adjacent building where he would escape to think and sketch undisturbed. Because it was a private space, Grandpierre slightly relaxed his disciplined gray, white, and ormolu scheme. It was furnished with a mahogany Louis XVI desk and bookcase, white-framed Louis XVI chairs, sheer white curtains, antique *petits graveurs* (fashion plates) with puce mattes and gilt frames, and a bouillotte lamp with green tole shade. By 1957, Dior had even managed to cover the walls in a leafy wallpaper that was unequivocally homey.

The key to Grandpierre's modernism, like Piguet's, was in the edit: these rooms were elegant, of course, but also functional, reductive, and—most of all—relevant. While the prefabricated housing of Jean Prouvé and the space-saving sliding doors of Charlotte Perriand represented one form of modernity, Grandpierre offered an alternative vision. Simplicity, a grisaille palette, a subtle mix of Louis XV and XVI references, a hint of Napoleon III, and the absence of fussy carpets, baroque conceit, or surreal wit proclaimed the new era. To be sure, the clean design was intended to showcase ravishing clothes, but just as important, it created something new: classically inspired interiors unburdened with banality.

OPPOSITE

Showing clothes to best advantage was the objective of a couture salon. Gray and white, in an immaculate space, set off the flower hues and polish of every Dior collection. To maintain such poised perfection, workmen arrived before every collection to touch up walls and reinforce chairs. (Shown here, dresses from the 1957 Spring-Summer collection.)

ABOVE

Left and right: As discretion and elegance were central to the Dior identity, there were always restrained afternoon ensembles. However, exuberant red—Dior's lucky color—made a striking appearance in every collection. After 1955, red would also judiciously appear in the interiors of the Grande Boutique.

OPPOSITE

Referencing the eighteenth century, the façade of Dior's beloved childhood house, and the Belle Époque aesthetic of Helleu, gray spelled elegance to Dior. It appeared in the collections, the packaging, and the couture house, and became synonymous with the Dior brand.

A PHILOSOPHY
BEGETS A BRAND

3o, avenue Montaigne and Beyond

Christian Dior had one disconcerting habit: he dressed every woman with his eyes. In fact, he didn't merely wish to button up her gown; he wanted to slip on her shoes, clip on her earrings, drape her in furs, and tuck a gift for her accommodating husband in her hand. From this desire sprang an ever-widening web of boutiques, perfumes, and licenses, bound by Victor Grandpierre into one cohesive aesthetic. From Paris to Tokyo, in premises, packaging, and publicity, Trianon gray, white, and neoclassical motifs heralded the New Look. • To provide that final touch, and that all-important gift, Dior's plans for 3o, avenue Montaigne included a small boutique modeled along the lines of an eighteenth-century luxury vendor. In itself, a boutique was nothing new; by the interwar period, nearly all couture houses had small shops stocked with accessories, perfume, and novelties.

Their ubiquity was not accidental; beyond providing finishing touches or frivolous amusements, these collections of bed jackets, kid gloves, and powder puffs represented an important source of income to the haute couturier, whose profit on couture was, at best, slim. What *was* new at Dior was how skillfully the boutique and related activities translated ephemeral ambience into hallmarks.

Given Dior's plans for a small and exclusive couture house, the initial ground-floor boutique was proportionately petite, at first neatly tucked into one side of the entrance hall. As its success grew, it expanded into the cubicle under the stairs, where a concierge had once monitored comings and goings, and ultimately spilled out into the greater hall, where a round, skirted table and a few wicker mannequins created an enticing sense of plenitude. Grandpierre demarcated the original space with paneled counters and a canopy, and furnished it with oval-back Louis XVI-style chairs, which would be memorialized by fashion illustrator René Gruau in dashing advertisements, yet another example of consistent visual messaging at Dior. During a pre-opening tour of the renovations, Christian Bérard struck on the idea of decorating the boutique with toile de Jouy, a type of printed textile hovering on the edge of neoclassicism. Sepia toile de Jouy was duly sourced (conveniently, it was manufactured by Boussac, Dior's backer) and hastily installed on walls, counters, canopy, columns, and even the stock ladder in time for opening day.

But the toile décor was short-lived. A photo from the early 1950s shows the boutique, bountifully stocked and decorated for the holidays (following the example of Robert Piguet, who seasonally replenished and restyled his boutique to encourage frequent visits), and now painted in gray and white. Piles of Christian Dior boxes perched above the canopy and casually scattered throughout the boutique were another Bérard suggestion, and one that lasted. The eighteenth-century font created by Nicolas Cochin (the designer-engraver for Versailles' Menus-Plaisirs, the office of royal ceremonies and events) that spelled out "Christian Dior" literally became the house signature.

The boutique, with its distinctive visual framework, was a popular stop on the modern Grand Tour. With its offerings of costume jewelry, silk flowers, and baubles, it served as good-will ambassador, conveying Dior magic to those who could not venture to the haute couture salons upstairs. Many items were unique. Exclusive silk scarves were commissioned from artists Henry Moore and Graham Sutherland. Beginning in 1948, the boutique offered a few simplified versions of the current couture collection. Even the boxes proved adept emissaries of the brand. All over the world, a gift from Christian Dior in a graphic white box with stylish black lettering was synonymous with Parisian taste.

Grandpierre's aesthetic drew each new undertaking into the fold. For the salon of Dior muse and milliner, Mitzah Bricard, he supplemented the repertoire of portières and neoclassical chairs with white-columned hat stands, gray-skirted dressing tables, white wall-bracket consoles, an Helleu-inspired drawing of a woman in feathered hat, and trifold mirrors surmounted by Fontanges bows that allowed customers to analyze a hat from every angle. (The ubiquitous bow motif was inspired by the fetching Duchesse de Fontanges, a short-lived mistress of Louis XIV, who tied a ribbon with trailing ends above her pretty forehead.)

Whether beaded by Rébé, covered in feathers, or tipped with a satin rosette (the famous square silver buckles were yet to come), Dior shoes by Beaux-Arts-trained

ABOVE

The first boutique was restrained in size but long on style. Spilling into the classically austere entrance hall and hung with the same gray satin portières as the salons upstairs, it signaled the Dior aesthetic to all who entered.

OPPOSITE

The sublime creations of Roger Vivier, a former sculptor, were displayed like artwork in the shoe boutique. Naturally, gray and white and Louis XVI seating defined the space. In a time before computers matched paint colors, the formula for Dior gray was a strictly guarded secret.

sculptor-turned-cobbler Roger Vivier were celebrities in themselves. (Vivier in fact could never bring himself to use the mundane term "shoes" and insisted on calling his creations "slippers.") For the 1955 Vivier-Dior shoe boutique, Grandpierre gave these refined shoes (ahem, slippers) star billing in a calm environment. He added to the established neoclassical vocabulary only the absolutely necessary: a fluted fitting bench, arched display alcoves, and a white mirror with a Fontanges bow set on the floor to reflect daintily shod feet.

Crossing channels and oceans as well as the Seine, the elegance of Dior had passport papers too. Beginning in 1948, Dior established licensing agreements in England, Canada, Cuba, Australia, Chile, and Mexico, and opened a branch in New York, which resulted, not surprisingly, in increased demand for cocktail dresses. In an era when Elsie de Wolfe designed her own suite at the St. Regis hotel, and Cecil Beaton had much-photographed rooms at the Sherry–Netherland Hotel, a Christian Dior suite styled by Victor Grandpierre—swathed in toile de Jouy like the original boutique—was unveiled at the Plaza Hotel in New York. In 1952, in collaboration with Cartier, Dior opened a boutique in Caracas, Venezuela, with interiors virtually identical to those on the avenue Montaigne. The décor of Dior had gone international.

As the New Look exploded into an international phenomenon, the Louis XVI–circa-1910 style of Grandpierre crystallized into a brand. What had once been known

Dior's muse, Mitzah Bricard, reigned in the millinery salon that Grandpierre devised for her. The mysterious Bricard famously proclaimed that her favorite florist was Cartier.

as Trianon gray transitioned imperceptibly into Dior gray. Clever tongues now referred to Grandpierre's gray-and-white scheme, laced with neoclassicism and touches of Napoleon III, as "Louis-Dior." In fact, the influence of Dior, and the Louis-Dior style, reached beyond boutiques and closets to domiciles. Young matrons who had grown up in their mothers' Poiret-inflected drawing rooms now placed inherited furniture in gray-and-white Grandpierre-style environments. They even brought the new aesthetic to their country houses and decorated their children's bedrooms in Louis-Dior gray and white, not forgetting to add a little chandelier and lighthearted white pompons to gray curtains.

Meanwhile, the line of branded products multiplied: gloves, perfumes, stockings, and even ties, all neatly packaged in gray and white and affixed with the Dior cartouche, materialized in quick succession. Dresses produced for the boutique flourished too, resulting in an expanded Boutique Collection, which had its own unveilings as well as a design studio and three workrooms to support it. Success, coupled with all the new offerings, increasingly challenged the capacity of the little boutique.

Ever lucky with real estate, Dior managed to acquire the adjacent space, at 15, rue François-1ᵉʳ. Instantaneously—or so it seemed to the Dior client, for the transition happened in the course of a single night in 1955—the boutique grew into an emporium. Coats, knit suits, cashmere sweaters, and ski wear, in addition to dresses, were now available in the boutique, and Dior handbags, fine jewelry, and umbrellas completed, rain or shine, the head-to-toe Dior look. And as Dior's vision was as much an ethos as a way of dressing, the new boutique also addressed the art of fine living. Lamps, silver, crystal ornaments and other gifts, tableware, and even the occasional antique were among the offerings.

By 1955, memories of the war were fading, Paris had recovered its radiant glow, and even Versailles had a fresh new roof. The interiors of the new Dior boutique, supplied by the august Maison Tréherne, followed suit. The décor was a tinge more opulent, featuring a few more references to the plush Second Empire and a lot of silk fringe. Perfume counters, with swags of gray velvet atop mirrors, draped tables, signage, and hanging shelves ornamented by Fontanges bows, were as sophisticated as the aldehydic scent of Miss Dior. In the oval room, where assorted gifts, objects, and porcelain were displayed, neoclassical pilasters and console tables with tailored skirts played off a festooned center table, recapitulating the signature interplay of Napoleon III and eighteenth-century styles. Grandpierre also added a second shade of gray to the palette and copied the practical eighteenth-century convention of marble baseboards, here in witty faux marble.

To ensure that the décor didn't dissolve into commonplace prettiness, Grandpierre specified a substantial modillion cornice for the room and handsome nailheads rather than delicate gimp trim to finish the oval-backed Louis XVI-style chairs. He also incorporated the same tailored houndstooth check that he had used for the packaging of Miss Dior, which added a crisp note to the feminine rooms. Touches of crimson, a color employed in every Dior collection, contrasted with the serene gray while tacitly highlighting the introduction of Dior lipstick.

In spite of Dior's prominent role in the fashion world and flair for publicity, he and his couture house epitomized restraint. Though he had flouted family convention by starting a business with the family name on the door, he was inherently averse to showy merchandizing. Accordingly, Grandpierre discreetly covered the windows of the new boutique in half curtains and Austrian shades; only two small display windows flanking the main entrance provided any indication of the riches within. But, much like Dior, who could turn a demure debutante into a sexy sensation, nineteen-year-old window designer Jean-François Daigre (who later teamed with Valerian Rybar to design flamboyant balls for the Patiños in Estoril and the Baron de Redé at the Hôtel Lambert) fully exploited the dramatic potential of these windows with spectacularly showy fantasies. Once past these glittery sentinels, however, the orderly universe of Christian Dior, with its grisaille palette, crystal chandeliers, and oval-backed neoclassical chairs, prevailed.

Now the boutique was more than a luxurious amenity; it was influential. Its wares and gifts, commissioned by Jean-Pierre Frère, manager of the gift and tabletop department, were invariably coveted by trendsetters. No less a personage than the Duchess of Windsor purchased a dessert service of faux-bois Limoges porcelain exclusive to the Dior boutique. Like the old boutique, the new one was seasonally restocked and redecorated. When designing these fanciful displays, Frère often received help at night from Dior's twenty-year-old assistant Yves Saint Laurent, an imaginative boy en route to becoming a maestro of fantasy.

At Christian Dior, Grandpierre was the decorator without whom nothing could happen, a role that became increasingly important with time. After Dior's death in 1957, his personal friendship with the couturier and long history with the couture

OPPOSITE

From the very beginning, Dior's vision transcended mere fashion—it was a way of thinking, a way of being, a refined elegance. In the enlarged premises, Dior could now sell the accoutrements of a lifestyle, as well as accessories for clothes.

ABOVE

At the perfume counter, the Dior design vocabulary is evident in bottles and packaging. The message of Dior was seamless, elegant, and unforgettable. Dior's new lipstick line, also introduced in 1955, graces the counter in both glass obelisk containers and more traditional portable tubes.

A PHILOSOPHY BEGETS A BRAND ■ 121

La Boutique de Baby

house provided a unique link to the vision of the founder. Well into the eras of Yves Saint Laurent and Marc Bohan, Grandpierre continued to breathe the spirit of Dior into its spaces and brand.

Designed by Grandpierre, the Baby Dior boutique at 28, avenue Montaigne was simultaneously innocent and urbane, its gray-and-white palette paired with pristine piqué and white wicker. Sales counters featured neoclassical pilasters, glass, and wicker; shopping bags had their own youthful version of the Cochin lettering. A stylish, tongue-in-cheek white knit stork had pride of place in a display window that glinted with chic copper trim. Princess Grace of Monaco, once famous for breezy double entendres in Hitchcock films, now decorous and dressed by Marc Bohan, cut the white satin ribbon for its 1967 opening.

For a new client who dispensed, perhaps by choice, with the time-consuming fittings and rigorous craftsmanship of haute couture, the house of Dior developed a prêt-à-porter line, Miss Dior, in 1967. And for the new Miss Dior boutique, located around the corner at 11, bis rue François-1ᵉʳ, Grandpierre jazzed up the classic gray-and-white palette with stainless steel, laminate, and recessed lighting, creating a mod interpretation of Louis-Dior. Similarly, when men's tailoring entered the Dior empire in 1970, Grandpierre created the masculine variation of the Dior interior: mahogany molding (a recurring

Grandpierre motif in his residential work) on gray walls, glass cases banded in stainless steel and mahogany, leather and metal club chairs, and probably a whiff of Eau Sauvage.

The design of perfume bottles and packaging also received the Grandpierre touch, a consistent vocabulary that gave the entire line of Dior scents, ranging from woody to rosy, seductive to sweet, a unified look. His first contribution, in 1947, was the addition of ringed handles to the amphora under consideration for Miss Dior. Though this might seem to have been a slight modification, it was significant. The handles reinforced the nascent neoclassical brand of Dior, keeping the Dior identity on message, and distinguished the Dior perfume bottle from other curvy perfume bottles on the market, such as Rochas's Femme.

When Grandpierre appropriated houndstooth for the packaging of Miss Dior, he departed from the conventions of pretty perfume boxes. Like the Miss Dior fragrance, which blended delicate white flower notes with virile chypre, the visual presentation he conceived, marrying houndstooth with a white satin bow, was a prescient blurring of masculine and feminine. Both worldly and well bred, the black-and-white check,

OPPOSITE

The perfume Miss Dior was worldly, à la Marlene Dietrich. To reflect its subtle crossover appeal—as well as that of Dior's tailored day suits—Grandpierre suggested the houndstooth motif for packaging and bottle. Houndstooth is now part of the iconography of Dior.

ABOVE

Gray walls, mahogany trim substituting for the traditional white, stainless steel, and a whiff of Eau Sauvage brought the Dior aesthetic to a manly plane in the men's boutique.

Le Salon
de Thé.

V. Grégoire

which had appeared repeatedly in the first New Look collection, was Dior's abstracted variation on leopard, the decorative talisman of 1950s glamour. Over the years, as the perfume packaging has been updated, houndstooth has been a continuous motif on boxes, bottles, and perfume labels. Stamped in relief on Dior's glass perfume bottles, houndstooth aligns sophistication with Dior perfumes. The simplicity and consistency of Dior perfume boxes—neoclassical oval cartouche, gray, white, houndstooth, and the occasional identifying hue, such as the romantic, Granville-evoking pink for Diorissimo, made a Dior perfume immediately recognizable. Just as future perfumes Diorama, Eau Fraîche, Diorissimo, Diorling, and Diorella adhered to this stylistic program (while occasionally incorporating new Grandpierre motifs such as obelisks, caning, or wicker), so, too, did men's fragrances. An early edition of Diderot's *Encyclopédie* inspired Grandpierre's mottled-brown box (many erroneously think it was inspired by tortoiseshell) with a dramatic carnelian cartouche for Dior's first men's fragrance, Eau Sauvage, introduced in 1966. Again, the masculine-feminine duality of fragrance and packaging triumphed: Eau Sauvage was an immediate hit with suave men about town as well as a favorite of preppy ingénues.

At Parfums Christian Dior, Grandpierre, as artistic advisor, was looked up to by the entire staff. A master of conceptual design, he consulted on the packaging and presentation of perfumes nearly to the end of his life. In keeping with his natural reserve, he did this quietly, listening attentively, reflecting, and then producing, minutes later, a fully developed, flawless concept, accompanied by a deft illustration sketched on the spot. He was also regarded as a keen editor; in a split second he could spot what was wrong, identify false notes, point out what was missing, and suggest the perfect refinement.

As in the Louis-Dior style, there was never an extraneous detail in his packaging designs. The former director of development and packaging at Parfums Christian Dior, Marie-Christine de Sayn-Wittgenstein, remembers the design process for the container of a new, apricot-infused cream. She had found a silver box with bas-relief fruit on the top in an antiques store, and thinking that it might be a good starting point for the design, brought it to Grandpierre. She recalls that Grandpierre responded gently but firmly with the words "Dior is never trivial" and tactfully took over the direction of the project, steering it in a less prosaic direction. His solution was a polished white container with the embossed monogram CD in an oval cartouche with a beaded border. It was but a suggestion, a whisper, of the implied elegance of Dior.

Grandpierre also applied his talent to the fine, if now disappearing, art of presentation. Once upon a time, before duty-free bazaars and internet sales, luxury perfumes were merchandised with refined displays. Department stores such as Bergdorf Goodman and Galeries Lafayette had elaborate counter presentations. The hallways of glamorous hotels, such as the Ritz and Plaza Athénée, were lined with vitrines filled with luxury goods, including Dior perfumes, to entice guests. Grandpierre was a master at conceiving these displays, called *presentoirs* in the business. He always considered them haute couture projects, impeccably made by hand, so his *presentoirs* were expensive to produce and invariably caused consternation in the business office. But Grandpierre, who considered his first duty to be faithful to the spirit of Dior, would calmly stand his ground. And, when compared with the competition (and Guerlain and Chanel were no slouches), the Dior *presentoirs* were standouts.

Though consistently representing Dior's philosophy, Grandpierre's designs accommodated every iteration of Dior. His influence rippled across the face of Dior, directly and indirectly, from the high-profile perfume bottles and interiors with limestone floors and gray satin curtains to the smallest details such as white Cochin lettering on gray letterhead, a neoclassical cartouche found inside a pair of gloves, or a Fontanges bow embossed on the packaging of Dior stockings. The litany of gray and white, the interplay of tradition and audacity, the dialogue of masculine and feminine, proved, time and again, then and now, apt and adaptable. Invisible elegance, as Dior and Grandpierre always knew, ranks as a modern classic.

OPPOSITE
Louis-Dior style incarnate, in a red chalk sketch by Victor Grandpierre: pilasters and palms, Louis XVI fauteuils and Fontanges bows, and a tufted center ottoman in a study for an unrealized Dior tea salon. What was popularly referred to in fashionable precincts as the Louis-Dior style prevailed not only in Dior interiors but in chic residences throughout Paris.

Diorella

Christian Dior

THE NEW LOOK
IN RESIDENCE

7, Boulevard Jules-Sandeau

With fine furniture and silk portières, Dior's townhouse in Paris ushered interior design into a new realm of luxury. Radical notions infiltrated classic restraint. Voluptuous Napoleon III banquettes flirted with linear pilasters. A Matisse drawing hung next to a Gothic tapestry. Florists in felt slippers noiselessly updated flower arrangements. Befitting ball gowns and business dinners, Dior's new house at 7, boulevard Jules-Sandeau was the latest iteration of Louis XVI. Its balance of opulence and cool, swagger and nonchalance, neutrals and singing colors influenced interiors as far away as Jackie Kennedy's White House. • If avenue Montaigne looked back to Louis XVI circa 1910, boulevard Jules-Sandeau brought Louis XVI squarely into the celebratory 1950s. Louis-Dior gave way to an assault of color, comfort, and personality. Gray and white blossomed into floral and jewel tones. Napoleon III, a subordinate at Maison Dior, emerged as a full design partner with an entourage of fringes, ferns, and flounces. Not so long before, a French interior disdained the comfort of a down-filled sofa or the ready convenience of a small drinks table; now American and British notions of comfort insinuated their presence. Amid Dior's eighteenth-century furniture, the increasingly cosmopolitan air of the 1950s—the era of Beistegui's ball in Venice, the Windsors enthroned in Neuilly, and Americans imported with the Marshall Plan seemingly everywhere in Paris—had found its way into this very French house.

The bohemian days in a walk-up with a turbaned cook had run their course. By the early 1950s, as the preeminent couturier in the world, Dior needed a dignified background for quasi-official entertaining. After looking in the desirable faubourg Saint-Germain and concluding that only Americans could find houses there, Dior cast his eyes farther afield. Though he had avoided his childhood neighborhood, Passy, one particular villa was irresistible: not only did it have a gracious floor plan and the all-important winter garden but it had also captivated him since childhood. From his family's apartment across the street, he had spent hours gazing at the villa's colonnaded façade and contemplating its mysterious actress occupant. Forty years later, as he filled it with velvets and Aubussons, Buffets and Bérards, mementos and objects acquired in the course of his pursuits and travels, the 1905 house fulfilled childhood fantasies and professional requirements alike.

Given Dior's visibility and the fact that few townhouses had been decorated from top to bottom since the war, Paris watched with anticipation. As it was common among the fashionable to divvy up the design of private and public spaces among decorators, Dior's hiring of both Victor Grandpierre and Georges Geffroy caused no eyebrows to lift—except, perhaps, those of the two designers in question, who had a chilly relationship at best. The reasons for their selection were obvious: Grandpierre could channel Dior and Geffroy was capable of grand. (And not to be forgotten, of course, was Geffroy's providential introduction of Dior to Piguet.) Less clear is how Maison Jansen's Pierre Delbée came to the project. Be that as it may, the pasha-like luxury of Dior's townhouse certainly provided Delbée with ample training for his most famous commission: Shah Pahlavi's multiday celebration of the 2,500th anniversary of the Persian Empire, which included golden tents for guests fitted with chandeliers, tapestries, marble baths, and silk tassels in the desert near Persepolis.

Perhaps the flamboyant Pierre Delbée, in charge of overall continuity of woodwork, upholstery, and curtains, raised the bar on sumptuous, because Geffroy exuded a new exuberance in this house. The sensuous salon, so appropriate for Dior, master of the pretty, romantic dress, was unusual for the decorator, whose work to this point tended toward glacial poise. Though the walls upholstered in sober sage velvet are textbook Geffroy, he replaced his repertoire of mahogany antiques and earth tones with eye-candy furniture—Louis XVI fauteuils with spiraling column legs, gilded bergères, a Sèvres athenienne, a Louis XVI table with delicate bronze mounts—and brilliant cherry red, Prussian blue, and emerald silks. There was an Aubusson rug, an elegantly veneered card table, and a splendid chandelier. Tufted satin, gilt, mounted porcelain, lapis, and fringed lampshades ratcheted up the luxury quotient and required all of Geffroy's cerebral composure to hold such abundance in elegant check. Such splendor, which

PRECEDING PAGES

Of his sumptuous house in Passy, Dior reflected: "I like an atmosphere which has been built up little by little out of the whims and fancies of the inhabitant. If I *had* to name my favorite style for a house, I would choose Louis XVI, but it would be a resolutely 1956 Louis XVI, a contemporary and therefore sincere version."

OPPOSITE

Dior's fashions and couture house emanated from the same vision. Now, silk faille and satin, Aubusson rugs and lacquered fingertips combined to usher Dior's inspiration into a polished home. Here, a model reclines on the window bench in his drawing room (for other views of Dior's drawing room, see pages 2 and 132).

would reappear in his work for the Guinnesses, Felloweses, and Patiños, defined sophistication for the era.

As dramatic, if more consistent with Geffroy's earlier projects, were the designs for the limestone vestibule and marble stair hall. Two commanding Egyptian funerary figures towered over arrivals in 1953. A slightly later photograph of the hall shows an Empire chandelier, a chair à *l'antique*, a mahogany armoire, and a bust majestically presiding atop a truncated column; a judicious use of color adds zing. Off-white portières, reminiscent of the curtained doorway to the salons at 30, avenue Montaigne, are edged with red Greek key–patterned passementerie, echoing the red in the Bessarabian rug. The opposite side of the curtains is emerald silk shantung to match the classical drapery on the stair rail, a full-out riff on the daintily draped banister in the fashion house of Piguet. The dash of green against white marble acts as a gust of cool air.

Nearly outdoing Grandpierre at Louis-Dior, Geffroy's dining room provided an intermezzo in a menu of riches. As in the vestibule and stair hall, Geffroy used little color, but whereas the vestibule is dramatic, the dining room is reserved. In Geffroy's idiom, of course, reserved did not mean without detail—or good furniture. Though the paneled walls were white, he employed three shades of white: lilac-white, rose-white, and white-white. On one long, paneled wall, a white console inspired by the eighteenth-century designs of Jean-Charles Delafosse fronted a mirrored recess surmounted by a gilded cartel clock. The console was flanked by bronze putti holding gilt candelabra shaped like sprays of flowers. The mahogany pedestal table was surrounded by white Louis XVI side chairs upholstered in cherry velvet. An Aubusson rug added visual texture, and a pale porcelain stove broadened the geographical references. There were few accessories: a pair of candlesticks on the console, sprigged and lightly gilded Porcelaine de Paris plates, and floral arrangements in the distinctive pyramids of Paule Dedeban. Countess Cristiana Brandolini remembers Dior's table, presided over by a butler, as being in the best tradition of the haute bourgeoisie. Set with a heavy white tablecloth and silver and glasses of simple design but excellent quality, the table was but a platform to receive the culinary feats of the white-toqued chef and sous-chef. It was not the least bit odd that old French values and traditional French cuisine coexisted with dernier cri dresses and design—for the moment, time-honored French culture was the font of all things fashionable.

Grandpierre's decorating, like that of Geffroy, took on new dimensions at the boulevard Jules-Sandeau that reverberated beyond Passy. The stylized elegance of avenue Montaigne relaxed and became personal. In Dior's winter garden, the masculine-feminine insouciance that juxtaposed silk bows and tailored houndstooth now spawned the frothiest of smoking rooms. After assembling the familiar Trianon gray, limestone, and Austrian shades. Grandpierre opened the window wide to the nineteenth century. Portières parted to reveal a panel of Chinese silk embroidered with birds and peonies, creating a virtual aviary. Fringe dripped from every portière, lampshade, curtain, and Austrian shade. A kentia palm in a Chinese pot was a holdover from the old apartment on the rue Royale. Twisting the conventions of camellia-filled conservatories—and not unlike branding floral perfume with a manly check—tobacco-colored leather on a tufted sofa and Louis XVI bergères, a humidor, and brandy snifters transformed a feminine solarium into a masculine smoking room. Recalibrating its taste to this audacious room, *Maison et Jardin* magazine lauded the mix of white-lacquered chairs, leather upholstery, gueridons, chinoiserie, and luxe, and decorators commenced cross-dressing Chesterfields in chintz and fauteuils in flannel. A decade later, international taste embraced Victoriana and the Peacock Revolution.

If the downstairs was a showplace to entertain Stanley Marcus and Laurence Olivier, and a showcase of New Look interiors, the upstairs rooms were a relatively understated haven. Red—the lucky color of the superstitious Dior—ruled in these quarters. In the high-ceilinged white bedroom, crimson silk taffeta draped a painted Directoire bed, which was flanked by a small gilt chair upholstered in cherry velvet

BELOW

Left: In Dior's restrained dining room, designed by Geffroy in three shades of white, the (reputedly) tallest, finest-looking butler in Paris presided over dining arrangements. Right: For quiet dinners with close friends such as Jean Cocteau or René Gruau, a smaller table was laid.

(an achingly beautiful color combination that Bettina Ballard also noted in flower beds planted by Dior at his country house in Milly) and a bedside table holding flowers, books, and notebooks. An Empire chair with majestic carved eagles pulled up to a Louis XVI desk littered with correspondence, reading material, and mementos. With its spacious dimensions, expanse of clean white walls, fine antiques, simple crimson carpeting, scattering of Persian bronzes, and personal paperwork, the room personified the man who declared that his favorite period was Louis XVI circa the present.

Nowhere was the Louis-Dior aesthetic more present than in the couturier's up-to-the-minute bathrooms. A plush dressing room lined with a French document fabric and faux-bois doors connected the bedroom to a regal bathroom that paid tribute both to Empire party girl Madame Tallien via Emilio Terry and Elsie de Wolfe, who had wowed Oswald Mosley before the war with her avenue d'Iéna bath, which boasted silver lamé curtains and an L-shaped sofa. Chez Dior, green silk faille portières protected a silver-plated bathtub with trompe l'oeil panels and swan faucets in a mirrored and paneled alcove decorated with framed drawings. Polychrome terra-cotta floor tiles added old-fashioned charm. Long window curtains, a tasseled and tufted green chair, and a gueridon topped by a silk-shaded urn lamp, a bisque figure, and assorted bibelots, upgraded the bath into a boudoir. Not so long before, one had settled for drafty bathing

OPPOSITE

In Dior's winter garden-cum-smoking room, Grandpierre riffed on his hallmarks for Dior couture. Louis XVI chairs, fringed portières, and limestone floors now became sumptuous. The easy interplay of masculine and feminine elements anticipated new design trends.

ABOVE

Left: Grandpierre's bedroom for Dior mirrored the restraint of the couture house, while enriching it with crimson silk bed hangings, cherry velvet upholstery, and a garnet-colored rug. Right: Dior's stylish neoclassical bath, also designed by Grandpierre, was his private escape.

quarters and de Wolfe's posh bathroom seemed outlandish; now, with more Americans entering the scene, baths became luxurious.

Grandpierre's whip-smart study, sometimes attributed to Delbée, reinterpreted the themes of 30, avenue Montaigne for an opulent retreat. Grandpierre's usual leitmotifs—Trianon gray walls, white trim, and mahogany moldings—established a handsome framework for two alcoves covered in crimson linen velvet and lined with banquettes. A predominantly red, floral-patterned Agra rug added to the richness of the room. Cards and music, Dior's favorite pastimes, dictated a card table and a piano. On the walls hung numerous drawings and paintings by Cocteau, Bérard, Dalí, Buffet, and Derain, and a Flemish tapestry. Tiers of shelves held sets of leather-bound volumes, odd pieces of bric-a-brac, fragments from antiquity, and family photos. It may have well been this room that prompted Cristiana Brandolini to remember the house as "very red and very velvet," but it was also the personal sanctuary that Dior's *Vogue* friend Bettina Ballard described as one of the happiest rooms she had known.

For decorators, Dior's house was a watershed. The more colorful and less rigid approach that Geffroy took in Passy would soon inform his best projects. Grandpierre's residential work graduated from well-bred style to sensuous self-assurance. Portières enjoyed a postwar renaissance that would be embraced by Charles de Beistegui, Madeleine Castaing, Gérard Mille, and Fred de Cabrol. The deep-seated, tufted upholstery and cosseting curtains on the boulevard Jules-Sandeau resuscitated nineteenth-century notions that became common currency in French design and beyond. And though the house was most certainly about style, it was even more adamantly—and radically—about the individual.

Equally novel was the way Dior approached antiques. As antiques dealer Alexis Kugel notes, Dior did not acquire antiques to form a collection but to re-create a manner of living. Motivated by connecting with the past, rather than by prestige, Dior happily browsed the shabby salesrooms of Drouot as well as the most tasteful dealers in Paris. He held antiques to the same standard of pleasing his eye as his dresses, recalls Olivier Kraemer, whose family owns one of the longstanding antiques establishments in Paris that Dior frequented. When Marcel Boussac first accompanied Dior to the Kraemer Gallery, the designer was looking for a tall cabinet but impulsively purchased a console and a Chinese vase instead, preferring, he explained, to acquire what spoke to his eye rather than his reason. For Dior, antiques represented a patrimony to be integrated into daily life.

Although Dior's house was French in aspect, it was unconventional and individual, befitting one who had come of age in the iconoclastic 1920s. Historian Alexandre Pradère points to the long tradition of elegant austerity in French design; for centuries, wit, conversation, reason, and breeding enhanced a beautiful room, not comfort or warmth. As a tastemaker, Dior exploded this notion, creating a house in keeping with his own concepts of comfort, individuality, and luxury. Applying to interior design the same open, independent, and confident taste that allowed him to pair plunging necklines with sedate gloves, he now integrated long-established savoir faire with new ideas of how to live. The house on the boulevard Jules Sandeau had roots in tradition but planted seeds of modernity, liberally watered by new international influences. Here, café society design made a very public debut.

Dior preparing for the day in his study. The Napoleon III-inspired red velvet banquettes and portières signaled the revival of Belle Époque style, largely initiated by Dior and Grandpierre, while the linen velvet art mats were the height of café society chic. Bernard Buffet's portrait of Dior over the fireplace now hangs in the Dior boutique in Paris.

PART THREE

French Tradition, Modern Glamour

MEASURED ELEGANCE

Georges Geffroy, 1948–1971

Few have had as keen an eye or as adventurous an aesthetic as Georges Geffroy. He could offer perfection to a duchess in an unassuming stone, place porcelain stoves in Louis XVI dining rooms, and mix rustic Finnish rugs with Jacob chairs. His designs were strict, his standards and techniques ancien régime, but his eye was unconstrained. All the while, his passion for eighteenth-century French furniture never diminished. Indeed, he is remembered for exclaiming "Exquis, *exquis, EXQUIS!*" to describe a new find, as well as for interminable discourses on French furniture that could set a dinner party yawning. In the worldly environment of postwar Paris, he embodied café society décor, incorporating influences from Russia, England, Sweden, and America that revitalized French neoclassicism. He was the long-sighted decorator of the 1950s.

After the war, the doors of *tout Paris* opened wider and wider. Money, taste, beauty, wit, and intelligence were the keys to admittance, while bloodlines became less important. The tight little circle of *le gratin*, familiar to readers of Balzac, had become international, resembling English café society. The old nobility of France, with their fine châteaux and ancestral furniture, often found themselves pushed to the sidelines as the guano kings and dime-store heiresses arrived in Paris. The Duc de Mouchy counseled a well-received young American (the kind to whom Dior lent dresses for the publicity she would generate) to spend less time with straitened old aristocrats such as himself; all the fun was to be had with the plentiful, new money.

The change was palpable. Everyone from Marie-Laure de Noailles to pretty arrivals from South America now spoke with the same distinctive cosmopolitan accent, a sort of English-accented French, the kind one heard in Switzerland. Some of the most influential tastemakers—Charles de Beistegui, Emilio Terry, Arturo López-Willshaw—may have passed as de facto Parisians but had roots in the Americas. Alexis de Redé, another aesthete, had even hazier origins, but had gone to the fashionable Swiss boarding school Le Rosey. Plus, he was beautiful, had exquisite manners, and was protected by López-Willshaw, which added up to more than the price of admission.

The new group floated above convention, courting no approval except their own, answering only to the dictates of style. While Parisians fled from the Occupation, joined the Resistance, or soldiered on stoically, Mexican silver-mining heir Charles de Beistegui blithely renovated his newly acquired Château de Groussay. Thanks to his Spanish diplomatic passport, Beistegui went through the war untroubled, decorating and entertaining in grand style at Montfort l'Amaury. His insistence on fashionable attire for his guests—despite the shortage of materials and drab tenor of the times—kept couturiers like Antonio Castillo afloat during the lean years.

The traditions that a mincing countess from the provinces may have revered were irrelevant to this glamorous group; what mattered was style, often, but not necessarily, coupled with quality. While Christian Dior adorned his models with strass and the Duchess of Windsor wore jewels by Jean Schlumberger and Fulco di Verdura, carefully conserved family jewelry languished in the vault. When Beistegui, the aesthetic ringleader who emphasized overall decorative harmony over authenticity, inherited a Greek sculpture from an uncle, he was nonplussed. "For the first, and perhaps only, time," he marveled, "I see a work of quality that surpasses a decorative object." Meanwhile, Coco Chanel and the Noailles continued to define their own styles, mixing Coromandel and suede, Balthus and bergères, the likes of which had never been seen before.

Thus, interior design evolved. Before the war there had been two strains of classicism: the historic, of course, and a new, modernist vein, with Jean-Charles Moreux, Jean-Michel Frank, and Serge Roche at the helm. Rigid canons of taste kept these two styles from blending until the ebullient newcomers arrived. Writing their own rules, concerned only with beauty, they blithely converged the two styles. A well-traveled, cosmopolitan air entered salons, along with the fashionable new accent. Geffroy's clients were, by and large, this fashion-forward crowd with roots on both sides of the Atlantic: Gloria Guinness, Daisy Fellowes, Arturo López-Willshaw, the American-born Vicomtesse de Bonchamps—those who were fabulously stylish and thoroughly indifferent to degrees of consanguinity or to fussing over an inherited, commonplace Louis XVI armchair as if it were the Throne

of Charlemagne. Though some, like Antenor Patiño, opted for magnificent interiors that harked back to Old France, the new high style, as dispensed by Geffroy, was most often a chic, dynamic blend of sculptural lines, tiger velvet, and ingenuity.

Of course, the internationals liked French aesthetics for the same reasons that they came to Paris: both offered beauty, sophistication, and a storied past that one could only dream about in San Francisco or Santiago. But looking with fresh eyes, they did not approach French furniture or interiors in a traditional way, did not recognize the old rules, and saw no reason why an English mahogany chest or a Gustavian commode—or a Gilbert Poillerat console, for that matter—could not coexist with chairs signed by Sené.

Modus Operandi

Geffroy, despite his idiosyncratic, somewhat affected patois, grand demeanor, and appreciation of old furniture, was thoroughly of his time. And though he lacked first-class social credentials, his talent, wit, and connections eased his entrée into fashionable circles. The art critic Waldemar-George described Geffroy as a young Palladio who introduced a new classical order of refined richness and subtle elegance. He was also up to date on modern art, mode, and mores. If you were an international sophisticate, you wanted Geffroy.

Geffroy had undeniable flair. He filled his rooms with faux painting, leopard, portières, gilt, and glamour. Neoclassicism was his native tongue; the rococo of Louis XV was, at best, his second language. He insisted on fine furniture, exhibiting a particular preference for Jacob, Roentgen, x-frame benches, and English mahogany. Hard surfaces of mahogany, mirror, metal, and stone contrasted with rich, sensuous fabrics. His color palette was entirely his own; despite all the Louis XVI furniture, there was barely a neoclassical pastel in sight. Instead, he opted for the emerald greens, russets, golds, crimsons, oranges, and ultramarines of the Empire, which gave heft and splendor to his rooms. Like Dior, he married Old World methods to modern glamour. His clients embraced his perfectionist standards and extravagant techniques. They wanted exceptional design, not run-of-the-mill good taste. In such a climate, a room of boiserie could be built, reviewed, and then wholly rebuilt if it wasn't quite right, to achieve optimal results.

For all his extravagance, Geffroy had the gift of measure, doing a little bit more with a little bit less. His fabrics, even the silks, tended toward the understated; rarely shiny, most had light-absorbing matte finishes. Sparkle was supplied by impressive mirrors, costly gilt bronze, and highly polished wood. Though known for his attention to detail, be it a passementerie border with a Greek key motif or custom-made Chinese fretwork, he did not waste time with dainty trivialities. There were no pillows with witty aphorisms or Porcelaine de Paris figurines. Nor was there the flashy effect of faux-tortoiseshell walls with metal banding. Instead, there were daring insertions of originality: Tibetan rugs, Thai silk, porcelain stoves, and plaster strapwork accompanying the fine ormolu, mahogany veneers, and silk velvets.

Generous but mannered, gifted but insecure, grandiose but human, considered a snob but capable of profound feeling, Geffroy was just as subtle and complex as the rooms he created. While doyennes at Dior, worldly playwrights, and many Parisians considered Geffroy an insufferable arriviste, others found him to be deeply caring.

The widow of novelist Roger Nimier remembers the letter that Geffroy wrote to her after her husband's fatal accident as the most moving of the hundreds she received. Antiques dealer Jean-Marie Rossi of Galerie Aveline recalls Geffroy's daily visits and his chatter over tea, which never touched on furniture—that was saved for business transactions—but on friends, fashion, and goings-on in Paris. Geffroy's contribution to the wedding of Gloria Guinness's daughter, Dolores von Fürstenberg (the bride dressed, naturally, in Balenciaga), was to arrange personally the masses of flowers in the church on the avenue Hoche.

Significantly, younger friends who had nothing material to offer Geffroy also found him kind and charming. Michel Guéranger, a promising artist, appreciated not only being included in the urbane cocktail gatherings and occasional ball under the eaves but also the interest Geffroy took in his painting. He listened attentively, too, to the Vicomtesse de Bonchamps's daughter over cozy lunches when she was home from Foxcroft. His godson, Nicolas Petitjean, recalls many lunches—just the two of them—on the rue de Rivoli. After the invariably delicious meals prepared by Odette, his devoted maid, Geffroy would give Nicolas a curated tour of his objects, carefully explaining their qualities, their provenance, and the reason he had selected each piece. And then there were the gifts of a thoughtful, and extravagant, godfather: a Breguet watch (suppliers of timepieces to Marie-Antoinette, incidentally) for First Communion, a monogrammed child's suitcase from Goyard on the eve of a voyage, a naïve painting— age-appropriate for a young boy—by Louis Roy, which was specifically earmarked for Petitjean at Geffroy's death.

Yet, as Bettina Ballard had suspected, Geffroy's life was an uneasy one and he was often despondent, turning to confidants like the Vicomtesse de Bonchamps or the Duchesse d'Harcourt to pour out his woes, disappointments in love, disillusionment with friends, and trials with tricky clients. He could run in rough company too, once turning up for lunch with Pamela Churchill, Babe Paley, and Jean-Marie Rossi sporting a black eye. Fooling no one, he insisted he had bumped into a door.

None of this angst dampened his decorative flair one iota. (In fact, it may have fueled it.) With little staff, no office, no training, and elementary drawing skills, his asset was his eye. Assuming the role of artistic director, he established the "look" of a project, but left its execution to others, while vigilantly monitoring every step in the process. Geffroy relied on Decour, the old-school *ensemblier* (a versatile hybrid of decorative consultant and upholsterer who assembled fine, inherited pieces into cohesive rooms) in the 16th arrondissement run by the elegant Madame de Grandsaignes, to produce the plush tufted sofas, fabricate the richly draped curtains, and collaborate on the precise details of upholstered walls with swagged detailing and fabric-covered architectural moldings (*gainage des moulures*), in which Geffroy took great pride. Decour even famously sewed colored strips of silk together to create a striped fabric that Geffroy had envisioned for curtains for the Philippe Durand-Ruels but couldn't find in the market.

Maison Tréherne, whose reputation was built on purveying and retrofitting eighteenth-century boiserie and parquet de Versailles floors, was the other pillar of the Geffroy empire. Though Jean Roche oversaw some architectural renovations for Geffroy in the 1950s, by the 1960s, the distinguished Tréherne was, in effect, Geffroy's exclusive contractor, hiring and overseeing the necessary plumbers, electricians,

painters, cabinetmakers, masons, and plasterers, and meeting with Geffroy three times a week to review drawings. Tréherne's elite École Boulle–trained draftsmen, accustomed to detailing neoclassical cornices and pilasters for specialized installers, now added indulgent baths and witty bookcases to their repertoire. The arrangement proved so beneficial that Tréherne made a car and driver available to Geffroy to facilitate, among other things, *Le Tour Geffroy*, his famous rounds of antiques dealers with clients, which, naturally, generated more business for all. Of course, stops were made along the way at jewelers, dressmakers, and florists too, for Geffroy—like Dior—had definite opinions on all aspects of *manière de vivre*.

Redé and Rochas Redux

Geffroy reached the height of his powers in the late 1940s and 1950s, and his ever-more-confident designs pleased ever-more-glamorous clients wanting a fillip of the extraordinary for their landmark residences, couture houses, and swank boats. The piano nobile in the Hôtel Lambert for the Baron de Redé was the first beneficiary of his mature eye. Built in 1640, Louis Le Vau's parlaying of a tricky triangular site into a glittering townhouse with tranquil garden showered

fame on the twenty-seven-year-old architect, who went on to design Vaux-le-Vicomte and ultimately to transform Versailles from a hunting lodge into a regal palace. Equally influential were the interiors, where the delicate brushwork and subtle tonalities of painters Charles Le Brun and Eustache Le Sueur resulted in Le Brun's appointment as chief decorator for Louis XIV and brought royal commissions to Le Sueur. The 75-foot-long Galerie d'Hercule, filled with Le Brun's allegorical paintings and ending in a windowed rotunda overlooking the garden, was the centerpiece of the house. Its antechamber led to the stretch of reception rooms that Baron de Redé occupied: Le Sueur's Salle des Muses (whose five paintings now hang in the Louvre), the Grand Salon, and the Salon d'Amour. They were, however, in tatters.

As soon as Redé heard from Victor Grandpierre that an apartment in the Hôtel Lambert had become available, he swapped his pied-à-terre at the Meurice for rooms in this historic house on the tip of the Île Saint-Louis. Happily, the enigmatic baron had the means to indulge his desire. The restoration of the house—once described by Voltaire, a former tenant, as worthy of a sovereign who dreamed of being a philosopher—was no small matter, but Redé, the fellow who had captured the fancy of Arturo López-Willshaw, was the Madame de Pompadour of his time.

The renovation of the Hôtel Lambert, culminating in the 1969 Oriental Ball, was Redé's life work, and it earned him a medal from the French government. Though

LEFT

The first version of Redé's library, rendered by Alexandre Serebriakoff. The reclining figures atop the bookcase had been inspired by Michelangelo. Geffroy, a consummate perfectionist, was unhappy, however, with the way that the figures crowded the beam. As it was a time when clients also insisted on standout design, regardless of time or cost, Geffroy would reconfigure the pediment.

the baron enjoyed antique scouting as much as spritzing his flower arrangements to simulate dew, he knew when to call on the professionals for specialized services. After the structural upgrades were completed, Redé commissioned Geffroy, flush from his success at the British Embassy, to design a library. Once again, Geffroy fashioned a bookcase with freestanding colonettes. But, given the difference in style between the neoclassical eighteenth-century Hôtel de Charost and the baroque seventeenth-century Hôtel Lambert, the new bookcase, of plum-pudding mahogany, was monumental rather than ethereal. A grand broken pediment separates dead center on a Le Brun-painted beam, with Michelangelesque figures reclining atop each half. The columns have elaborate gilded bases and Corinthian capitals. There were further stylistic differences between the two projects even in small decorative details; whereas Beistegui in his role as eminence grise of the embassy library had proscribed books turned outward, Redé proudly displayed beautiful tooled bindings. The date of completion, 1948, is inscribed in gilded roman numerals on the entablature and may well have inspired the inscription along the entablature of the embassy library, which was added in 1958.

But a tour de force is rarely arrived at instantaneously—a fact still appreciated in an era that hovered on the cusp of handcraftsmanship and industrial design. The bookcase required alteration to achieve its final form—and stands as an example of Geffroy's relentless pursuit of perfection, no doubt encouraged by Redé and underwritten by López-Willshaw. Initially built with an unbroken pediment (close in spirit to that in Michelangelo's Medici Chapel, where the reclining Day and Night figures rest close together), the bookcase nearly abutted the beam, creating an uneasy sense of compression. By 1954, Geffroy had fully rebuilt the pediment and widened the separation between the pediment's halves. Only then—six years later—did the room find its equilibrium.

The colors in Redé's library are wholly Geffroy, which is to say completely in sync with that fluid, trans-Channel moment when Violet Trefusis, Pamela Churchill, Diana Cooper, and the Windsors were dashing about Paris. As a matter of record, Cecil Beaton suggested blue for the bookcase interiors, but Geffroy surely would have proposed blue himself, as it echoes the faux-lapis scagliola on the columns and octagonal panels on the base of the bookcase, as well as the cerulean baguette border and acanthus-leaf motif in the eighteenth-century Savonnerie rug, reputedly one of a series made for Versailles. The strong use of blue accents in the crimson-walled room assured that despite inevitable changes of furniture over the years, the library would maintain its visual continuity.

In 1949 Alexandre Serebriakoff, the artist of record for the chic set's interiors, painted Redé's library in its first incarnation, when the furnishings included a double-sided sofa, Consulat table with griffon supports, and bergères in the manner of Percier and Fontaine, and the bookcase pediment was in its original form. In its final iteration, about 2004, high-backed, magnificently studded Louis XIV-style chairs made by Geffroy are accompanied by Directoire tub chairs with painted backs in the antique manner, curule benches, and a simple contemporary low table with a banded granite top and metal base. Small brass tables by Lucien Toulouse stand ready to receive the champagne glasses of the baron's ever-thirsty crowd. In contrast to the realist vein of Chanel and Saint Laurent, who kept their twentieth-century technology unapologetically visible, Redé hid his telephone discreetly in a Turkish ottoman. But who quibbles over nuances when surrounded by perfection?

ABOVE _____

Stairs, like bookcases, would
distinguish Geffroy's work.
The flowing staircase at the
couture house of Marcel
Rochas referenced Beistegui's
at the Château de Groussay
and prefigured Geffroy's work
for Jacques Kugel (see pages
188–89). The fringe detail
on the rail may have been
inspired by the passementerie
on the staircase at Piguet's
couture house.

OPPOSITE _____

Always in quest of the
unexpected, Geffroy triumphed
with passementerie-laden
sconces for the couture house
of Marcel Rochas.

After Victor Grandpierre and Dior unveiled the interiors of 30, avenue Montaigne,
every other couture house looked out of date. Marcel Rochas, sharply attuned to
image, felt the need to make Maison Rochas au courant—that is, to fill it with cool
gray neoclassicism and a few Napoleon III references—and hired Geffroy to do so. But
Geffroy, never one to follow a style slavishly, injected elements of surprise, even into
gray-and-white interiors. His entrance combined a classic limestone-and-black floor
with an audacious flying staircase. Pale blue fringe adorned the stair rail, and gray moiré
walls and tufted seating created a sense of anticipation in the presentation room. In
the boutique, chandeliers were smothered in passementerie with silk jasmine-laden
tiebacks cascading from the arms, and a wicker tiered table and side tables by artist-
artisan Lina Zervudaki, who had also provided mannequins for the little boutique at
Dior, mixed insouciantly with tufted velvet slipper chairs, ferns on pedestals, and ruched
awnings in a festive gazebo environment. Maison Rochas was luminous and airy, but the
neoclassical restraint at Dior had evolved into a worldly bazaar.

Richness Meets Measure

As the memory of war receded, Paris reclaimed its grandeur. In a burst of patriotism,
the city decided to commemorate the 250th anniversary of the place Vendôme in May
1950 and appointed Geffroy to oversee the decoration. In the role of Denis-Pierre-Jean

Papillon de la Ferté, the mastermind behind the eighteenth-century fêtes at Versailles, Geffroy set the stage with the sensibility of a couturier and drama of a set designer, translating the pomp and patterns of Versailles into modern form. Streamers waved from the Austerlitz Column; swags of red velvet with gold bullion fringe draped balconies and the pediment of Jacques-Jules Gabriel's Hôtel de la Fare—the largest, and central, building on the east side of Hardouin-Mansart's octagonal square—to create a proscenium that dominated the festivities. During five nights of fireworks, ballets, concerts, speeches, and fashions, concierges and cobblers gathered with the likes of *saloniste* Marie-Louise Bousquet and diplomat-dramatist Paul Claudel to celebrate their shared heritage.

Individuals like Arturo López-Willshaw, the Chilean collector and patron of the arts, also invested life with Versailles-like luxury. In fact, it was said that with his ring-covered fingers, imperious ways, and couture-clad wife adorned with rubies and diamonds, López-Willshaw resembled Louis XIV, minus the wig. His impeccable eye was unconstrained by a bank account. At his house in Neuilly—designed by architect Paul Rodocanachi—guests dined on royal eighteenth-century silver and danced in a mother-of-pearl ballroom. And while magnificence was as much a daily routine for López as for Louis XIV, nights were spent cozily with Redé at the Hôtel Lambert.

Like Geffroy, López-Willshaw married reverence for the eighteenth century with modern mores—when it suited him. On his yacht, *La Gaviota IV*, López-Willshaw mixed museum quality with caprice, while remaining intractable on other standards (women were forbidden to wear trousers onboard, for example). Like Redé, López-Willshaw was an active participant in his decorating projects, but the responsibility for filling in the gaps on *La Gaviota IV* and implementing them on a tricky schedule fell to Georges Geffroy. Appreciative of quality and usually willing to wait for it, in this instance López displayed a touch of Beistegui impatience; he wanted to sail his new, 200-foot-long boat, with a service ratio of twenty-six crew to nine passengers, to Venice and Biarritz that very summer.

Neither Geffroy nor López-Willshaw had any intention of falling into maritime clichés of teak and blue, although they did have the good sense to avoid delicate marquetry, which would have disintegrated in the salt air. Instead, Mrs. López-Willshaw's Louis Vuitton trunks were sent to a stateroom appointed with satinwood Restauration furniture, just as in her boudoir in Neuilly, and upholstered in a blue-and-pink floral stripe. Arturo's stateroom was, literally, stately with gilt-wood armchairs believed to be from Marie-Antoinette's theater in Versailles and a secretary signed Garnier-Dautriche, all enhanced by considerable gilt on the crown molding, doors, and portholes. The wood-paneled office had mahogany and gilt-bronze chairs and file drawers made by the bronzier Lucien Toulouse, who also furnished most of the seaworthy brass lighting on board. An article in *Connaissance des Arts* marveled at the extreme finesse and quality of workmanship—finer, in fact, than that found in many a good house.

For López, who had a lifelong fascination with China, Geffroy designed a lounge with bamboo and fretwork around a series of Chinese paintings acquired from Princess Marina of Greece. He also created an Ottoman salon, replete with a tented divan upholstered in Turkish carpet and heaped with pillows made by artist Margarita

OPPOSITE

Geffroy's theatrical style easily lent itself to designing the 250th anniversary celebrations of the Place Vendôme in 1950. Like Dior, Geffroy was becoming a French institution.

TOP LEFT

Romantic Restauration furniture and feminine chintz graced Patricia López-Willshaw's stateroom on *La Gaviota IV*.

BOTTOM LEFT

Strictly business for Arturo López-Willshaw's office meant neoclassical lines, mahogany furniture, and chic touches provided by the smart set's favorite metalworker, Toulouse.

OPPOSITE

Geffroy's use of bamboo treillage in multiple scales for the yacht's chinoiserie salon pleased López-Willshaw, a great admirer of Chinese culture. Geffroy's keen eye for proportion and detail specified hefty mahogany fretwork to outline the walls.

OVERLEAF

Charles de Beistegui in his private theater. Though the neoclassicist Emilio Terry directed most of the architectural work at Château de Groussay, Beistegui's theater was a baroque fantasy. Geffroy, channeling his love of fabric as a former couturier, embellished the theater with ruched damask and bows. The balustrades and staircases were copies of those in the Margravial Opera House in Bayreuth. Overhead, a trompe l'oeil ceiling included a surrounding shelf of blue-and-white Chinese porcelain pots.

Classen-Smith (who had executed Bérard's trompe l'oeil panels at the Institut Guerlain on the Champs-Élysées by meticulously sewing ribbon on yellow felt). To amuse this particularly world-weary client, Geffroy added a handsome blackamoor and tub chairs with flagrantly faux animal motifs (so faux that the spotted species cannot be identified) and gilt lion's-paw feet. Every bit a nightclub, the salon's whimsy evidently pleased López; he engaged Geffroy to design a similar room in Neuilly, featuring an awning over a seating alcove, leopard-print pillows, and lacquer tables, that appeared in *Maison et Jardin* in 1960.

For a breath of fresh air, guests escaped to the deck, which Geffroy furnished with mahogany-and-brass Edwardian-style deck chairs from Jean-Pierre Hagnauer, the rue de Seine dealer who was Geffroy's first stop for neoclassical and mahogany pieces. Scattered among these distinguished chairs—copies of a pair Hagnauer had sold to Jean Marais—were willow chairs and wicker tables, a saucy Geffroy juxtaposition reminiscent of his work for Marcel Rochas.

Le tout Paris anoints its tastemakers, then vies for their approval. Postwar style arbiters included the Duc d'Harcourt, the Vicomte de Noailles, and, later, the hypercritical Feray brothers, Jean and Thierry. But the most-feared arbiter of all was Charles de Beistegui, the man with the steely blue eyes behind the shift in taste to neoclassicism. Disdaining museum perfection and liberal with decorating rules (he wasn't technically French, after all), Beistegui fashioned his own highly personal response to the eighteenth century in his house, the Château de Groussay.

For his new theater at Groussay, Beistegui cast aside the classical eighteenth century in favor of the baroque seventeenth. Geffroy, who handily circled in the Beistegui orbit, was entrusted with the decoration of the theater, along with decorator Antoinette Bernstein, wife of playwright Henri Bernstein. The swagged, bowed, fringed, and tasseled results in the manner of Daniel Marot-meets-Margravial Opera House, would have fulfilled any couturier's wildest draping fantasies. In the tradition of Louis XIV, Beistegui commissioned a play to mark the opening, Marcel Achard's *Impromptu de Groussay*, which was performed by the Comédie-Française, the prestigious theater established by royal decree in 1680. Though decades later his grandniece would host school plays in the theater, Beistegui himself never mounted another production. Like all great master builders, he grew bored once a project was completed.

If anything could out-dazzle Beistegui's opening of his theater at Groussay, it was his unveiling of the Palazzo Labia, his pet restoration project in Venice. Once satisfied that the palazzo, filled with frescoes by Tiepolo, Raphael, and Reni (in typical Beistegui fashion, some were original, some acquired), had regained its proper luster, he threw the ultimate housewarming party, the Beistegui Ball. Instructed to wear eighteenth-century costumes, as well as masks and dominos, enterprising guests assembled entourages, ordered costumes at their couturiers, and carefully choreographed their entrances.

The López-Willshaw ensemble, with costumes designed by Geffroy and sewn in the workrooms of Nina Ricci, was considered the most spectacular of all. Once again, Geffroy's designs reflected his patron's fascination with China. Dressed as a resplendent emperor of China, Arturo led the delegation, followed by Patricia as empress, Redé, ever diplomatic, as courtier, Geffroy as a bird catcher, and costumed supernumeraries to carry the litter. Legend has it—and one wonders exactly who began the story—that

Geffroy's costumes were exact copies of clothes depicted in the Beauvais tapestry series *The History of the Emperor of China*. There is, in fact, no discernible similarity. However, though Geffroy may have occasionally been lax in the fact department, he was never lax on detail; a Chinese junk spectacularly delivered the López-Willshaw contingent to the party on the Grand Canal.

Redé, however, was more impressed by the elegance of Daisy Fellowes, dressed by Christian Dior as America, 1750. As she entered the room, she turned into a queen, he recalled, admiring her regal bearing. In fact, Daisy Fellowes's immaculate style was wholly self-invented. Unlike Arturo López-Willshaw, who opted for the finest and the most lavish, Fellowes's acquired taste favored the ostensibly simple. Paradoxically, her preference for understated cotton dresses was accompanied by a love of jewelry, which she would wear as readily with bathing suits as ball gowns. Insistent on symmetry, she placed copious orders at Boivin, Herz, Van Cleef & Arpels, Cartier, and Schlumberger for bracelets and rings in pairs, to balance her arms and hands. Her eighteenth-century house in Neuilly, originally built for the Comte d'Artois and done up for her by the architect Louis Süe, reflected her hard, streamlined taste: curtains of green glass beads, a bedroom of quilted white satin and mirror, a dining room of glass with door frames by Lalique, a garden of metal tube sculptures by Jean Cocteau.

Over the years, though, Fellowes's predilection for studied simplicity waned. In the 1930s, her clothing veered from the minimalist Chanel to the provocative Schiaparelli. By the 1950s, when she moved to a house at 69, rue de Lille, behind what is now the Musée d'Orsay, her interiors became theatrical and quirky, filled with old furniture (as the only child of the Duc Decazes, she had access to plenty) and Napoleon III-style sumptuousness. Drama, it seems, was the weapon of this essentially plain-looking woman against boredom. She amused herself by hosting dinners for guests who despised one another and flustering young brides—such as Diana Cooper—by bedding their husbands. Given this malicious streak, the story recounted by Philippe Jullian, chronicler of taste and decoration for *Connaissance des Arts*, of Fellowes's giving Geffroy four days to decorate her house, has a ring of plausibility. Off Geffroy went to rent hangings, chandeliers, and little gilded pieces of furniture, assuming that he would soon be tackling proper decorating after meeting this arbitrary deadline. Fellowes, apparently, found the temporary décor rather charming and decided, to Geffroy's chagrin, to make it permanent.

Permanent, fortunately, is a short-lived concept for followers of fashion. Eventually, Geffroy got the decoration in hand; photos of the house published in 1952 show swaying portières, silk curtains, unusual lanterns, and rare rugs, all of which require long lead times and laborious effort. Even the classic hallway with its severe paneling, black-accented limestone floor, and noble Régence caned chairs, was warmed by heavy portières and a giddy tole-and-porcelain flower lantern. Fellowes's drawing room was Peking blue, for like many with blue eyes, her favorite colors were gray and blue. Certainly not created in haste were the seven pairs of lavish curtains dressing two windows and five doorways, including pink silk undercurtains, blue silk striped curtains, and Louis XVI-style swagged valances. Mirrors inset in the Louis XVI paneling, an Empire Savonnerie rug, a gilt-wood chair signed Sené, and a settee by Jacob created an air of richness, while busts of two ancestors by Caffieri made it undeniably Daisy.

OPPOSITE

Geffroy meticulously designed and orchestrated the entry of the López-Willshaw contingent (left to right: Alexis de Redé, Arturo López-Willshaw, Patricia López-Willshaw, Georges Geffroy) at the Beistegui Ball in Venice. Dressed as the emperor of China and his court, the group pulled up to the Palazzo Labia on a Chinese junk. Costumed supernumeraries then carried them on a litter into the party. The empress wore exaggeratedly long false fingernails. The costumes were executed at Nina Ricci.

LEFT

Daisy Fellowes poses in the Tiepolo Room at the Palazzo Labia. Her costume for the Beistegui Ball, designed by Christian Dior in yellow and leopard silk, was accessorized with her famous "Hindu" necklace from Cartier. Her umbrella carrier was James Caffrey.

ABOVE

The combination of Daisy Fellowes's temperament with Geffroy's talent spelled drama. Portières and curtained doors made for dramatic entrances and added coherence to her drawing room.

In the ten years that she lived in the house, Mrs. Fellowes turned to writing, producing several novellas little remembered now. The more literary she became, the less she cared about shocking clothes and the more thrillingly mannered the house's décor became. (Jewelry, however, remained a constant.) In the drawing room, the richness increased: the pale blue ceiling alchemized into gold, more and more family paintings—by Nattier, among other artists—filled the walls, and the seating became an imperial mix of striped-silk divans with leopard silk velvet seat cushions, heavily ruched striped skirts, and buttoned bolsters. Busts of her Besenval ancestors greeted her as she came home. Louis XV marquetry tables amassed collections of snuffboxes and chatelaines. Chinese porcelain animals conversed with ostrich eggs. Imari mixed with faux-jasper urns of Apt faience. Such splendor was a worthy setting for Daisy's seventeen-carat pink Potemkin diamond.

The rest of the house became rich and exotic as well. The once-gray walls of the dining room turned russet; the austere black leather Louis XVI chairs were re-covered in warm red leather with gold tooling. Over time, too, the library walls took on more and more paintings, a damask screen displayed a collection of miniatures, Charles of London chairs were re-covered in crimson velvet with moss fringe, and a slipper chair upholstered in tiger silk velvet appeared. Trinkets from all over the British Empire, bits of ormolu, and porcelain wares covered the tables. With its mid-tone colors, theatrical curtains, and fine furniture, the house was a beguiling period piece of 1950s decorative style. But in its eclecticism and blithe disregard for convention, which had its own inner consistency, it was a testament to the style of Fellowes superimposed on that of Geffroy.

Like Beistegui and Fellowes, Gloria Guinness followed no dictates but her own. She arrived in Paris in 1945 as Gloria Rubio von Fürstenberg, a dark Mexican beauty with an aura of mystery and a possible past, elegantly attired in black and white Balenciaga clothes, her long, slender feet shod in Hellstern & Sons' slimmest last, and her diamonds very white and discreetly worn. That season, she was the rage of Paris, yet curiously resistant to being lionized by society. Geffroy, perhaps recognizing a natural flair and discernment tantamount to his own, befriended this elusive star.

Many travels and two marriages later, gliding from Countess von Fürstenberg to Princess Fakhry to Mrs. Loel Guinness, Guinness hired Geffroy in the early 1950s to design a two-story flat at 18, avenue Matignon. Her chic stemmed from her knowledge of exactly what suited her and led to her sobriquet, "The Ultimate." She never deviated, never ordered in excess, never fell for novelty. She was likely to wear the same black Balenciaga dress over and over with two strings of superb pearls and a black mink Balenciaga coat. Such self-aware, disciplined chic and such indifference to bourgeois convention, coupled with Georges Geffroy, produced a smashing apartment.

Sobriety and drama joined forces in the double-height living room, which Geffroy studded with four bays (entryway, fireplace, bookcase, and doors to the wraparound balcony) centered on their respective walls. Each bay was swagged with heavy curtains of silk cannetille that matched the golden walls and were trimmed with a Greek key border of crimson cut velvet. The bookcase and the alcove around the mantel were lined in red velvet, the same fabric that covered the tufted sofa and two chairs from Decour. A massive crown molding added architectural vigor. A Tang dynasty camel (Tang horses

OPPOSITE
Old world, new look. The confluence of styles after the war flowed into the library of Daisy Fellowes. A French aesthetic, now laced with English, Russian, and American accents, reigned in Paris. The bookcases had decorated the Tuileries Palace office of her ancestor the Duc Decazes, a minister for Louis XVIII. The Victorian clock on the English table had been made for a maharajah. Overhead, a Louis XVI zodiac chandelier.

RIGHT

Opulence and shadows,
mirrors and ambiguity. With
Louis XVI seating and rococo
sconces, Turkish bolsters and
ruched skirts, a Nattier portrait
above the fireplace and a
bronze dragon guarding it, the
drawing room of Daisy Fellowes
was a mosaic of time and
place. The chair in the left
foreground is stamped Sené.

were much too common) brayed on a verre églomisé coffee table. There was a turn-of-the-century Empire Revival rug, a smattering of very good French furniture, and a pair of curule benches painted white, but the room did not read as old-fashioned French. Symmetry, assertive color, and understatement rendered it as clean and sleek as the latest Jaguar XK.

The private rooms benefited from the same rigor and mix of French rarities, English neoclassicism, and personal style. Guinness's magnolia-white bath, a study in luxurious simplicity, was a prime example of the well-considered bathrooms that arrived with the new internationals. A bull's-eye window was centered over a tub handsomely encased in diaper-patterned woodwork on a pale blue ground. Under the window was a console shelf awaiting well-chosen toiletries and photos. Diaper-patterned woodwork also enclosed her vanity. A neo-Louis slipper chair graced a corner and, sometimes, a fur rug warmed the floor.

As like attracts like, many motifs of Geffroy's own apartment made their way into the Guinness flat. The reception rooms were separated by a long corridor that was lined, as in Geffroy's dining room, with glazed doors backed with silk, punctuated at both ends with ruby faille portières. The walls and ceiling of the anteroom to the bedrooms were decorated with intricately interlacing strapwork. The corridor leading to the terrace had the same red floor tiles as Geffroy's entrance hall.

The women in high-visibility transatlantic marriages, notably the Duchess of Windsor and Mona von Bismarck, and reinforced by Gloria Guinness, were exceptionally stylish. Though slightly more discreet, the Vicomtesse de Bonchamps did not lack for pizzazz either. Her husband, the Vicomte de Bonchamps, was an old-school aristocrat and former Free French officer who zipped about town in a Jensen and lunched with Alexis de Redé. She was a pretty heiress from California who wore only Givenchy, the new designer with the light touch who dressed Audrey Hepburn. That is, she wore Givenchy when she wasn't dressed as a pagoda for Redé's Oriental Ball, to which she was transported by truck, as she couldn't sit in her wood armature. Though they hired the fashionable decorator of their friend Redé, their interiors displayed little of the dark romanticism of the Hôtel Lambert or the textured richness of Daisy Fellowes's house. Instead, Geffroy's eye once again looked forward, stamping classicism with originality and reaching new summits of style.

Givenchy's 1955 "Les Muguets" (lily of the valley) ball dress, worn by the vicomtesse and now residing in the Victoria & Albert Museum, parallels the modern spirit that Geffroy brought to his designs for the Bonchamps apartment. The strapless white silk organdy dress, worn with long black satin gloves, was hand embroidered with white and cream silk and sequins from bodice to hem. The sequins, it must be noted, were modern plastic disks, a playful touch typical of the irreverent Givenchy. Drawing on classic traditions of workmanship, Geffroy, like Givenchy, reworked old ideas on a clean slate for the avenue Foch apartment, where he pared down and simplified, emphasized volume and negative space, and admitted light and fresh air into rooms filled with antiques. Surprises such as painted walls bereft of paneling, curtains with neither swags nor trim, expanses of blank wall, and outdoor ornaments used for interior decoration, though not compromising quality, were novelties in grand apartments in the early 1950s. These ideas proliferated in the decades that followed.

The entrance sequence transitioned from dark to light: a moody vestibule of blue stamped-velvet walls, an eighteenth-century tooled-leather box, and a gilded neoclassical console unfolded into an airy gallery with unadorned, pale gray walls, parquet de Versailles floors, mirrored doors, and rustic wood vases, faux-painted to look like marble, from the Château de Meudon. A capacious twenty feet in width, the gallery was large enough, as the vicomtesse's daughter remembers, that, when combined with the dining room, nearly two hundred could be seated for dinner. Separated from the gallery by white Ionic columns was a windowed anteroom, bathed in sunny color. A long—so long it was in two pieces—Louis XVI settee made for the Château de Saint-Cloud, dressed in buttercup-and-white taffeta, coral-lacquered side tables, Louis XVI chairs upholstered in tangerine velvet, and a small floral Aubusson sparsely filled the space. The walls, in the same pale gray faux marble as those in the gallery, were devoid of ornament except for a single overscale sculpted cartouche. The curtains, unembellished but buoyant, matched the silk stripe on the settee.

In the adjacent drawing room, richness met measure. Having few distinguished architectural features to work with, Geffroy fashioned character out of fabric. The material he chose was a made-to-order bronze-green silk velvet (only twenty-seven inches wide, as the width of a handloom is dictated by the span of the human arm) from Prelle in Lyon, suppliers of silk to royalty since 1752. For architectural interest, Geffroy had Decour upholster the deep cove molding and doors in the same fabric, and create curtains with no decorative hardware.

To emphasize the room's impressive height, he furnished it with a Boulle armoire, a pair of towering Italian marble columns, a glittering Régence mirror, and a pair of tall eighteenth-century *cartonniers* (file cabinets) with tooled-leather drawers that had belonged to Louis XV's minister of finance. The parquet de Versailles floor was largely covered by a seventeenth-century East Turkestan, probably Kashgar, rug, shot through with silver and gold yarn. The tawny velvet sofa, so magnificent that Hubert de Givenchy hoped to acquire it when the apartment was dismantled, had seat cushions edged with tiger silk velvet and grapefruit-sized tassels dripping from the corners of both the back and the seat cushions. (Inevitably, the dogs eventually got the better of these alluring tassels.) By eschewing bulky coffee tables and placing small tables or benches for resting a drink conveniently close to seating, Geffroy achieved an easy circulation in the room. Six pairs of sconces from the Château de Champs lit the room in candlelight; electric light was supplied only by torchères.

While funds from California covered the cost of the decorating, the vicomte provided ancestral paintings. For the vicomtesse, who loved English furniture, mahogany coaching tables and a demilune card table made their way into the drawing room. In the center, a grand Louis XV writing table held her collections—astrolabs, stone specimen eggs in an agate bowl, pomanders, and a head of St. John the Baptist. It was the era of table collections. As Philippe Jullian, the waspish chronicler of taste and decoration, advised, personal collections should cover the surfaces of a well-designed room to hide the hand of the decorator: "Tabletops should be garnished with evidence of pastimes . . . Fabergé for the truly rich," he counseled, ". . . mixed with photographs of Barbara [Hutton] and Arturo [López-Willshaw]." For the merely rich, he magnanimously added, eggs in marble and semiprecious stone would do.

In the blue, white, and blonde dining room, Geffroy brought the focus back to light and continued to mix periods and provenance. Seventeenth-century Chinese export wallpaper, rumored to have been in the inventory of Brighton Pavilion, set the stage for a blue-and-white Mongolian rug, English consoles and dining table, raw silk curtains, and a faience stove. Antique Chinese wallpaper typically has an all-over floral pattern (as in Gloria Guinness's bedroom) or scenic panels, but the wallpaper here was unusual for its graphic border of bamboo. The flat doors, with stainless-steel hinges (most likely sourced at Maison Fontaine, Geffroy's preferred locksmith-metalworker), were wittily painted with trompe l'oeil paneling. The nearby butler's pantry repeated Geffroy's handy trick of glazed doors backed with silk. The surface of the counters consisted of a mosaic of azulejo shards, the result of a shipping accident with the blue-and-white Portuguese tile Geffroy had ordered for the vicomtesse's bath.

Fortunately, enough of the azulejos survived intact to cover the walls, ceiling, and floor of the bathroom. Cleverly, Geffroy placed the tub in the center of the room and added paneled walls inset with mirror at either end of the tub to separate the bath area from the plush dressing area, where, once again, glazed doors, here backed with blue silk, made a graceful appearance. High ceilings made it possible to hang a very large crystal galleon chandelier, also much admired by Hubert de Givenchy. The adjacent bedroom was predominantly blue and white, with unadorned off-white walls, an antique parquet floor rescaled to suit the room's proportions, and a bed alcove lined with peach velvet and hung with blue-and-white flame-stitch curtains. Louis XVI chairs upholstered in Havana-colored suede and a low bench covered in Indian red leather near the fireplace provided a tailored contrast. A guanaco rug invited bare feet.

By 1958, Geffroy's own salon had also acquired a lighter countenance. It glowed with new wall upholstery of custom-made golden velvet with a wavy stripe motif and countless gilt-bronze sconces and candelabra, which he lit in the evening. Persimmon silk velvet portières, rose silk on the Pluvinet benches, and cherry damask on a gilt-wood Louis XVI screen imbued the room with a pretty blush. He moved the Bessarabian rug from the dining room to the salon, adding warmth to the salon while the dining room assumed a studied coolness. A leopard silk velvet sofa, trailing bullion fringe, replaced the former sofa, which had tiger velvet only on the seat cushions.

More furniture, of course, had accumulated over the years: Jacob lyre-back mahogany music-room chairs with suede seats and an elegant gueridon by Charles Topino. The Riesener desk moved from study to salon. Once the large elements of the apartment were in place, Geffroy focused his attention on acquiring objets d'art, with results that rivaled Daisy Fellowes's object-laden tables. Ming porcelain dogs and porcelain urns with gilt-bronze mounts now flanked Marie-Antoinette's clock on the mantel; pre-Columbian, Egyptian, and Augsburg trinkets rested on a Riesener table; a Kangxi

OPPOSITE

In a luminous anteroom in the apartment of the Vicomte and Vicomtesse de Bonchamps, Geffroy introduced elegant architecture and an antique parquet de Versailles floor, confidently limiting the decoration to expanses of unadorned wall, an oversized cartouche, and an unusual settee. Garden ornaments and mirrored doors, not seen here, completed the adjacent gallery space.

OVERLEAF

Left: Much admired by Hubert de Givenchy and Mark Hampton, the Bonchampses' silk velvet-lined drawing room balanced French and English antiques, scale and intimacy, luxury and restraint, elegance and sex appeal. Right: The dining room, with its unusual bamboo-bordered scenic Chinese wallpaper (Arturo López-Willshaw surely would have been envious), also featured an unexpected blue-and-white Mongolian rug.

Always part of the fashion
world, Geffroy (left) exults with
Yves Saint Laurent and Dior
pillars Suzanne Luling (right)
and Marguerite Carré (center)
after Saint Laurent's debut
collection for Dior in 1958.
Years earlier, Geffroy had
recommended Carré to Dior.

Geffroy's own living room,
circa 1958. Though his aesthetic
was strict, his personal
approach to collecting avoided
dry academicism. His godson
remembers Geffroy fondly
explaining each and every object.

porcelain cat and gilt-bronze dogs with the Rohan–Medici coat of arms sat on the
Weisweiler desk. François de Bigorie's portrait of an impish Geffroy wearing a high
starched collar presided over the desk, conveying the subject's obvious pleasure in the
events unfolding before him.

Though he added a few spectacular touches to the dining room—most notably
green velvet Austrian blinds and a trompe l'oeil coffered ceiling—at the Château de
Daubeuf in Normandy for the Duc d'Harcourt's sister, Geffroy tended to reserve his
boldest strokes for deep-pocketed internationals. Indeed, his renovation for Georges
Litman, an entrepreneur of Romanian origins, was so remarkable that *Maison et
Jardin* featured the work in progress in 1957, marveling at the plaster coffered walls,
carved-mahogany doors, bookcases with the familiar freestanding colonette motif,
elaborate trompe l'oeil grisaille swags and knots in the dining room (much in the spirit
of the festooned theater at Groussay), and plaster urns covered in trompe l'oeil semiprecious stone. The finished reception rooms appeared in print a long six years later.
The paneling, moldings, and domed ceiling upholstered in gold-verging-on-saffron

silk velvet in the round study were a testament to the skill of Decour. In the salon, conceived around a Directoire tapestry running the length of the room, Louis XVI neoclassicism and the candlelight palette Geffroy increasingly favored were enlivened with crimson and subtle gray-blue, elegant Louis XVI chairs, a tasseled divan, and the shimmer of ormolu.

Luxury Reimagined

As the 1950s segued into the 1960s, Americans from both hemispheres continued to call on Geffroy. A 1962 photograph in *Vogue* of Elizhinia Moreira Salles with her two young sons seated on a deep sofa entirely covered in tiger silk velvet, leaves no doubt about who decorated her apartment. Coiffed by Alexandre, dressed by Balenciaga, and bejeweled by Schlumberger, Madame Moreira Salles, wife of a Brazilian financier and diplomat, epitomized the bold, reductive luxury now à la mode in Paris. Like her personal style, her Paris apartment, with its trompe l'oeil Corinthian pilasters, paneling, and crown molding in the library and bedroom upholstered in sumptuous hand-embroidered yellow silk, eased its way into the aesthetic of the new decade.

Jimmy Douglas's arrival in Paris—as well as his apartment—also created a stir. Wealth, charm, chiseled good looks, and the calling card of Barbara Hutton, whom he protectively escorted around the world, gained the young American access and attention everywhere. In Paris, he acquired an apartment with fine beams, an aristocratically scuffed black-and-limestone entrance, and a view over a garden, in a townhouse owned by the Comte de Beaumont. He set to work on its decoration with Geffroy, and the results appeared in *L'Oeil* in 1962. Fifty-five years later, Mr. Douglas still lived amid his Geffroy trappings—all a little faded but still remarkably handsome—and recalled Geffroy's unfailing eye for composition, quality, and style. In his opinion, Geffroy was the only decorator who mattered.

As in the Bonchamps apartment, Geffroy's furniture plan for Douglas allowed for easy circulation. Large expanses of wall, interrupted only by the occasional old master painting, and open interiors created a Zen-like calm that ushered the eighteenth century into a new chapter of modernity. Geffroy effortlessly blended Japanese, Jansen, and Jacob tables with gingham and handwoven silk. (As Douglas was the nephew of Thai silk entrepreneur Jim Thompson, Geffroy enjoyed the cachet of introducing the exotic silk to Paris.) Crystal candlesticks and Siamese silver boxes, Tibetan rugs, and even eighteenth-century busts looked jet-set new.

The entrance hall retained its smart austerity and black-and-bone scheme. A Jansen Royale table with steel legs, caned Louis XV chairs with black velvet cushions, a banquette, and sober black-and-white prints on the walls were its only furnishings. The

OPPOSITE

Geffroy conceived the classical living room for Georges Litman as a royal stop in Neuilly en route to the Trianon.

ABOVE

With every architectural detail faultlessly executed in velvet, Geffroy's oval salon for Georges Litman exemplified great French craftsmanship. Preserving longstanding artisanship in a modern age was a priority for both Geffroy and Dior.

drawing room was similarly spare: walls upholstered in greige velvet, a pale blue Tibetan rug, side tables draped in tailored taupe suede tied at the corners with suede thongs, and sofas without tufting, scrolls, or poufs, their only embellishment a discreet bullion fringe on the skirt. Two towering Jacob bookcases, an impressive writing table with an assertive Greek key frieze, attributed to Garnier, a Louis XV chair upholstered in deep blue velvet, and imposingly large oil paintings, school of Van Dyck and Richard Wilson, established virile authority. A low, upholstered screen, a now-neglected decorative device, gracefully enclosed a sofa near a door.

By adding a wall to the drawing room, Geffroy carved out a library, which he decorated in cognac, russet, gold, and brown—the fall colors that he personally preferred. The bookcases, as in the Guinness and Redé libraries, were lined with fabric—here green moiré taffeta, with a clipped fringe on the shelf edges. A daybed, in a quilted, ochre-and-white windowpane check, casually held its own against the backdrop of a Spanish-style screen of brown figured velvet studded with nailheads. A Greuze portrait of a young girl and an original plaster cast of the bust of the writer Jean de Rotrou by Caffieri flanked the window. A tidy Louis XVI desk and chair, an English wine cooler, and a bamboo tripod table completed the room, where drinks were customarily served before dinner parties.

In the silvery blue bedroom, Geffroy avoided the tedium that can plague pale, essentially monochrome rooms by variations of tonality. Dark and light, assertive profiles, and reflective glints of crystal, ormolu, silver, and lacquer added verve to the subdued palette. Covered in a silk gingham check, the bed, pillows, and round bolsters

With pitch-perfect scale and mastery of tone, Geffroy inserted innovation into a poised drawing room for Jimmy Douglas. Thai silk and a Tibetan rug added subtle surprise amid the greige velvet, Jacob cabinets, and neoclassical urns. The eighteenth-century English landscape is by Richard Wilson.

were sheltered in a curtained alcove. A varnished portrait of Queen Henrietta Maria, a Queen Anne writing table of handsomely figured walnut, topped by pairs of blue obelisks and crystal candlesticks, polished off the space.

In the late 1960s Geffroy took his campaign of simplification to the apartment of his friend Robert Ricci, son of Nina Ricci and a past president of the Chambre Syndicale de la Haute Couture. The apartment near the Champ de Mars (the green space behind the Eiffel Tower that had once served as the drilling field for the École Militaire) had a classic Parisian layout of a square entrance hall with doors opening to the public rooms as well as a long corridor leading to the bedrooms. Geffroy stripped Ricci's entrance hall of frippery, lined the walls in golden fabric, and furnished it with a Greek key–ornamented console and an x-frame folding chair. A portière now separated the entrance hall from the hallway to the bedrooms. Often a neglected tunnel in Parisian apartments, Geffroy extravagantly refashioned the hall as a luxurious gallery that became the conversation piece of the project.

With a vanishing-point perspective under a vaulted, velvet-covered ceiling, velvet moldings, and the suggestion of paneling created by a grid of nailheads, the creamy hallway was Renaissance in its conception but contemporary in its aura of hushed luxury. (It was also the panne velvet successor to Geffroy's all-velvet architecture for the drawing room of the Vicomte de Bonchamps.) Simple Louis XVI brass lanterns drew the eye upward and forward in the space. Opposing mirrors lightened and widened the hallway. A Persian runner added visual texture.

In the salon and library, Geffroy continued to eliminate detail and work in a neutral palette with Thai silk. Furnishings included his own design for a stainless-steel table base, a now-predictable colonnaded bookcase, and a Spanish rug from Sami Tarica. Once again, the walls were plain expanses; no mirrors or paintings hung over the mantels. Though the Ricci apartment was refined and luxurious, the exuberance of the New Look had vanished.

Ever keen to shifts of fashion, Geffroy embraced the new mood with more reductive designs. Luxury, however, never vanished: curtains were now subtly but sumptuously lined in suede. Antiques never disappeared entirely from his work either—indeed, his own apartment changed little after 1958, testifying to his enduring love of the eighteenth century—but they became less prominent, serving as accents, rather than as primary furnishings. To replace classic pieces with modern furniture that met his standards of quality and aesthetics, Geffroy resorted to his own handcrafted furniture designs, instead of industrially produced pieces. In addition to the abstracted tree-root table base and the versatile folding chairs he designed for Ricci, as well as the one-off side tables that he

ABOVE

The chic restraint of Jimmy Douglas's entrance hall derived from the same aesthetic as Grandpierre's austere entrance hall at 30, avenue Montaigne. The library can be seen in the background.

had made by Maison Toulouse over the years, he designed a wrought-iron neoclassical version of a teak deck chair. Upholstered in natural suede, it was decidedly not for deck use. By 1969, both the table base and the chair were available for sale at his long-time associate Jean-Pierre Hagnauer's antiques shop. Editors at *Plaisir de France* praised his designs as a turning point in modern French furniture, and his gueridon base was used in a project by François Catroux, then a young decorator increasingly in the news.

Geffroy also aligned with the antiques dealer Jacques Kugel over the bold and unexpected turns of classicism. Their affinity is hardly surprising as Kugel, who grew up in a family of antiques dealers in Saint Petersburg, had the wide-ranging openness of taste and eye typical of the cosmopolitan city that boasted groundbreaking neoclassical interiors, most notably those at Pavlovsk Palace. For Kugel's store on the rue Saint-Honoré, Geffroy designed a double flying staircase that was executed by ironmaster Raymond Subes, who had made the deco railings for the French ocean liner SS *Normandie*. Connecting modernity, fine craftsmanship, and the past, its slender steel balusters with gilt-bronze fittings snaked theatrically through antiques-laden rooms upholstered in ochre velvet.

Whereas the 1971 Kugel staircase was a direct descendant of Geffroy's fringed staircase for Marcel Rochas, circular staircases, like bookcases with colonnettes, were a recurring theme throughout Geffroy's career. They appeared in the 1960s as an elegant spiral, enclosed in ingenious trompe l'oeil coffering, in an apartment on the square des Écrivains-Combattants-Morts-pour-la-France and, slightly later, as a circular staircase that masterfully reorganized the distribution of space in the townhouse of the actor Alain Delon on the avenue Messine.

Though architecture and modernity increasingly preoccupied Geffroy, his renown as a decorator-connoisseur led to his last large-scale project, the apartment of Antenor Patiño at 9, avenue du Maréchal-Maunoury. Like the American Vicomtesse de Bonchamps, whose apartment was also near the Bois de Boulogne, the Bolivian-Parisian collector and museum benefactor was a confident client, and his 1930s-era apartment, like hers, had little architectural interest. Geffroy, working with Tréherne and Decour, compensated with brilliant color, luxurious textiles, rare Savonneries, and the museum-quality Louis XV furniture Patiño preferred. The entrance gallery, featuring walls lined in gauffraged gold velvet, animal paintings by Oudry, and tortoiseshell and ormolu Boulle cabinets, set a tone of warm magnificence. In the grand salon, rock crystal chandeliers, gilt-wood brackets, lacquer case pieces (a Louis XV parquetry commode with black Chinese lacquer, an ebonized and black lacquer writing table with sumptuous mounts by Dubois, cabinets signed BVRB with Japanese lacquer panels and foliate ormolu mounts—adapted to fit the space), glittering mirrors, and sofas from Decour were resplendent amid velvets and suedes in rose, ochre, gold, rust, and tiger against a backdrop of white boiserie. A smaller salon, with upholstered red walls, featured a Savonnerie rug and bergères signed by Tilliard, carved with his signature flowers, volutes, and heart cartouches. Mounted porcelain, gilt-wood wall brackets, and ormolu sconces abounded. In the library, between bookcases, Geffroy reprised the alcove theme of the Guinness apartment, here boldly upholstered in tiger silk velvet. A Louis XV gilt-wood canapé upholstered in emerald silk velvet in one alcove faces a velvet sofa with tiger velvet accents and scalloped skirt in another. Apparently, there can never be too much of a good thing.

OPPOSITE

Borrowing liberally from Brunelleschi, Geffroy employed Renaissance perspective to achieve quiet drama in the hallway of Robert Ricci's home. Nailheads translated velvet into boiserie.

OVERLEAF

For antiques dealer Jacques Kugel, Geffroy designed velvet walls and a flying stair executed by ironmaster Raymond Subes, creator of Art Deco staircases for the SS *Normandie* and SS *Île de France*. Geffroy clearly adhered to the words of Auguste Perret, architect of the Art Deco Théâtre des Champs-Élysées: "A civilization is judged by its staircases."

The Final Curtain

Eighteenth-century splendor for Antenor Patiño and a steel staircase for Jacques Kugel, though widely divergent in style, were fitting final projects for Geffroy. Since the beginning of his career, versatility had been his hallmark. Back in 1949, *Vogue* had noted his trailblazing originality, unrelenting search for the rare, and quest for perfection. In fact, his taste was so demanding that when visiting Lady Kenmare and Rory Cameron at La Fiorentina, reputedly the most beautiful house on the Côte d'Azur, he could muster only a few faint words of praise. "Pretty still life," he murmured halfheartedly as he passed some ostrich eggs in a basket.

Such perfectionism does not make for happiness. By the end of his life, though he was the finest decorator working with antiques in Paris and exerted worldwide influence, Geffroy had become disillusioned. This careful synthesis of dandy, wit, and aesthete regretted the artistic compromises and the ephemeral nature of decoration. In his most cynical moments, he declared that his most enduring accomplishment had been Alain Delon, whose career he claimed to have launched. He was bitter, too, at the passing of time, the stress caused by devious clients, the hangers-on who cluttered his life, and the futility of nightlife.

The relentless rigor, personal disappointments, business anxieties, and socializing that had fueled his business had taken their physical toll. Fragile since his early bouts with tuberculosis, now, thanks to late nights and countless Gitanes, Geffroy coughed between sentences when holding forth at evening cocktails. Though the painter Michael Wishart remembered Geffroy's mention of several strokes and Pierre Le-Tan suggested that whisky had hastened his demise, other friends do not recall any specific illness. Yet, at the relatively young age of sixty-six, in April 1971, the curtain dropped on the life of Georges Geffroy. His apartment, lovingly assembled over three decades, was dismantled within months and sold at auction by his family.

Not even death quashed Geffroy's instinct for drama, however. After his demise, the famous car and driver took one final *Tour Geffroy* through Paris, this time to drop off bibelots and works of art that he had designated for friends, suggesting that Geffroy had had a premonition of his end. Accompanying each delivery was a black-and-white portrait of him, dubiously attributed to Cecil Beaton. An obituary ran in *Le Monde*, impressive but inaccurate, stating that he had designed the Beistegui Ball and worked for the Windsors. The source of this bit of revisionist history is not clear; perhaps a well-intended but uninformed family member—none of them had been given a ringside seat to Geffroy's life, after all—furnished facts in haste as best as he or she could.

What might have been said in Geffroy's obituary instead was that he rewrote the rules for classic French design, banishing old-fashioned paneling, standard notions of appropriate colors, and what goes with what. He combined raw Thai silk with Jansen tables and statues by Caffieri. He mixed Louis XV chairs with stainless-steel tables. He made a cramped garret a showpiece. He decorated public monuments, edited a singular book, and dipped into early experiments with film. He made French style—not the stuffy one of codified rules, but the self-confident one that instinctively knew how to mix, adapt, and move its aesthetic heritage forward—exciting in its reinvention and relevant to modern living. Where scrubbed pine and gilt mirrors collide today, the spirit of Geffroy is alive.

LUXE, CALME, ET VOLUPTÉ

Victor Grandpierre, 1948~1984

Though his work for Christian Dior represents a landmark in twentieth-century design, measuring Victor Grandpierre by neo-classical ribbons and gray and white understates his impact. Cool and cerebral when defining the look of Dior, he was a romantic when it came to homes. To established doctrines of good taste, he brought unimagined comfort and individuality. As design in the mid-century careened from fussy classicism to self-conscious stage sets, high-minded industrial design to shoddy mass production, Grandpierre's design barometer remained firmly fixed on his clients. The results—refined rooms that reflect individuals more than theories—earned him the reputation as the subtlest designer of his era. • Though his warm, humanist approach to design never flagged, his style varied considerably. With a few yards of leopard velvet and a dozen tassels, he turned Madame Jean Ralli's polite living room into a romantic boudoir. In the library of the stately Château de la Motte-Tilly, he swathed velvet sofas with fur throws that beckoned one to curl up with a book. In the apartment he designed for Yves Saint Laurent and Pierre Bergé, bookcases, leather doors, and a wall-to-wall banquette combined with Eames chairs, crystal obelisks, Sudanese sculpture, and Renaissance bronzes to bring the eclecticism of Marie-Laure de Noailles to the era of de Gaulle.

Whether installing Rouaults or Rembrandts for Liliane de Rothschild, Grandpierre, like Dior, knew that the present was the sequel to the past. While Dior reinterpreted the hourglass silhouette of Charles Worth, Grandpierre adapted bergères and Napoleonic tents for twentieth-century life. Though he often tossed in a hedonist touch of Napoleon III tufting, portières, and silk velvet, making his work all the more delectable in a pleasure-seeking age, he could just as deftly place a Parsons table in an eighteenth-century house. At other times, he simply let sparse château halls and attic apartments eloquently speak for themselves.

Classic or Belle Époque, eclectic or austere, Grandpierre worked with lofty precedent. When Philippe d'Orléans established himself at the Palais Royal, away from the censorious eyes of his uncle, the Sun King, French design entered the modern age. Though royal and ritualized, life at the Palais Royal favored pleasure and amusement, which led to notions that have gained ground ever since. Function, as much as convention, drove design. The plethora of small tables designed specifically for reading, card games, coffee, sewing, jewelry, makeup, backgammon, correspondence, and coiffing reflected this new, eighteenth-century response to individual needs. The poufs and pillows of the nineteenth century expanded on it. Grandpierre, whose clients always came first, was its postwar avatar. He pleased a convalescing Baron Élie de Rothschild, accustomed to a certain formality, by adding a small dining table in his private sitting room, then went on to design the Belle Époque restaurant of the Rothschild-owned Hôtel Saint-Jacques.

Even the most pampered of his clients were impressed by Grandpierre's attentiveness and, decades later, still speak of it. He took charge of his projects, editing an impulse into a polished statement, locating every element, from antique boiserie to key tassels, but acknowledged that final decisions were the prerogative of the individual who would reside in the space. Unsurprisingly, his best work was for the innately stylish (Lilia Ralli, Patricia and Arturo López-Willshaw, Jean Dessès, Yves Saint Laurent, and Pierre Bergé), the worldly (Prince and Princesse Matei de Brancovan, Monsieur and Madame Jacques Politis), or those who floated serenely above the fray (the Baron and Baronne Élie de Rothschild, Cécile de Rothschild, and the Marquise de Maillé). Yet, being of open mind and artistic bent, more scholar than snob, he did not restrict himself to the *gratin* and willingly advised up-and-coming publishers in converted mansard apartments and fashion editors with more dash than cash.

When it came to comfort and convenience, Grandpierre was a pacesetter with perfect timing. Comfort—the idea of a lamp near a chair, or even more shocking, of a throw on a sofa—was, at best, a foreign English concept. At worst, it was petit bourgeois. In the finest homes, the telephone was traditionally installed in a drafty hall, never next to a sofa or on a desk where one might conceivably wish to use it. In 1947 the magazine

PRECEDING PAGES

Directoire paneling and a neoclassical stone floor brought high-style Louis-Dior to an apartment on avenue Foch. The boiserie is believed to be by Clérisseau, who had worked with Robert Adam in St. Petersburg for Catherine the Great. The floor was designed by Grandpierre.

OPPOSITE

Gray-green moiré, red silk, and a touch of leopard produced a seductive living room for Lilia Ralli—also known as the "Pocket Princess" for her diminutive size and royal connections. Elegant pleating, rosettes, and fringe on the curtained sofa alcove amplified the sense of luxury.

Plaisir de France deemed worthy for publication a home renovation with the bathroom *farther* from the bedrooms after construction was completed. At Baron de Cabrol's tasteful country house, as well as at the converted mill that served as Dior's weekend retreat, one had to go outside to reach the bedrooms and the kitchen.

The arrival in Paris of English, North Americans, and South Americans challenged these ideas. When Princesse Laure de Beauvau-Craon—accustomed to the restrained French table such as at Dior's home—dined at the Windsors' and encountered a table laden with silver ashtrays, cigarette holders, place-card holders, nut dishes, saltcellars, and figurines for every imaginable and unimaginable purpose, she was amazed by the microscopic attention to detail. Grandpierre's similar consideration of creature comforts, tempered by his respect for traditional French savoir vivre, wove these foreign notions into accepted French practice.

Comfort purveyed by Grandpierre, however, did not mean a wholesale letting go of aesthetic standards. It meant deep sofas, extravagantly canopied beds, hushed hallways, velvet in all forms (especially the silk and animal varieties), and having the things one loved and used—books, mementos, decanters of cognac, and card tables—close at hand. Such practicality may seem elementary to our twenty-first-century sensibility, but the influence of Grandpierre can be judged by photos of the way things used to be. Well into the 1960s, design magazines featured rooms with seating too far away for conversation, minuscule rugs scattered at random, and no convenient tables flanking chairs. Grandpierre's classicism, softened by Napoleon III voluptuousness and nodding to the modern realities of fewer servants, new technologies, and a quicker pace brought comfort, sensuality, and beauty into balance. This comfort, by the way, was served up in a pristine package with no sticky fingerprints.

Before the war, one valued patina; a maid could be fired for over-polishing a gilt-bronze clock. After the war, as if to banish all traces of German officers from one's château, or psyche, one was driven to fastidious housecleaning. Brilliant, sparkling effects had become desirable; the veneer of life was démodé. One yearned for the past, but beautifully maintained and romanticized, minus the battle scars. Grandpierre's work followed suit; bronzes gleamed, French polish glistened, colors were clear, slipshod workmanship was never acceptable. A Grandpierre room was impeccable.

One didn't adjust to a Grandpierre room; Grandpierre tailored a room to the client. Whereas a René Prou apartment on the Quai d'Orsay was designed down to the last accessory, so that the clients could move in with little more than a minaudière, Grandpierre left plenty of room, not just for books and collections but also for the expression of the client's personality. In the tradition of the Noailles' Hôtel de Bischoffsheim, where a 1920s parchment-lined salon by Jean-Michel Frank coexisted next to a rococo ballroom installed by the owner's grandfather, Grandpierre created polished spaces in the longstanding French fashion that allowed for additions and modifications as time, interests, and taste evolved. In comparison, those studied, sleek rooms that lost their poise the minute their occupant left an errant piece of mail on a table or shifted a chair closer to the window, were, paradoxically, old-fashioned.

An international beauty greatly appreciated that her Grandpierre-designed apartment on the avenue Foch was gorgeous and accommodated her diplomatic entertaining needs, but she equally valued the fact that it was inviting and comfortable.

OPPOSITE

Even old French families embraced New Look interiors. In the library of Prince Jean-Louis Faucigny-Lucinge, Grandpierre housed books amid Parisian architecture, Louis XVI chairs, and an Empire pedestal with the added surprise of jaunty tassels on the curtains.

ABOVE

Glowing boiserie and an emerald velvet banquette, impeccably ruched and banded, invited confidences. An antique floor, Aubusson rug, and paintings by Kees van Dongen and Ten Cat added richness to this warm and welcoming living room (see page 16 for another view of the room).

Even with two children, who brought home friends, there was no need for such a thing as a family room; the oak-paneled living room and the book-lined library with its Degas drawing and Greek key detailing were welcoming and functional whether she was entertaining twenty for dinner or spending a quiet evening with her family. Grandpierre's colleague at Parfums Christian Dior, Marie-Christine de Sayn-Wittgenstein, describes the apartment in the faubourg Saint-Germain that he designed for her with luxurious brown velvet walls and a rare seventeenth-century Isfahan carpet as, first and foremost, a home in which to raise two sons. Because Grandpierre's work gleamed with contemporary style, nodded to the past, recognized everyday reality, and reflected each client's taste, Pierre Bergé likened him to Mario Praz, the Italian scholar and design theorist who saw homes as both archives of individuals and mirrors of an age.

Sensuous color, upholstered walls, tented rooms, scenic wallpaper, portières, upholstery ruched à la *turque*, Austrian shades, scagliola, metal tables by Lucien Toulouse, and eighteenth-century furniture were staples in the magic kit of Victor Grandpierre. The tactile, hushed richness of velvet, which Pierre Bergé recalled as Grandpierre's favorite fabric, enveloped rooms in luxury. And clients could count on perfection in every detail, for Grandpierre was not only a careful executor, but understood how his clients lived. As antiques were often part of the package, Grandpierre frequented Kraemer, Aveline, Segoura, and Kugel with the best of them, but impressiveness was beside the point. Beauty, interest, warmth, and continuity were what drove the Grandpierre aesthetic.

Certain rooms had a distinctive look. Grandpierre bedrooms, like the fashions of the time, celebrated *la différence*: women had sybaritic sanctuaries with elaborately draped beds, whereas men had military-precise dressing rooms furnished with narrow

BELOW

Grandpierre's talent was to make luxury livable, even for two little boys. In the faubourg Saint-Germain, brown velvet walls, a rare Isfahan rug, and old master paintings (selected by the client) belied an actively used—and forgiving—drawing room. Rendering by Alexandre Serebriakoff.

Empire beds. As at Dior's house, baths frequently became elegant hideaways. For bedrooms and breakfast rooms, Grandpierre showed a taste for Charles X furniture, which he acquired at the brother dealers-of-the-moment Roger Imbert on the rue du Faubourg Saint-Honoré and Jean Imbert at his store, Chélo, on the rue Lamennais. Directoire-inspired mahogany moldings on walls and doors—as in the couturier Jean Dessès's dining room (1952), Prince Matei de Brancovan's gallery (1952), Dior's library (1953), Prince Faucigny-Lucinge's foyer (1955), and Dior's men's boutique (1970)—are another telltale sign of a Grandpierre project.

   In the postwar era, as society flattened, staffs were reduced, and construction resumed, grand old houses often gave way to soulless apartment buildings, even in the most desirable areas of Paris. Grandpierre, fortunately, had a knack for creating character. He routinely thickened postwar walls to establish a sense of solidity, upgraded flimsy doors to weighty ones, recalculated proportions, adjusted light, unearthed antique parquet, paneling, and mantels, designed marble floors, added pilasters, wired antique chandeliers, and oversaw architectural details down to the last window pull to create timeless refuges.

OPPOSITE

For Patricia López-Willshaw's Restauration sitting room in Neuilly, Grandpierre added a punch of marigold yellow to his customary calm gray.

ABOVE

A Murano chandelier, a corona bed canopy, painted furniture, and fanciful pink paneling suggested dreams of Venice along the Seine.

Grandpierre's projects of the early 1950s—following the cool classicism of the Dior couture house on the avenue Montaigne and before he became synonymous with luxurious French interiors—revealed the range of his taste. His modernist interests were on display in the Meudon manor house of collectors Monsieur and Madame Claude Hersent (née Maillé de la Tour-Landry), where he mixed cerused paneling, contemporary iron sconces, framed acrostics by Christian Bérard, Jacob benches, a porcelain stove, and paintings by Tanguy and Balthus in a house that welcomed Marie-Laure de Noailles to bohemian kitchen dinners when the chef was away. In contrast, Chateaubriand's—and Grandpierre's—Romanticism held sway in Patricia López-Willshaw's sitting room in Neuilly, with its matte gray walls bordered with nineteenth-century wallpaper, Restauration furniture, and an insouciant mix of dog paintings and needlepoint. Twentieth-century chic polished a living room for the Marquise de La Falaise to lapidary brilliance in 1951 with contemporary paneling in two shades of gray, gilt-wood marquise chairs, a skirted table, an Aubusson rug, and a mantel graced with a pair of perfume burners. Grandpierre was capable of fantasy, too, creating a shell-pink, baroque-mirrored, Murano-chandeliered Venetian bedroom that appeared in *Connaissance des Arts*, and transforming the Cirque Fanni into a fairy realm of floral garlands, Napoleon III chairs, and paper lanterns for Prince Sturdza's ball, described by *Vogue* as the most beautiful and discussed event of the season.

Case Study: Décor for a Prince and Princess

But what Grandpierre is most associated with today, apart from his deep imprint on Dior, is a hefty portfolio of gilt-edged Parisian residences. An early commission in the grand manner was his architectural and decorative transformation of an imposing, but architecturally indifferent, nineteenth-century apartment at 91, avenue Henri-Martin for Prince and Princesse Matei de Brancovan in 1952. Possibly his family connections came into play, as the Brancovans figured among the worldly Romanian clique in Paris (and were, coincidentally, cousins of the poetess Anna de Noailles, née Bibesco Bassaraba de Brancovan, in whose memory Emilio Terry designed the Temple d'Amphion). The three-story apartment for the Brancovans, who could be found chatting with Daisy Fellowes and Baron de Redé at parties at the Hôtel Lambert, was designed specifically for the grand entertaining so dear to café society. The Brancovans' young daughter, Princesse Eugénie, and her brother were relegated to the children's quarters on the third floor, where the decorator hung Redouté prints and reverently housed the doll

Classicism recolored. The salon
of Prince and Princesse Matei
de Brancovan was among the
first to display the new palette
of fresh, clear colors associated
with New Look interiors. Through
the portières, the tented smoking
room can be seen.

collection. She recalls the excitement of sitting on the stairs and watching costumed
guests as they floated from entrance hall to smoking room, salon, and the small and
grand dining rooms. (Despite the two dining rooms, the children took meals upstairs
with the Swiss nanny until packed off to Le Rosey—or a suite at the George V.)

Nearly all of Grandpierre's themes emerged in this one apartment. In the salon,
filled with eighteenth-century furniture (by the likes of Jacob, Lelarge, and Boudin),
he rejected conventional pastels for a vivid Savonnerie rug, cerulean cannetille on
the walls, and gold silk and cherry lampas, and proceeded to arrange the furniture in
convivial seating clusters. The more intimate of the two dining rooms featured antique

Zuber scenic panels on the walls, a screen, and Charles X table and chairs. The more formal—and daring—dining room had gray Louis XVI chairs upholstered in natural leather and grisaille canvases inset into rose faux-marble panels.

The smoking room, tented in a greige, green, rose, and black silk imberline stripe, lined with bullion-fringed velvet banquettes, and hung with landscapes and miniature paintings updated Orientalist chic for the 1950s. Though *Maison et Jardin* commented that Delacroix would have loved being in this room, one man must have felt distinctly uncomfortable here. It was to this room, during a dinner party, that Arturo López-Willshaw summoned the young playwright Jean-Pierre Gredy to outline the terms of the young man's friendship with his wife, Patricia. It seems a bit unfair, given that Arturo spent most of his time with the beautiful Alexis de Redé, but such, perhaps, were the times.

The Princesse de Brancovan wore Schiaparelli before the war, Dior after the war, and jewels to rival Daisy Fellowes until stock in the Suez Canal collapsed. In what

BELOW

Empire-inspired tents were all the rage, and none was more chic than Grandpierre's for Prince de Brancovan. With its strong, clean lines, neoclassical furniture—from Louis XVI to Directoire to Empire—lent itself easily to the cosmopolitan taste of postwar Paris.

Princesse de Brancovan's
double-curtained bed alcove
would have equally appealed to
her couturier, Christian Dior,
who famously favored cozy
beds. Using green and white
toile de Jouy, floral plaques
of Sèvres porcelain, and
needlepoint, Grandpierre re-
created the atmosphere of a
château in a Parisian apartment.

was probably a coincidental alignment of taste with her new couturier (but they did,
after all, share the same decorator), she slept in a toile de Jouy–covered bedroom with
a curtained bed alcove. Though frilled, flounced, and filled with eighteenth-century
pieces, nineteenth-century needlepoint on a Louis XVI chair, memorabilia, art, and
a few mahogany pieces made the room personal, rather than precious. For his part,
the prince retreated to a room that epitomized a gentleman's bedroom as envisioned
by Grandpierre: a narrow sleigh bed embraced by hangings handsomely trimmed with
green braid and suspended from rings on the walls. Passementerie-bordered walls, a
needlepoint rug, a Karelian birch chair, dark, romantic paintings, and a bust made the
room worthy of a grand field marshal. Except for a door (with the requisite Directoire
moldings, of course) substituting for a tent flap, one might believe one was on campaign.
Grandpierre designed similar soldierly bedrooms for couturier Jean Dessès (a Jacob
bed, greige bourette-lined walls, trademark mahogany moldings, and a Persian rug),
the Marquis de La Falaise (Louis XVI daybed, English leather chair, military prints) and
for Eugène Weinreb (a Percier and Fontaine Empire bed with important bronze mounts,
red faille coverlet trimmed with red and yellow passementerie, gray velvet upholstered
walls, horse paintings by Alfred de Dreux, a tufted green leather chair, and a blue,
yellow, and ruby petit-point Charles X rug).

Great Houses in the Grand Tradition

It wasn't only so-so Haussmannian or new avenue Foch apartments that benefited from Grandpierre's ministrations; magnificent old buildings required renovations too. And just as Grandpierre and Geffroy had both worked on Dior's house in Passy, tolerating (and carefully avoiding) each other, they found themselves both working for the Baron de Redé at the Hôtel Lambert. Redé referenced both decorators in his memoirs, noting that Grandpierre helped him considerably in his efforts to bring the whole place back to life, particularly the upstairs rooms.

These were a challenge. Redé's apartment on the piano nobile had grand reception rooms—a salon, a library, a study—but no obvious place to sleep. And although there was an unoccupied gallery on the top floor, the architecture could not be altered because the building was a classified monument. Further complicating matters was Redé's own gilt-wood Louis XVI bed, in the heavy manner of Delafosse, and mahogany secretary by Roentgen, both to be incorporated into the design. Auspiciously, Grandpierre discovered François-Joseph Bélanger's 1785 designs for the bedroom of the Comte d'Artois in the Bagatelle in the Bibliothèque Nationale. Tented, domed, and full of grandiose gilt furniture, the drawings suggested a clever solution—a tent within a room.

ABOVE

Prince de Brancovan's bedroom with its satinwood sleigh bed, draped à l'antique with braid-trimmed hangings, epitomized the tailored, martial men's bedrooms Grandpierre favored. The chair at the desk is Karelian birch; mahogany moldings on the door (unseen) accent the military aspect of the décor.

Working around tricky beams and difficult proportions, Grandpierre designed a blue-and-yellow-striped tent on the top floor of the Hôtel Lambert that was a far cry from his usual tailored men's bedrooms. Instead, he reinterpreted Artois's elaborately draped martial bedroom, even incorporating a nearly illusionistic dome (the ceiling height was a mere nine-and-a-half feet), delicate carved and gilded tiebacks, and a cameo that featured a Fontanges bow, all executed by Decour. A panther-skin coverlet and a chair in tiger velvet (Delafosse, whom Grandpierre and Redé were channeling, frequently employed animal motifs too), tufted upholstered walls in the adjacent stairwell, and a lacy dressing table inspired by Bélanger visibly connected the dots from eighteenth-century design to the dense interiors of the nineteenth century. Fortunately for the room, Redé later abandoned the cumbersome bed for a fine-limbed Louis XVI model, and with the exception of this change, the room remained more or less intact for fifty years until it was dismantled and sold off in the Redé auction.

Several years later, in 1956, the death of Comte Étienne de Beaumont, modern art patron, costume-ball impresario, and jewelry designer for Dior, marked an end and a beginning for the Hôtel de Masseran. In Beaumont's time, the former Spanish Embassy, with its elegant garden, was renowned for costume parties orchestrated by artists, often attended by Victor Grandpierre. Beaumont's guest lists were deliberately, and famously,

BELOW

Baron de Redé's sumptuous bedroom defied Grandpierre's predilection for tailored gentlemen's bedrooms. Working in the landmarked Hôtel Lambert necessitated fabricating a tent within the existing structure. The grandiose late-Louis XVI furniture was selected by Redé.

exclusionist. He would typically leak a party date well in advance, then watch social aspirants tremble in the hope of receiving an invitation, and smile at their chagrin when they realized they had not made the cut.

The next occupants, Élie and Liliane de Rothschild, decorated the Hôtel de Masseran in appropriate eighteenth-century fashion, bringing with them spectacular inherited Boffrand paneling. Brogniart's neoclassical architecture, combined with Liliane de Rothschild's preference for the eighteenth century (she chaired the Friends of Versailles), Baron Élie's interest in twentieth-century art (a rarity in his family), and the assistance of Victor Grandpierre, left little room for traditional Goût Rothschild. The family paintings, armorial silver, Boulle cabinets, and Victoriana found in Waddesdon Manor and Château de Ferrières ceded to Aubussons, silk curtains, and contemporary art on the rue Masseran.

Working with plentiful Gainsboroughs, Picassos, and Rembrandts, as well as fine French furniture, Grandpierre consulted, coordinated, and filled in the gaps in the reception rooms. Though his sense of color and scale animated these elegant rooms, the private rooms upstairs afforded greater scope. The baronne, cultivated, witty, self-confident, and more inclined to focus attention on French furniture than clothes (she was described as looking like a cook, speaking like a queen, living like

BELOW _____

Good design gets better with time. Over the years, Redé replaced his bulky bed with a slender neoclassical model more to Grandpierre's taste, and added a fur throw. The Consulat table and desk chair from the library (see pages 152–53 and 155) moved upstairs too.

an empress, and thinking like a philosopher), was fond of the refined Grandpierre and his classicism. Baron Élie, who had enough style for two—after polo matches, he donned custom-made white canvas redingotes to conceal his rumpled polo clothes—appreciated Grandpierre's aesthetic latitude and attention to practical detail. With few calls to exercise his modernist leanings, Grandpierre happily assembled square-armed sofas, a Parsons table, and a pony-skin rug amid works by César, Miró, and Ernst in Baron Élie's personal quarters. Before the nineteenth century invented the concept of a room dedicated to dining, dining tables were set up where and when needed. In the baron's study, Grandpierre dispelled with doctrinaire convention to revive the eighteenth-century notion of placing a dining table at the convenience of the occupant. The finicky Baron Élie, it was said, loved it.

Color Theory

Grandpierre occasionally resorted to his Dior-gray-and-white palette, which he described poetically as the interaction of shadow and light. Though he frequently paired gray with variations of yellow—saffron velvet for the living room of the Marquise de La Falaise, mustard for the drawing room of the Franco-Greek couturier Jean Dessès, buttercup for the sitting room of Patricia López-Willshaw—gray in his hands, like a stormy sky, enhanced virtually every color. For Saint Laurent's and Bergé's gray-and-white library on the place Vauban, he hung tobacco-colored curtains and installed a bronze-green velvet banquette to complement the Sudanese sculptures, sleek contemporary wood furniture, Egyptian masks, quartz, and jasper in the owners' collection. For Lilia Ralli's salon, he combined gray velvet walls with cerise and leopard in 1956. When Dessès opened a showroom near the Acropolis in 1960, Grandpierre brought Paris style to Athens, designing a couture salon reminiscent of Dior's, complete with tasseled swags and kentia palms. The persuasive combination of Parisian chic and Dessès apparently worked magic; shortly after attending the opening, Princess Sofia asked Dessès to design the gown for her upcoming wedding to Juan Carlos of Spain.

More often than not, however, Grandpierre reached for pinks, reds, greens, and blues—saturated, clear colors that set off marquetry furniture, gilt bronze, and Aubusson rugs to perfection and reflected the optimism of the postwar period. Like Beistegui, Grandpierre used many colors in a single room and did not confine himself to a strict palette. Seemingly natural, but in fact complex—not all colors blend together, it is always a question of tone—this ostensibly random use of color lent an unforced quality to Grandpierre's designs.

By mid-career, there seemed no limit to the colors Grandpierre could combine with dexterity. In 1958 he mixed emerald, periwinkle, rose, Chinese red, maize, and leopard (indeed, a color in the lexicon of Grandpierre and Geffroy) with Regency, Louis XV, and Louis XVI seating and paintings by Vernet and Demachy to create a welcoming and unaffected salon overlooking the Bois de Boulogne. In 1961 *Connaissance des Arts* published an apartment in the 16th arrondissement where, in a warm setting of light oak paneling and paintings by Utrillo and van Dongen, Grandpierre assembled cherry silk curtains, a forest-green velvet banquette, a crimson velvet canapé, a tiger silk velvet

In 1962 Yves Saint Laurent opened his own couture house and moved to the 7th arrondissement. His eclectic apartment, designed in collaboration with Grandpierre, reflected the same modernity as his clothes: extraordinary colors and pure lines, mixed with primitive and exotic elements.

Left and right: Pierre Bergé, Saint Laurent's partner, noted the ease with which Grandpierre handled old and new, periods and provenance in his work with Saint Laurent on the apartment. Although Grandpierre had spent most of the preceding decade immersed in Louis XVI and Napoleon III, his artist's eye had not narrowed.

Turkish ottoman, blue and yellow lampas, parrot-green damask, rosy stripes, and jewel-colored scagliola into one of the prettiest rooms in Paris.

Pale blue walls, a saffron rug, and an emerald sofa emerged from his collaboration with Yves Saint Laurent, an extraordinary colorist in his own right, in Saint Laurent and Pierre Bergé's living room. For the 1965 living room in the home of Yves Lanvin, president of Lanvin, Grandpierre's palette intensified to Technicolor: cherry red, ultramarine, emerald, yellow, and French blue created a shimmering backdrop for a secretary stamped Saunier and chairs signed Lelarge and Tilliard. Elsewhere in Paris, one year later, Grandpierre combined shell-pink walls, moss curtains, lettuce-green silk faille undercurtains, pale blue lampas, chocolate velvet, and leopard with a faded mocha and rose Aubusson, forming an elegant setting for a Riesener desk, Tilliard chairs, a Deshayes portrait, and a Leleu commode. Bravo, Victor Grandpierre, applauded the editors of *Maison et Jardin*, for fresh, surprising, and intelligent design.

When socialite and confidant of royals Lilia Ralli moved from her Grandpierre-designed apartment on the rue Jean-Goujon, with its gray-green velvet and cherry silk living room, to a terraced duplex apartment on the Boulevard des Invalides overlooking the dome of Saint-Louis-des-Invalides, she turned again to Grandpierre. Ralli, a cosmopolite of Greek descent with Parisian taste, was a beloved member of café society, a fixture on the López-Willshaws' cruises, and a fashion insider who suavely handled public relations for Molyneux in the 1930s (she made sure Molyneux dressed her childhood friend Princess Marina of Greece and Denmark for her wedding to the Duke of Kent) and for Jean Dessès and Christian Dior after the war. Her distinctive style, delineated by Cecil Beaton in *The Glass of Fashion*, was consistent with her personal sensibilities and petite frame.

Ralli's new apartment was as charming as its owner. An inviting pair of velvet chaises longues flanked a fireplace stacked expectantly with firewood. A magazine table (which also served for dining), glowing Louis XV and XVI marquetry, oyster-colored raw silk curtains with vivacious peony-pink undercurtains, and a well-stocked bar made the room a magnet to anyone seeking a drink and the latest news of Paris. Though no one remembers now if it was Saturday or Sunday, Madame Ralli had a "day" for receiving, when everyone passed through, from visiting royals, Cecil Beaton, Prince Matei de Brancovan, the Marquise de Ravenel, and Pierre Bergé to the Dior crowd—Suzanne Luling, Marc Bohan, Roger Vivier with Michel Brodsky, and Victor Grandpierre with Jean-Claude Donati.

In chilly weather, the appeal of velvet chaises by a roaring fire was undeniable. But when the weather turned warm, Madame Ralli's terrace was irresistible. The amateur landscaper Charles de Noailles, whom Grandpierre had encountered in the 1930s on the Côte d'Azur (and the man who preferred flowers to women, or men, according to his wife), framed the romantic view of the Invalides' dome with treillage by Lemaire, to this day provider of trellises for Versailles. Black iron furniture, a white awning, and a bust of Nero completed the furnishings. The palette of Noailles, who advocated green-on-green gardens, was as controlled as Grandpierrre's was loose. Ivy, Virginia creeper, mugho pines, dwarf cedar, *Cotoneaster*, *Pyracantha*, and box tree (shaped into cones and spheres) created a textured green garden, relieved only in spring by a few flowering white dog roses. In 1964 Noailles also introduced a novelty: avant-garde

OPPOSITE

Bathed in rosy light, contemporary upholstery mixes with an Aubusson rug, Leleu commode, Riesener writing table, and a portrait by Deshayes. Other treasures in this living room for an anonymous client are by Tilliard and Lancret. Grandpierre also specified the architectural details of pilasters and gilt baguettes.

ABOVE ────────────────────────────────

Dressed by Molyneux and behatted by Suzy,
Lilia Ralli (left) and Princess Karam of Kapurthala
(in Mainbocher and Reboux) attend Lady
Mendl's tea for the twelve most glamorous
women in the world. Sketch by Eric for *Vogue*.

RIGHT ────────────────────────────────

The duplex apartment Grandpierre designed
for Ralli was as enchanting as its owner. In
the living room he assembled velvet chaises
longues, eighteenth-century tables, inherited
Meissen, and Italian paintings given to Ralli by
Paul of Yugoslavia into a welcoming tableau.

green plastic grass, of which both landscaper and client were said to be inordinately proud.

Though Grandpierre handled gray with elegance and floral colors with aplomb, red was his trump card, as it had been for Dior. It rippled through earlier projects like the Michard-Pellissier drawing room on the avenue Foch, which featured a portrait of the Comte d'Artois, and came to full flower in Arturo López-Willshaw's *cabinet des gemmes*, where the connoisseur displayed his Renaissance crystal reliquaries, enameled chains, jeweled stone tazzas, coral sculptures, and cabochon fantasies in a setting modeled after Bramante's Tempietto of San Pietro in Montorio in Rome, with domed ceiling of cut velvet, niches banded in marquetry of rare wood, and red velvet walls ornamented with a fish-scale motif in gold. This life-size jewel box was originally designed by Grandpierre to exhibit López-Willshaw's collection at a fundraiser for the Louvre, the *Cabinet de l'amateur* exhibition at L'Orangerie. After the exhibition closed, the vignette was reinstalled at the López-Willshaws' Hôtel Rodocanachi in Neuilly, where the prettiest guests were allowed to try on the jewels. (When the house was dismantled, it was relocated to the Dalí Museum in Spain, where it remains the last intact design of Victor Grandpierre.) Running as a leitmotif through projects for Ralli, Brancovan, Serge Heftler-Louiche (Dior's childhood friend from Granville who ran Parfums Christian Dior), Politis, Lanvin, and Sayn-Wittgenstein, red hit its apotheosis in the 1960s, when the erudite Thierry and Jean Feray, the brothers who assumed Beistegui's mantle as prickly arbiters of good taste, covered the walls of their own drawing room in *rouge d'Andrinople* (Turkey red). Grandpierre continued to use it, to dramatic effect, until the end of his career.

Inquisitiveness and Understatement

Over the course of his decorating career, Grandpierre lived in the patrician 7th arrondissement, first on the rue Oudinot and later, about 1958, at 8, rue de la Chaise, in an old, low-key building where he also maintained an office. Dior publicist Jean-Claude Donati, very much a part of Grandpierre's life, lived around the corner on the rue de Grenelle. Joël le Moal remembers when, as a twenty-five-year-old, he first saw Grandpierre's rue de la Chaise apartment. Inspired by the breadth of vision, the erudition, and the luxury on display, the young man immediately began to collect antiques himself, ultimately amassing a collection that would appear in *The World of Interiors*. Somehow, somewhere, Grandpierre ran into a young Nicky Haslam, who was also wildly impressed by what he perceived as Grandpierre's "very grand, very *français* apartment." Very French, indeed, but it also managed to be idiosyncratic and unpretentious: Pierre Bergé remembered the entrance hall, which doubled as a dining room for small, urbane dinners. Decorative arts historian and artist Jean-Louis Gaillemin also recalled dinners

ABOVE

Jean-Claude Donati, the suave head of Dior's press department, attended Ralli's salons with Grandpierre. Years earlier, Grandpierre had introduced the young man to Dior, who originally engaged him to catalogue drawings and documents at the couture house.

OPPOSITE

Amateur landscaper extraordinaire Charles de Noailles equipped Ralli's terrace with treillage from Lemaire, supplier of trellises to Versailles, and gave it a disciplined green, black, and white palette. Panels opened up to reveal a view of the dome of Les Invalides. The grass was in fact a plastic facsimile, considered at the time a technological advance.

OPPOSITE

For a prestigious exhibit to benefit the
Louvre, Grandpierre reinterpreted Bramante's
Tempietto as a red velvet and gold-threaded
fantasy to showcase Arturo López-Willshaw's
collection of sixteenth-century jewels.

ABOVE

López-Willshaw later relocated his *cabinet
des gemmes* to his house in Neuilly. The
elaborate niche, moldings, and dome were all
executed in velvet and gold. The geometric
floor reflected Renaissance principles.

with far-ranging topics of conversation, and, surprisingly for a decorator known for a light eighteenth-century touch, an apartment of robust, neoclassical furniture, in particular an imposing Empire settee.

Courteous and considerate, Grandpierre could be counted on for observant, well-informed, and upbeat conversation, but he typically refrained from speaking of himself, his projects, or his accomplishments. Only years later might an interested young aesthete learn about the surrealist photos that Grandpierre had created to accompany Louise de Vilmorin's poetry. His proper Parisian upbringing allowed him to slip into the social whirl of *le tout Paris*. Like anyone who mattered, he attended Beistegui's Venetian ball in 1951, arriving with Christian Dior as part of Salvador Dalí's Entrée des Géants. As the catalyst behind Alexis de Redé's residence at the Hôtel Lambert, he naturally attended Redé's inaugural dinner in the Galerie d'Hercule. From time to time, *Vogue*'s photographers still captured him out and about—at a party given by Étienne de Beaumont that stipulated tiaras and tailcoats, or at the Bal des Oiseaux with Christian Bérard and Patricia López-Willshaw—but his party-going days were largely in the past.

Though he had access to the inner group in Paris, he edged toward its artistic fringe, lunching with Ned Rorem and painters one day, Dior, Boris Kochno, and the old crowd the next. With Dior, he visited Dalí in Barcelona and dined at the picturesque Los Caracoles. And though he preferred a quiet life to a flurry of parties, he didn't cocoon himself in a velvet-lined drawing room. In the 1960s and 1970s, he stopped in almost nightly at Fabrice Emaer's Club 7, predecessor of Le Palace, on the rue Sainte-Anne, where the artistic, the beautiful, and the outré came together. He is remembered, always amiable, chatting at the Op Art bar, silk handkerchief gracing his tweed jacket, and nursing a nightcap among models, artists, and the hip. Modest by all accounts, Grandpierre's one apparent concession to vanity was an aquamarine signet ring that matched the color of his eyes. As he spoke and gestured, it often appeared flatteringly near his face.

The Worldly and Sublime

While Grandpierre frequented Club 7 at night, he was busy with design commissions by day, including a luxurious household linen boutique for Dior at 28, avenue Montaigne and an apartment for Maria Callas. Considered by many the greatest living actress of her time, the soprano had raised opera to new heights with her interpretation of *Norma* at the Paris Opera in 1964. For the production, director Franco Zeffirelli had fused voice, orchestra, sets, and costumes into a total theatrical experience for Callas, who emphasized the drama of the libretto as much as the beauty of the music. Now celebrated in

Paris and a style icon (Aristotle Onassis had long ago taken her to Dior and upped her game), Callas purchased an apartment in 1966 at 36, avenue Georges-Mandel, across the street from Henri Grandpierre's chef-d'oeuvre, the Hôtel Singer-Polignac. Jean-Paul Faye, Grandpierre's assistant, recalls that the decorator also worked for Onassis at 88, avenue Foch, which may explain how he came to the attention of Callas.

Spectacular on stage, la Callas in life was tailored and refined. Her decorating style, however, had not quite kept up with her wardrobe. Her former home in Milan, partially influenced by the director Luchino Visconti, had been filled with Italian marble, mirrors, antiques, and dark paintings, and had been likened to a grandiose, even somewhat tacky, hotel. In Paris, Grandpierre turned down the glitz and fashioned an apartment at once as understated and operatic as his client. Grandpierre and Callas matched each other in perfectionism. (Perhaps he had witnessed her uncompromising standards in action during the fourth, controversial, performance of *Norma* at the Paris Opera, when, having muffed a high C, she imperiously raised a finger and recommenced, to triumph on the retake.) The salon, accessed via a pair of Venetian lacquered doors, had walls upholstered in velvet and hung with dark Italian, French, and Spanish old masters. A mix of Italian, French, and Asian furniture, some gilded, some lacquered, some walnut, some signed, some not, bespoke sophistication. Porphyry and Brescia lamps, rare Qianlong vases, gilt pagodas studded with semiprecious stones, and Chinese, Persian, and French rugs referenced her traveled, worldly existence. In the music room, to accompany the black Steinway (number 399040, to be exact), an eighteenth-century Italian lacquer music stand held operatic scores.

It is said that Grandpierre worked for the Paris Opera, which may explain the Zeffirelli-caliber exuberance in Callas's pink-and-white marble bath. As in Dior's Empire boudoir-bath, Grandpierre added an upholstered chair, as well as a cushy settee. Banks of tiger lilies, telephone, phonograph, rugs, and heavy white curtains elevated the bath into a bona fide sitting room where Callas planned her day, made phone calls, listened to recordings, and received friends, clad in the exotic caftans she wore at home, like a glamorous Violetta. Fortunately, her career made her independent of Greek financing, for soon she, like the *Traviata* heroine, would be shelved. As frequently happens, a friendship developed between client and decorator. Grandpierre would be devoted to Callas up to her solitary ending.

Worldly taste cast its eye farther and farther afield, but French aesthetics—sophisticated, perfected, timeless—persisted as its heart. Though Regency tables, spare white walls, and American-style bars made guest appearances, settees and silk, with accents of Porthault and Rigaud, remained indispensable to the canon of high design. Châteaux were the touchstone. Unlike Paris residences or villas on the Côte d'Azur, where one had carte blanche to create one's own design statement (invariably competing for the approval of style arbiter Charles de Beistegui), one did not tamper with a château, a shrine of family history, not a stage for individual style. As châteaux had their architecture, comfortable or not, and their inherited furniture and art, liked or disliked, there was simply no need for decorators in this world of legacy. Instead, *ensembliers* were called in to upholster furniture, make curtains, perhaps hang fabric on walls, or locate a rug. For the Rohan-Chabots' Château de la Motte-Tilly, in the Champagne-Ardenne region, Grandpierre assumed this role, much as he had at the Hôtel de Masseran.

RIGHT

In the library, where the
Comte de Rohan-Chabot
had previously installed Louis
XV-style bookcases and
seventeenth-century still lifes
by Jean-Baptiste Monnoyer,
Grandpierre added and
reconfigured furniture to create
a cozy afternoon room for
reading, cards, and tea. In his
day, opulent chinchilla throws
engulfed the velvet sofas.
Curtains were classically simple,
held back by tasseled cords.

OVERLEAF

Left: Grandpierre added
sumptuous curtains and a
stylish velvet settee to the
blue salon, which retained its
original eighteenth-century
color, although the paneling
was refurbished. The settee,
with Turkish-cornered cushions,
plump tassels, and corded and
draped skirt reflects the late
eighteenth-century fascination
with the exotic. Pale blue
silk lampas was selected for
pillows. The caned chair is
Régence. Right: For his friend
Claire-Clémence de Maillé,
Grandpierre designed a
bedroom around a flowering
Indienne document fabric and
a château-appropriate mix of
painted and marquetry furniture.

Because he knew the Comtesse Claire-Clémence de Maillé, whose mother was the current chatelaine of the Château de la Motte-Tilly, it seems that Grandpierre was brought on to the project as a family friend. Neither the Dior-wearing daughter—another favorite of Arturo López-Willshaw—nor her mother, the marquise, had to explain the rules to him. Operating with discretion, Grandpierre shepherded the perfectly scaled Louis XV monument into the mid-1960s. While gently spiffing up its contents, he enhanced its livability (including an upgrade of its electrical capacity, as film director Milos Forman was able to shoot footage for *Valmont* here).

In the library, Grandpierre replaced the late Comte de Rohan-Chabot's stiff arrangement of chairs with a pair of deep blue velvet sofas flanking the fireplace, an ivory, gold, and blue Chinese rug, and gold silk curtains, tied back simply with cords, to create a light-filled reading room. At one end of the room he placed the Migeon card table of the Marquise de Maillé and at the other, an inviting round table with chairs, perfect for afternoon tea bathed in sunlight. In Grandpierre's time, chinchilla throws were draped over both sofas; some forty years later, in shreds, they had to be removed.

In the adjacent Salon Bleu, hand-sewn blue silk curtains with swagged and corded valances graced the windows, and a chic settee with neoclassical legs and seductively rolled arms, covered in putty-colored velvet, Turkish pillows, and generous tassels joined Louis XV bergères and Régence armchairs now upholstered in blue and gold lampas. Bedrooms were made over, fresh and pretty, with canopy or alcove beds and traditional floral fabrics from Prelle or Braquenié. In Claire-Clémence de Maillé's bedroom, Grandpierre covered the walls, bed, corona, curtains, and chairs in a single eighteenth-century document fabric of flowering branches and birds, its light ground a perfect foil for the dark furniture and antique rugs.

Dangerous Beauty

Rich and suggestive, visceral yet refined, red was the go-to color for the new avenue Marceau headquarters of Dior's artistic heir, Yves Saint Laurent. Whereas both Dior and Saint Laurent turned to the rustling skirts and rich taffetas of the Belle Époque for inspiration, Dior's vision was a lament for the well-mannered memories of his childhood, while Saint Laurent sought to re-create a world he never knew. For day, Saint Laurent designed supple interpretations of modern street style; for night, his sumptuous evening clothes emanated from the realm of dark fantasy and beautiful escape. The disciplined décor of Saint Laurent's first headquarters on the rue Spontini proclaimed his commitment to modernism. By 1974, his reputation as the most innovative couturier had been secured by his appropriation of the pea coat, pantsuit, and "Le Smoking" for stylish women. In Paris and the fashion press, Saint Laurent reigned supreme.

With new headquarters in a posh Napoleon III *hôtel particulier* and no further need to broadcast his modernity, Saint Laurent could now indulge his romanticism. Underscoring his connection to Christian Dior, Saint Laurent called on Grandpierre, architect of Maison Dior and, conveniently, the decorator of his old apartment on the place Vauban. Just as Saint Laurent had coaxed the highly structured Dior dress into the swaying Trapeze line of 1957, Grandpierre now conducted the decorous Dior interiors into the moody, vaguely dangerous territory of Proust. For the main showroom,

OPPOSITE

When Yves Saint Laurent moved his couture house to the avenue Monceau, he affirmed his connection to his mentor by hiring Grandpierre, Dior's decorator. His new office, as conceived by Grandpierre, channeled the Belle Époque—the era that had profoundly inspired the artistic vision of all three men.

Grandpierre re-created pale gray walls but replaced all traces of Louis XVI with Napoleon III. Red silk Austrian shades, as ruched and tasseled as a gown for la Dame aux Camélias, crimson damask on the tufted center ottoman, gilt-wood ballroom chairs, corded club chairs, and a chandelier suspended with a red sleeve ushered the visitor into the world of nineteenth-century aesthetics. Statuary depicting the four seasons alluded to the passage time. Saint Laurent's own office—like Dior, he worked in an atelier but needed a more private retreat as well—with its moiré rug, dense mauresque wallpaper, and foliage-patterned gilt-wood mirror, might well have been airlifted from the onyx exoticism of the Hôtel de la Païva, that monument of nineteenth-century taste on the Champs-Élysées that now houses the Travellers Club.

Saint Laurent's homes mirrored the course of his fashions. While his new rue Babylone apartment teemed with worldliness, the house he and Bergé acquired in Normandy in the late 1970s sprang from the poetic otherworld that balanced Saint Laurent's aesthetic. Like ostrich ruffs and panels of black lace, the nineteenth-century Château Gabriel spoke to an ephemeral vision. Named for the park where Proust's narrator meets Gilberte Swann, the country house would become a reliquary of Proustian sensibility, full of portières and palms, velvet and tassels, Napoleon III furniture and tapestries, the territory Victor Grandpierre had explored in the avenue Marceau headquarters.

At the Château Gabriel, Grandpierre transformed the dark interiors of an uninhabited nineteenth-century neo-Gothic house into flowing spaces of ethereal light, reworking spatial distribution and opening walls so that light penetrated to its core, all the while respecting the character of the house. He widened the doorways of the reception rooms to make the first floor more expansive and slipped pocket doors into walls to close off rooms when needed. In the dining room, he installed a handsome new black-and-white floor and demarcated the space with columns to create a more intimate dining area at one end. The luminous winter garden of the Princesse Mathilde Bonaparte was the model for the château's own renovated winter garden, a room essential to a Proustian existence, to Christian Dior, and to Yves Saint Laurent.

After the architectural renovations, Grandpierre moved on to the decoration. With his understanding of country house tradition, his literary bent, and his affinity for tufted poufs, he might have fashioned extraordinary interiors, but health issues intervened. When he resigned from the project, Jacques Grange, who had been entrusted with the bedroom floor, took over the decoration of the reception rooms. Like Saint Laurent's "Le Smoking," the decoration of Château Gabriel resonated with its time. The corded slipper chairs and majolica that had captivated the virtuoso from Oran would set the tone for Denning & Fourcade's interiors for leveraged-buyout titan Henry Kravis and influenced every doyenne who lunched at Mortimer's.

One suspects that Grandpierre applauded Grange's success, for he habitually encouraged young talent. Years before, he had introduced a recent graduate of Parsons School of Design, Charles Sevigny, to Christian Dior, who commissioned a few renderings; shortly thereafter, Sevigny's own international career ignited. Grandpierre also brought a young hotelier, Jean-Claude Donati, to Dior's apartment on the rue Royale, which led to Donati's first job archiving and, ultimately, running public relations at Dior. He polished his own assistant, Jean-Paul Faye, who came from a humble background,

into a sophisticated decorator who went on to work for connoisseurs, collectors, and princesses and publish in the best European glossies. Grandpierre understood that life, like a successful interior, constantly evolves. Being calm, philosophical, and inclined to see humor in a decorating crisis served him well when juggling commissions for Dior, private clients, and press engagements; now, these same qualities helped him to handle the vagaries of time.

What appears to have been a stroke, belatedly treated, slowed Grandpierre's pace and critically impacted his spatial perception in the mid-1970s. Whereas he had easily circumvented seventeenth-century beams to tent a bedroom for the Baron de Redé in 1953, dealing with the lovely old beams in Marie-Christine de Sayn-Wittgenstein's new home in Paris perplexed him in 1976. Although many of the sofas, bergères, commodes, and case pieces from her old apartment transitioned effortlessly to the new house (and the house therefore displays the indelible hand of Grandpierre), the decorator felt sufficiently challenged by the architecture to decline the project. As at the Château Gabriel, Jacques Grange would fill the void.

Though diminished, Grandpierre maintained a professional presence for a few more years. He designed two new Dior boutiques in Paris, which opened in 1979. (Befitting a new era, the youthful Princess Caroline of Monaco presided over their openings.) He also continued his association with Parfums Christian Dior, where the directors of marketing and product development valued his insight, judgment, and eye, which took in equally the new and the old. Faye continued to assist him on ongoing residential projects, and Grandpierre himself still visited antiques galleries and auction rooms. Junior specialists who were once captivated by his gracious presence now found Grandpierre dark and forbidding. At the twentieth anniversary of the House of Saint Laurent in 1982, held at the Lido, a fragile-looking Grandpierre sat next to the exuberant Margaux Hemingway, then retreated from sight. On August 1, 1984, at the Hôpital Saint-Antoine, in the quarter of Paris that housed its furniture craftsmen, the final chapter closed on the life of Victor Grandpierre, gentleman, hotelier, photographer, journalist, illustrator, decorator, and architect of Louis-Dior.

A New Look: Seduction and Elegance

In Grandpierre's hands, couture houses became institutions, châteaux became intimist canvases, and stilted apartments became gracious homes. For Dior, he translated well mannered into relevant and elegant. His subtle balance of cerebrality and sensuousness, heritage and iconoclasm, is evident in the palette and packaging, boutiques and bottles, iconography and ambience he created for Dior—all of which is still visible today. His gift for color elevated Trianon gray to iconic status, revitalized private residences and enlivened eighteenth-century furniture. Combining tobacco leather and Austrian shades, houndstooth and cabriole legs, Grandpierre introduced subtle, slightly subversive sexuality into refined interiors. He softened a harried world with velvet, fashioned boudoirs out of practical bathrooms, and made bedrooms into private havens. Like Mario Praz, who chronicled the significance and pleasures of personal interiors in *The House of Life*, Victor Grandpierre used material culture to transform the everyday into a celebration of life.

OPPOSITE

Château Gabriel was conceived as an homage to Marcel Proust. The luminous winter garden of Princesse Mathilde Bonaparte was the model for the château's renovated winter garden, a room essential to a Proustian existence. In many ways, the house paid tribute to Dior and his influence on Saint Laurent: in his bedroom, inspired by Monsieur Swann, Saint Laurent kept a photo of Dior on his writing table.

EPILOGUE

Modern Romance

Aesthetics evolve. Every shift of politics, economy, mood, and sentiment turns the visual kaleidoscope, twisting fixed contents into ever-new configurations. Since the era of Christian Dior, Victor Grandpierre, and Georges Geffroy, a succession of trends — hip, futuristic, socially responsible, high-tech, deconstructed, ancestral, international, minimal, and street cool—have glided through living rooms and wardrobes. But however a given moment redefines beauty, the need for it doesn't change—which explains why, in 1945, attendees stood in line in frigid Paris to see an exhibit of fashion dolls, *Le Théâtre de la mode*. And just as the world held its breath to see how Christian Dior would decorate his new house, it now waits for a table at Restaurant Guy Savoy, the Jean-Michel Wilmotte interiors (in an eighteenth-century landmark) as much a draw as the 3-star cuisine. Clothing and interiors, as well as cuisine and the arts of the table, fold beauty into the routines of every day.

The more intense life becomes, the more valuable the lessons in the rustling dresses of Dior and velvet-hung rooms of Grandpierre and Geffroy. Of course, the signatures of Dior, Grandpierre, and Geffroy are rarely out of sight. Leopard, fluted legs, accentuated waists, and Miss Dior are now established classics, routinely revived and adapted for new settings. But it is their approach, as much as their glamour, that matters. The soul of the past weaves threads of continuity and heritage into the fabric of daily life. A couture coat infuses tactile pleasure into the act of staying warm. A Caffieri bust reminds us of other visions, modes of beauty, and aspirations. An Uzbekistani textile brings breadth to a living room and opens new vistas. Reaching beyond the mere mechanics of fashion and furnishings, drawing inspiration from humanism and history, Dior, Grandpierre, and Geffroy show the present how to embrace something greater, and grander, than an isolated moment.

The enduring chic of Dior, Grandpierre, and Geffroy—what keeps them from being mere time-capsule stylists—is rooted in their ability to fuse postwar reality and eighteenth-century inspiration to create contemporary solutions. They knew that if not set off by contrast, modernity exists in a vacuum. But inserted into a timeline, modern anything becomes instantly interesting, often head-turning. Geffroy was onto this when

he designed a steel chair to mix with Directoire furniture. Today, mixing concrete floors and gilt-wood consoles, or a wedding dress with sneakers, is the new New Look.

The perfect tilt of a hat, the exact shade of blue, even a beguiling arrangement of flowers infuse texture and grace into every day, hour, and minute. Dior and his decorators show that knowledge is the key to getting it right. Looking at cultures, both past and present, our own and others', provides more options, more insight, and more apt choices. And though history does indeed offer perspective, Dior, Grandpierre, and Geffroy never took it as a dictum. Just as Grandpierre willfully hung Austrian shades without heavy accompanying curtains and Dior lopped inches off the Belle Époque hemline, tradition can be embraced, modified, or even consciously rejected when fashioning the present. At second glance, that gilded mirror frame or patinated chair is an invitation more valuable than any from the Comte de Beaumont—it is an invitation to view, understand, and connect to the continuum of human experience.

APPENDIX

Dior in the Country

Dior and His Decorators chronicles the emergence of the New Look and its sophisticated counterpart in interior decoration. These highly polished, worldly statements by Christian Dior, Victor Grandpierre, and Georges Geffroy were, at heart, Parisian phenomena. However, the story is augmented by a look at Dior's country houses, which reflect the abiding French sensibility that grounds this soaring cosmopolitan aesthetic.

Profound individuality, respect for architectural context, and understatement are the common threads that bind Dior's two country properties—one a former mill, the other an old coaching inn, one dating to the fifteenth century—into the aesthetic narrative of postwar French design. Dior's friend and gallery partner Pierre Colle and his wife, Carmen (soon, the director of the boutique at Christian Dior Haute Couture), first introduced him to the area near Fontainebleau, where they had a country house and where, incidentally, he sketched his groundbreaking New Look collection. Visiting the Colles quite naturally segued to the rental of a cottage in Fleury-en-Bière. The purchase of a sixteenth-century bailiff's house in nearby Milly by his friends Jean Cocteau and the actor Jean Marais added to the area's allure. Soon, Dior acquired a dilapidated mill surrounded by a cluster of outbuildings—"a ruin in a swamp"—whose very state of abandon stirred his latent architectural ambitions.

Personal associations also lured Dior to the outskirts of Grasse, where he had lived with his father after his discharge from the army. Despite the grim political situation and the primitive, unelectrified cottage that his father had occupied since his bankruptcy, Dior discovered calm and focus in tending a kitchen garden as well as in the landscape of Provence. Later, as the responsibilities of running the preeminent Parisian couture concern intensified, the serenity of Provence beckoned once again. A rustic former hostel in Montauroux, not far from Grasse, became another backdrop for Dior's architectural vision as well as his personal haven.

Le Moulin du Coudret

If the ormolu sconces and gray satin at 30, avenue Montaigne breathed Parisian sophistication, the gravel paths, armoires, and ticking stripes at Le Moulin du Coudret radiated the warmth of a Chardin painting. Dior's first country retreat, a reclaimed fifteenth-century mill in Milly-la-Forêt, not far from Fontainebleau, nurtured reflection and renewal amid rippling streams, relaxed flower beds, cozy rooms, and stalwart furniture.

With its confident lack of pretension, Le Moulin du Coudret encouraged bonhomie and homely pleasures. Close friends would come on Sundays to swim in the old mill pond, contribute a stitch or two to Dior's current needlepoint project, indulge in the good French cooking of Denise, the Martiniquan cook with a wardrobe by Christian Dior, and linger in the sun over the framboise liqueur that the couturier distilled from his own harvest. Dior himself was most often dressed in boots, tending the flower beds he had modeled on exuberant roadside gardens in Normandy.

Rusticity at the mill, a mere sixty-three kilometers from Paris, was a virtue and a charm, but hardly random. Following the success of his first collection, Dior rewarded himself with a rundown country property, rather than a villa or manor house, for its lack of affectation. With architect, Geffroy Schaison, he minimally restored the complex of former mill, stable, and barn, and retained the rubble-and-mortar façades, dormer windows, and faded shutters. The addition of multiple bathrooms was a sybaritic concession to modernity—and Dior's penchant for daydreaming in the bath.

With his Polish gardener, Ivan, Dior added a lawn in the former working courtyard, planted perennials against its low stone walls, and encouraged old vines to cling to the lichen-covered façade. In a snub to gentrifying parasols and patios, the pool where one swam remained unapologetically a mill pond. Plantings were as casual as the peasant gardens Dior admired: cosmos and zinnias spilled over gravel paths, an isolated yellow hollyhock framed a window. Behind the nonchalance, however, *Vogue* editor Bettina Ballard detected the sure touch of Dior in flower beds that were pure New Look poetry: dark red hollyhocks against gray stone with one heartbreaking pink rose blooming underneath.

The interiors, like the flower beds, were outwardly relaxed but carefully tended. Guests who visited in the 1950s recall a level of comfort, detail, and function that doesn't occur by happenstance. The house had in fact been professionally decorated, albeit with a light touch. Though no records survive, several believe that Victor Grandpierre consulted on the décor—its unaffected mien resembles the look of a country house in Meudon that he decorated at roughly the same time. In any event, the home-loving Dior oversaw the interior atmosphere with its scattering of rugs and bibelots just as closely as the draping in his atelier. Almost as keen on antiquing as gardening, Dior knew the local antiques haunts and personally selected much of the down-to-earth Louis-Philippe furniture, jardinières, and landscape paintings.

Flowers, books, and the odd painting infused Le Moulin with the warm, natural quality of a house lived in for a long time. Indeed, though Le Moulin was new to its role as a residence, it took part in longstanding French rituals. Leisurely Sunday lunches were a habit. And though Parisian friends—Henri Sauguet, Pierre Gaxotte, Christian Bérard, Victor Grandpierre, Bettina Ballard, and Dior's second-in-command Raymonde

PRECEDING PAGES

Dior at Le Moulin du Coudret. Though he found inspiration in the very air of Paris, it was in the country that he reflected on the lessons of the city: "The peace and quiet calm of the country are essential to me."

OPPOSITE

Le Moulin du Coudret comprised a converted mill, stables, and storage buildings clustered around a courtyard. Dior valued its rusticity, for in his view, simplicity was "indispensable to the standard of good taste of old France."

OVERLEAF

Top left: In the double salon, a beamed ceiling and polished terra-cotta floor set off unpretentious Louis XVI and Louis-Philippe furniture. Bottom left: A Louis-Philippe bed with swan carvings, bed curtains and an Empire sling chair, both with pompon fringe, furnished the ladies' bedroom. Right: In a former granary, Dior set up a summer dining room.

Zehnacker—came frequently, business rarely entered this sacred retreat. Like any good country squire, Dior integrated himself into community life: he not only knew the local *antiquaires* but refrocked the local priest, Curé Letellier, whose soutane, to Dior's eyes, lacked dignity of cut. Clothes, like houses, were conduits for a way of life.

Simplicity, Dior wrote, was at the heart of the good taste of the past—and, he might have added, the future. Le Moulin du Coudret complemented the bright lights of Paris and the shock of celebrity. In the calm of Milly, new collections came to life. Nature proposed color schemes that blossomed against the gray-and-white backdrop of 30, avenue Montaigne. Flower forms influenced silhouettes and details of dresses. The embroideries of the "Vilmorin" and "May" dresses are the flower beds of Milly rendered in silk. If the Swiss-born Jean-Jacques Rousseau found peace in majestic landscapes, Dior found it in country domesticity. Whether at table with friends, in repose amid simple surroundings, or with his hands in the soil, Dior drew inspiration from the rhythms of Milly.

Though his furniture and objects were varied and down-to-earth, Dior assembled them with the same trained eye that accessorized a dress, applying the same "art of pleasing" to his house that he had employed to revive Parisian couture. A bust on a mahogany stand completes a corner; a framed photograph, urns, and a potpourri burner balance a mantel; everywhere, glasses of dahlias, vases of lilacs, and posies in clay pots add charm. By drawing inspiration from familiar sources, Dior's taste in decorating, as in fashion, articulated a new mood. As if envisioning Le Moulin du Coudret, Solange d'Ayen, formerly of *Vogue* and now the editor of a new magazine, *Maison et Jardin*, noted that attempts to create a self-conscious period room or a studied masterpiece were out of sync with the times: truly contemporary decorating circa 1950 revolved around pretty and diverse objects assembled for comfort and charm. Elsewhere, for Dior and others, Georges Geffroy and Victor Grandpierre exemplified Ayen's comments with mixes of French furniture, comfort, and glamour. Whereas Dior's house in Passy would typify the cosmopolitan extreme, Le Moulin, with its aged surfaces and humble fabrics, was its rustic variation.

La Colle Noire

At physical remove from Paris and light-years from the action on the Côte d'Azur, the nineteenth-century bastide La Colle Noire, near Grasse, emanates the spirit of Dior. Its vineyards, olive groves, Renaissance stone lions, and shaded Italian garden mingle past with present. Cool tiled hallways, glimpses of linen velvet, and Emilio Terry influences add calm and charm. If the house in Passy was a civilized nest amid the demands of Paris and Le Moulin du Coudret represented an escape from the city, La Colle Noire, with its solid dignity, was Dior's chosen home.

Purchased in 1950, the coaching inn turned manor house was Dior's final domestic creation, and still a work in progress at the time of his death in 1957. Just as another of his last creations—the 1957 city dress "Palais de Glace," with tidy bodice, slender sleeves, and meticulously gathered skirt—signaled in its sobriety, beauty, and understatement a return to the vision of 1947, the stone house represented permanence. Its atmosphere of storied family house, mixing antiques with the occasional surprise, was gracious and unaffected. Dior, who planned to retire to La Colle Noire, was so dedicated to the house that he eventually sold the mill at Milly to underwrite the renovations, the cost of which, as typically happens, exceeded expectations.

Approached through an allée of cypress trees, the house sat on more than a hundred acres of pleasure garden and working land, accompanied by graveled terraces, a private chapel, and views across the valley. Dior installed a 150-foot reflecting pool that ran the length of the house. For parties, he illuminated the pool with fifty candled hurricanes around its perimeter. The faithful Ivan, maestro of the flower beds in Milly, now moved south to take charge of the gardens. Always practical, Dior planned for the grape vines and olive trees to generate income if his designing luck ran out. But for the moment, with neither retirement nor professional decline on the horizon, the vineyards, olive groves, and garden, planted with perfume flowers like jasmine and May rose solely for the pleasure of their scent, were opportunities to reconnect with the land.

André Svetchine, the Nice-based architect who had designed Raymonde Zehnacker's nearby country house, provided Dior with plenty of rein to play gentleman architect. In fact, Dior conceived much of the house on his own, often relying on Svetchine and interior decorator Michel-Jacques Marsan more for execution than conception. For construction, as for couture, Dior was a curator of time-honored craftsmanship. He required the use of old materials or, at least, materials made in the old-fashioned manner, whenever possible. Fortunately, Svetchine proved adept at sourcing local and antique elements that reinforced the ambience of an old manor house. Glazed Anduze planters flanked the door, and a new gravel forecourt greeted arrivals. Lanterns with wrought-iron arms ornamented with a Greek key motif, inspired by Emilio Terry but designed by Dior, illuminated the entry.

Throughout the house, white walls, gray paneling, and terracotta or white stone floors, or some combination thereof, weave simplicity and continuity into the décor. Following the notion of a provincial manor that has evolved over the years, formulas were relaxed, never strictly enforced. Periods, styles, colors, and types of rugs varied; the only cardinal rule was that the ambience remain polished but unpretentious.

Decoration proceeded slowly, in part determined by the renovation schedule. Because of a delay in the electrical hookup, only two rooms were habitable as of 1956. With such a leisurely pace, the loose accumulation of furniture gave the impression of having been amassed over generations. Except for one chair by Séné, the furniture was warm and burnished but far from museum quality, generally eighteenth- and nineteenth-century French, with the occasional Biedermeier chair or Continental piece for variety. Ditto the casual stock of old paintings, engravings, bas-relief plaques, fashion plates, and drawings, brought smartly up to date with a drawing by Saul Steinberg and several paintings by Leonid Berman.

With its waxed tiles and patinated furniture, La Colle Noire conveys Dior's response to postwar reality. Instead of falling back into familiar routines after the war, the world had rushed forward

BELOW

Like La Colle Noire, Dior's 1957 "Palais de Glace" dress affirmed his belief in time-honored values and established forms.

OPPOSITE

The timeless dignity of La Colle Noire represented security and permanence for Dior.

into uncharted territory. Europe integrated warily, colonies sought independence, the Soviet Union loomed as the new world menace, and the economy transitioned to industrial production. In this mid-century flux, as patterns changed and the pace picked up, Dior was a conservator of enduring custom.

A fashion genius coupled with conscientious businessman, Dior worked incessantly in this new economic climate, designing collections, developing perfume, and licensing new global products, leaving him less time to pursue the friendships, gardening, antiquing, music, and quiet he craved. Others found themselves with less wherewithal, and even less inclination, to observe the niceties of the past. Even *Maison et Jardin*, the glossy broadcaster of aspirational decoration, vaunted a plastic tablecloth that could be cleaned with the swipe of a dishcloth. Jewels, hats, and gloves, those precious accoutrements perfected by centuries of patronage, with techniques conserved from generation to generation, were called into question. Emblematically, the actress Grace Kelly, a Dior client, though engaged to a prince, was photographed for *Vogue* without adornment, just bare shoulders, blonde hair, and American *fraîcheur*.

OPPOSITE

Dior's office in 1956, featuring his cherished red palette, terra-cotta tile, and Louis XVI and Empire furniture, translated Parisian style for Provence.

ABOVE

Left: Simple ticking in Dior's boudoir defined a new chic that even Sister Parish would have embraced. Right: Panoramic wallpaper depicting Telemachus on Calypso's island introduced nineteenth-century exoticism to a room of imposing mahogany Empire furniture.

ABOVE

Dior's bedroom at La Colle Noire combined gauffraged linen velvet with chalky white walls, simple gray trim, and gleaming terra-cotta floors. Since his childhood in Granville, he had sought security in curtained and alcove beds.

OPPOSITE

Drawing on Directoire and Empire documents, Dior and architect André Svetchine sourced an antique marble tub and brass water cisterns for a smartly symmetrical, mirrored bath with custom-made swan's-neck faucets and faux-marble walls.

Quality, time, and heritage, those hallmarks of Dior, were the new luxuries. Now, interiors and clothes that were in sync with the time were comfortable and timeless, without gimmick or artifice. Frivolity, Dior determined, was passé, and as an artist, he reflected his time. His pet model changed from the aloof Renée to the accessible Victoire. He streamlined his 1954 collection into the quiet H-Line. Nevertheless, since its introduction in 1947, his tiny-waist silhouette had proved both flattering and versatile and had become a classic. Full skirts still turned up in his collections, as perennial and sure as snowdrops in the spring. His new country house, too, rejected showy effect in favor of simplification and tried-and-true refinement.

Dior was—both as a professional couturier and as an individual—a believer in the accomplishments of French civilization. The hand sewing, beading, embroidery, solid construction, and line of a Dior dress were rooted in French history. So, too, were Dior's courtesy, table, and interests in art, music, and antiques. La Colle Noire, indifferent to fad, drew on French crafts in its construction, history in its furnishings, and tradition in its seasonal rhythms. While timelessness emanated from the time-worn stone of Dior's last house, its modernity was in its ease, adaptability to contemporary life, loose appropriation of the past, and embrace of its time. Its appeal, like that of the New Look dress, was that it fulfilled a need for romance.

BELOW

A contemporary view of the southwest façade of La Colle Noire. Dior, who renovated the property with André Svetchine in the 1950s, differentiated little between his dresses and architecture. He wrote, "My weakness is architecture. I think of my work as ephemeral architecture, dedicated to the beauty of the female body."

CHRONOLOGIES

Owing to limited documentation, information listed here
is approximate and incomplete; dates are frequently based
on date of publication.

Georges Geffroy (1905–1971)

CLIENTS AND COMMISSIONS

1925: sets for the film *Les Aventures de Robert Macaire* (Jean
Epstein)

1930s: house, Duc François d'Harcourt, 53, rue de Verneuil,
Paris 75007

1938: private salon, Robert Piguet, 60, avenue Montaigne,
Paris 75008

1944–48: apartment, Monsieur et Madame Marcel Rochas, 40,
rue Barbet-de-Jouy, Paris 75007

1945: set design, *Le Théâtre de la mode,* Pavillon de Marsan,
Musée des Arts Décoratifs, Paris 75001

1946: library, British Embassy, Hôtel de Charost, 35, rue du
Faubourg Saint-Honoré, Paris 75008

1947: editor, *Le Calendrier des dames pour 1947*

1947: apartment, Alexis de Redé, Hôtel Meurice, 228, rue de
Rivoli, Paris 75001

1949: library and general counsel, Alexis de Redé, Hôtel Lambert,
2, rue Saint-Louis-en-l'Île, Paris 75004

1950: apartment, Palmyre Béglarian, 73, avenue de Breteuil,
Paris 75007 (redecorated in 1964)

1950: couture house, Marcel Rochas, 12, avenue Matignon,
Paris 75008

1950: event design, 250th anniversary, place Vendôme, Paris 75001

1950: yacht, *La Gaviota IV,* Arturo López-Willshaw

1952: house, Daisy (Mrs. Reginald) Fellowes, 69, rue de Lille,
Paris 75007

1952: apartment, Maurice Rheims, 12, avenue Matignon, Paris 75008

1953: entrance, salon, dining room, and stairwell, Christian Dior, 7,
boulevard Jules-Sandeau, Paris 75116

1953: apartment, Mr. and Mrs. Loel Guinness, 18 avenue Matignon,
Paris 75008

Mid-1950s: house, Nicole de Montesquiou, 31, rue Delabordère,
Neuilly

1956: house, Georges Litman, 35, boulevard du Château, Neuilly

1956: apartment, Monsieur and Madame Jacques Abreu, 73,
quai d'Orsay, Paris 75007

1957: theater, Charles de Beistegui, Château de Groussay,
Monfort-l'Amaury (Yvelines)

1958: partial redecoration, Marquis and Marquise (Armand) de
Pomereu, Château de Daubeuf (Seine-Maritime)

1960: sitting room, Arturo López-Willshaw, 14, rue du Centre,
Neuilly

1960s: residence, Alain Delon, 22, avenue de Messine, Paris 75008

1961: apartment, Vicomte and Vicomtesse (Guillaume) de
Bonchamps, 42, avenue Foch, Paris 75116

1961: apartment, Mr. and Mrs. André Rueff, boulevard de
Montmorency, Paris 75016

1961: duplex apartment, Pierre Le Blan, 4, square des Écrivains-
combattants-morts-pour-la-France, Paris 75016

1962: apartment, James H. Douglas, 44, rue du Bac, Paris 75007

1962: country house, Mr. and Mrs. Loel Guinness, Haras de
Piencourt, Bailleul-la-Vallée (Eure)

1962: apartment, Mr. and Mrs. Walter Moreira-Salles, 22, avenue
Foch, Paris 75116

1962–65: country house, Mr. and Mrs. Pierre David-Weill,
Gambais (Yvelines)

1967: apartment, Mrs. Descamps-Béghin, 5, rue Auguste-
Comte, Paris

1968: apartment, Prince Édouard de Lobkowicz, 30, avenue
Marceau, Paris 75008

1969: apartment, Robert Ricci, 14, avenue Élisée-Reclus,
Paris 75007

1968–70: apartment, Mr. and Mrs. Antenor Patiño, 9, avenue du
Maréchal-Maunoury, Paris 75016

1969–71: house (partial), Mr. and Mrs. Philippe Durand-Ruel,
Rueil-Malmaison (Hauts-de-Seine)

1970: staircase, Galerie Jacques Kugel, 279, rue Saint-Honoré,
Paris 75001

Victor Grandpierre (1906–1984)

CLIENTS AND COMMISSIONS

1930s: journalist and photographer, bylines and credits in *Le
Jour, Vogue* (Paris), *Vogue* (American), *Le Jardin des modes,*
and *L'Officiel de la couture et de la mode;* exhibited in
Chasseurs d'Images at the Carlton Hotel, Cannes

1942: photographer, *A Midsummer Night's Dream,* sponsored by
Comtesse Lily Pastré, Château de Montredon near Marseille

1946: cover illustration, *Art et Style* no. 4, April; photo reportage
on the rue Jacob, *Art et Style,* no. 5, October

1946–47: couture house, Christian Dior, 30 avenue Montaigne,
Paris 75008

1948: *L'écho des fantaisies,* photographs by Victor Grandpierre,
text by Louise de Vilmorin

1949: Christian Dior suite, Plaza Hotel, New York

1949: sitting room, Patricia (Madame Arturo) López-Willshaw, 14,
rue du Centre, Neuilly

1950s: apartment, Mr. and Mrs. Serge Heftler-Louiche, 3, rue du
Général-Appert, Paris 75116

1951: ball design, Prince Sturdza of Romania, Cirque Fanni,
boulevard Pasteur, Paris 75015

1951: country house, Mr. and Mrs. Claude Hersent, le Tour de
Villebon, Meudon (Hauts-de-Seine)

1951: apartment, Marquis and Marquise de La Falaise, Paris

1951–52: apartment, Jean Dessès, 17, avenue Matignon,
Paris 75008

1952: triplex apartment, Prince and Princesse Matei de Brancovan, 1 avenue Henri-Martin, Paris 75116

1953: millinery atelier, Christian Dior, 30, avenue Montaigne, Paris 75008

1953: winter garden, study, and private quarters, Christian Dior, 7, boulevard Jules-Sandeau, Paris 75116

1954: bedroom and stairwell, Alexis de Redé, Hôtel Lambert, 2, rue Saint-Louis-en-l'Île, Paris 75004

1954: Venetian-style bedroom, anonymous client (*Connaissance des Arts,* January 15)

1954: apartment, Maître and Madame Jean Michard-Pellissier, 88, avenue Foch, Paris 75116

1955: Boutique Christian Dior, corner of avenue Montaigne and rue François-1ᵉʳ, Paris 75008

1955: shoe boutique, Roger Vivier for Christian Dior, 17, rue Francois-1ᵉʳ, Paris 75008

1955: apartment, Prince and Princesse Jean Faucigny-Lucinge, rue de Presbourg, Paris 75008

1955: decoration, Baron et Baronne Élie de Rothschild, Hôtel de Masseran, 11, rue Masseran, Paris 75007

1956: apartment, Mr. and Mrs Eugène Weinreb, street address unknown, Paris 75016

1956: apartment, Mrs. Jean (Lilia) Ralli, rue Jean-Goujon, Paris 75008

1956: display for collection of Arturo López-Willshaw, *Le Cabinet de l'amateur* exhibition, L'Orangerie, organized by the Marquis de Ganay and the Friends of the Louvre (later relocated to the López-Willshaw house, Neuilly)

1957: living room, anonymous client, Paris ("Le Charme dans la maison d'une allure somptueuse," *Maison et Jardin*, September–October)

1957: apartment, Laurent Rombaldi, street address unknown, Paris 75007

1958: apartment, anonymous client, Paris 75016 ("Décor à l'ancienne dans un immeuble 1930," *Maison et Jardin*, November)

1959: country house, Mr. and Mrs. Serge Heftler-Louiche, Biarritz (Pyrénées-Atlantiques)

1960: apartment, Mr. and Mrs. Jean François Malle, 3, rue Courty, Paris 75007

1960: renovation, Vivier-Dior shoe boutique, 17, rue Francois-1ᵉʳ, Paris 75008

1960s: apartment, Aristotle Onassis, 88, Avenue Foch, Paris 75116

1961: boutique, Jean Dessès, Athens

1961: apartment, anonymous client, 32, avenue Foch, Paris 75016 ("Une vraie maison du XVIIIᵉᵐᵉ," *Connaissance des Arts*, December)

1962: apartment, Pierre Bergé and Yves Saint Laurent, 3, Place Vauban, Paris 75007

Post 1964: partial redecoration, Aliette de Rohan-Chabot, Marquise de Maillé, Château de la Motte-Tilly, la Motte-Tilly (Aube)

1965: duplex apartment, Lilia (Mrs. Jean) Ralli, 28, boulevard des Invalides, Paris 75007

1965: apartment, Marquis and Marquise de La Falaise, Neuilly

1965: apartment, Mr. and Mrs. Yves Lanvin, corner avenue Friedland and avenue Hoche, Paris 75008

1966: apartment, anonymous client, Paris ("Splendeurs et cadre en harmonie," *Maison et Jardin*, March)

1966: apartment, Maria Callas, 36, avenue Georges-Mandel, Paris 75116

1967: Baby Dior, 28, avenue Montaigne, Paris 75008

1967: Boutique Miss Dior, 11 bis, rue Francois-1ᵉʳ, Paris 75008

1970: Boutique Christian Dior "Monsieur," 13, rue Francois-1ᵉʳ, Paris 75008

1972: couture house, Yves Saint Laurent, 5, avenue Marceau, Paris 75116

1972: Café Français, Hôtel PLM Saint-Jacques, 17, boulevard Saint-Jacques, Paris 75014

1973: linen boutique, Christian Dior, 28, avenue Montaigne, Paris 75008

1976: apartment, Antoinette de Gunzburg, rue du Bac, Paris 75007

1978-79: partial renovation, Pierre Bergé and Yves Saint Laurent, Château Gabriel, Benerville-sur-Mer (Calvados)

1979: Boutique Miss Dior, 32, avenue Montaigne, Paris 75008

1979: luggage and leather boutique, Christian Dior, 26, avenue Montaigne, Paris 75008

NOTES

PROLOGUE

Page 11: The unveiling of the New Look . . . was a *succès fou*: Bettina Ballard, *In My Fashion* (New York: David McKay Company, 1960), 230.

Page 11: Overnight, the swagged hobble skirt . . . became outmoded: Susan Mary Alsop, *To Marietta from Paris 1945-1960* (New York: Doubleday & Company, 1975), 71-72.

Page 11: Well-bred Parisians morphed into lionesses: Alsop, *To Marietta from Paris*, 93.

Page 11: At the Jockey Club . . . members now spoke of nothing but Dior: Antony Beevor and Artemis Cooper, *Paris After the Liberation 1944-1949*, rev. ed. (New York: Penguin Books, 2007), 255.

Page 11: The memory of the Belle Époque . . . acquired mythical status: Christian Dior, *Christian Dior et moi* (Paris: Vuibert, 2011), 189.

Page 13, caption: Fashion was not merely "a sort of Vanity Fair": Dior, *Christian Dior et moi,* 171.

Page 14: A posh nightclub, À la belle époque: Anne Pierry, "Rythmes de Paris," *Plaisir de France*, February 1947, 50.

Page 17: Like Gaul, [the decoration of] Dior's townhouse was divided into three parts: *Vogue* (American), November 15, 1953, 92-93.

Page 17: A handsome Spanish butler: Françoise Giroud, *Christian Dior 1905-1957* (Paris: Éditions du Regard, 1987), 46.

Page 18: A single sewing machine sufficed for seventeen seamstresses: "Dior Celebrates a Decade at the Very Top," *Life*, March 4, 1957, 132.

Page 19: Georges Geffroy meticulously dismantled Louis XV corner cabinets . . . to re-create new cabinets: *The Patiño Collection*, Sotheby's New York, November 1, 1986, Lots 83 and 84.

Page 21: An enviable standard of living: *New York Times*, March 1, 2017. (Between 1945 and 1975, the purchasing power of the average worker in France rose 170 percent.)

THE ELEMENTS OF STYLE

Page 28: "L'engrais Dior, c'est de l'or!": Musée Christian Dior, *Christian Dior: Man of the Century* (Paris: Editions Artlys, 2011), 4.

Page 28: A winter garden would later be a criterion for his own house in Paris: Dior, *Christian Dior et moi*, 187 and 213.

Page 28: Dior would install canopied beds or sleeping alcoves that recalled the security of Les Rhumbs: *Maison et Jardin*, February 1958, 69.

Page 28: "Parc Monceau" and "Bonbon": Haute Couture Collection Spring 1947; "Eugénie": Haute Couture Collection Fall-Winter 1948.

Page 30: Dior would translate elements of the house's façade–as well as his stylish mother and glamorous Angevin grandmother: Jeanne Perkins, "Dior," *Life*, March 1, 1948, 89.

Page 31: The prevailing convention of attributing certain styles to specific rooms: Helena Hayward, *World Furniture* (London: Hamlyn Publishing Group, 1965), 242.

Page 31: When a journalist for *Time* found Dior in his velvet-walled library surrounded by fine paintings . . . and plaster statuettes: Stanley Karnow, *Paris in the Fifties* (New York: Times Books, 1997; reprint, New York: Broadway Books, 1999), 389.

Page 31: A style that Dior would refer to as "Louis XVI-Passy": Dior, *Christian Dior et moi*, 190.

Page 31: The quarter was in its prime: Jean-Louis de Faucigny-Lucinge, *Un gentilhomme cosmopolite: Mémoires* (Paris: Perrin, 1990), Avant-propos/ Foreword.

Page 31: The rue Richard-Wagner was renamed rue Albéric-Magnard after World War I.

Page 32: Madeleine Dior ditched her Japonisme for the eighteenth-century-inspired modernity: Dior, *Christian Dior et moi*, 190.

Page 32: Their florist, Orève: Marie-France Pochna, *Christian Dior: The Biography* (London: Duckworth Press, 2008), 33.

Page 32: Dior later acquired his own Helleu drawing: As seen in the Brassaï photo of Dior in his rue Royale apartment. Thank you to Perrine Scherrer of Dior for confirmation of this fact.

Page 33: The new street was oddly dark: Pochna, *Christian Dior*, 32.

Page 33: Shades believed to be much closer to the interiors of Versailles: Pochna, *Christian Dior*, 32.

Page 35: Dior embraced the architecture of Le Corbusier . . . and ended his nights at the bar of the Boeuf sur le toit: Dior, *Christian Dior et moi*, 193.

Page 35: Chanel devised sweaters in utilitarian jersey: Christian Dior, *Talking about Fashion to Elie Rabourdin and Alice Chavane* (London: Hutchinson & Co., 1954), 21.

Page 38: Christian Bérard, Max Jacob, Pavel Tchelitchew: Pierre Le-Tan, *Rencontres d'une vie 1945-1984* (Paris: Aubier, 1986), 70.

Page 38: An exhibition devoted to the architect . . . designer Emilio Terry: Pierre Arizzoli-Clémentel, *Emilio Terry: Architecte et décorateur* (Paris: Gourcuf Gradenigo, 2013), 29.

Page 38: Dior penned courtly notes: Dior Parfums Archives, *Dior et l'art*, 4.

Page 38: Bland country curate made out of marzipan: Cecil Beaton, *The Glass of Fashion* (New York: Rizzoli, 2014; first published 1954 by Doubleday), 298.

Page 38: Applauding talent from the sidelines: Dior, *Talking about Fashion*, 19.

Page 41: Nicholas Bongard–nephew of Paul Poiret: Pochna, *Christian Dior*, 51.

Page 41: Bongard was business partner of café society jeweler Jean Schlumberger: Obituary of Nicholas Bongard, *New York Times*, April 19, 2000.

Page 41: Jean Ozenne, a cousin of Christian Bérard: Pochna, *Christian Dior*, 67.

Page 41: Careful recording of his sales to Alix Barton (Madame Grès) . . . and glover Alexandrine: Alexandra Palmer, *Dior: A New Look, a New Enterprise* (London: V&A Publishing, 2009), 12; Pochna, *Christian Dior*, 69.

Page 41: Editorial work from *Le Figaro* and *Harper's Bazaar*: Ballard, *In My Fashion*, 233; Palmer, *Dior: A New Look*, 12.

Page 41: He moved into the Hôtel de Bourgogne: Dior, *Talking about Fashion*, 25.

Page 42: All navy with white linen: *L'Hebdo*, October 22, 2015, online edition (http://www.hebdo.ch/hebdo/culture/detail/robert-piguet-le-suisse-qui-r%C3%A9gnait-sur-la-haute-couture, accessed July 2, 2016; site no longer active.)

Page 42: There can be no elegance without simplicity: Dior, *Talking about Fashion*, 28.

Page 42: Referencing the illustrations of the beloved children's books by the Comtesse de Ségur . . . daring dresses that . . . spelled success: Dior, *Talking about Fashion*, 26.

Page 42: "Café Anglais" was Dior's first hit: Dior, *Christian Dior et moi*, 205.

Page 42: Brought him to the attention of the all-powerful Carmel Snow: Dior, *Talking about Fashion*, 26.

Page 42: The couturier Dior most admired, Edward Molyneux: Dior, *Talking about Fashion*, 20.

Page 45: He re-created the atmosphere of Les Rhumbs on the rue Royale: Perkins, "Dior," *Life*, 88.

Page 45: It looked provincial: *Vogue* (American), April 1, 1947, 146.

Page 45: An elegance that accorded well with the décors of a Jean-Michel Frank and the extravagances of Surrealism: Dior, *Talking about Fashion*, 29.

Page 45: Countess Nicole de Montesquiou and Mitzah Bricard contributed the feminine elegance that Dior adored: Ballard, *In My Fashion*, 234-35.

Page 45: Dior was content executing beautifully crafted clothes: Laurence Benaïm, *Dior: The New Look Revolution* (New York: Rizzoli, 2015), 63.

Page 45: Described by *Ce Soir* as looking like a fashion plate of the past: "Au Rideau de Paris: Captain Smith," *Ce Soir* (Paris), March 19, 1938.

Page 46: Piguet resorted to hiring a young fellow from Chanel, Antonio Castillo: Jean Pierre Pastori, *Robert Piguet: Un prince de la mode* (Lausanne: La Bibliothèque des Arts, 2015), 58.

Page 46: Paul Caldaquès . . . introduced him in 1941 to Lucien Lelong: Dates of Dior's engagement at Lelong—1941–1946—confirmed by Solène Auréal at Christian Dior, May 23, 2017.

Page 48: Sparks emanating from the house of Lelong: Ballard, *In My Fashion*, 231.

Page 48: Claire McCardell even designed a cotton "Kitchen Dinner Dress": Brenda Polan and Roger Tredre, *The Great Fashion Designers* (New York: Bloomsbury Academic, 2009), 93.

Page 49: Christian Bérard, appointed art director, orchestrated the talents of his friends: Edmonde Charles-Roux et al., *Théâtre de la Mode Fashion Dolls: The Survival of Haute Couture*, rev. ed. (Portland, OR: Palmer/Pletsch Publishing, 2002), 42.

Page 49: Sewing machines were moved about Paris several times a day: Charles-Roux, *Théâtre de la Mode*, 36.

Page 49: Full black silk surah skirt and a candy-pink crepe top: Charles-Roux, *Théâtre de la Mode*, 133, fig. 23.

Page 49: Turquoise garden-party dress with a white organdy collar: Charles-Roux, *Théâtre de la Mode*, 151, fig. 117.

Page 51: When the model breathed, buttons inevitably popped: Pierre Cardin, interview with author, January 2016.

A QUEST FOR GRANDEUR

Page 53: Geffroy alluded to maternal ancestry: Le-Tan, *Rencontres d'une vie*, 61.

Page 54: Entertaining a bejeweled Duchess of Windsor in his elegant walk-up apartment: Michel Guéranger, interview with author, May 2017.

Page 54: Liveried Morris-Wolseley with red leather interiors: Nicolas Petitjean, interview with author, May 2017.

Page 54: His grandfather and father were sober lawyers who served on the Superior Court: Grandfather: Louis Philippe Marie Geffroy, per death certificate on file in Paris, born 1804 in Liffré (Ille-et-Vilaine), deceased 1896 at 80, rue de Grenelle, Paris. Father: Paul Louis Geffroy, per birth and death certificates on file in Paris, born 1865 at 80, rue de Grenelle, Paris 7; died Rosporden, 1917.

Page 54: His Latvian-born grandmother, Wilhelmina Catherine Elisabeth Pinsa-Cruz: Per death certificate on file in Paris, born in Riga, Latvia, died in Paris at 80, rue de Grenelle in 1893.

Page 54: Madame de Pompadour had grown up at 50, rue de Richelieu: Jacques Hillairet, *Connaissance du vieux Paris* (Paris: Editions Princesse, 1956), 232 and 236.

Page 55: Both had oval faces with high foreheads, chestnut hair and eyes, rounded chins, and strong noses: Physical description of Paul Geffroy obtained from his military file, army roll number 415.

Page 55: *Goût qui chante* (taste that sings): Duchesse d'Harcourt, interview with author, November 2015.

Page 55: Could little imagine him in the confines of a school: Duchesse d'Harcourt interview, November 2015.

Page 55: Consider Geffroy to have been highly cultivated: Alain Demachy, interview with author, October 2015.

Page 56: Provided illustrations for two issues of Lucien Vogel's fashion journal: *Le Jardin des modes*, no. 61, August 15, 1924, and no. 67, February 15, 1925.

Page 56: With his sclerotic lungs . . . he was demobilized in 1929: Georges Geffroy military record, Number 501, opened May 10, 1925.

Page 56: Geffroy worked for the couturier Rolande: Jean-Baptiste Minnaert, *Pierre Barbe: Architectures* (Liège, Belgium: Mardaga, 1991), 68.

Page 56: Geffroy also worked briefly for Poiret and Redfern: Minnaert, *Pierre Barbe*, 68.

Page 56: Michel de Brunhoff . . . was doing his best to help the foundering Geffroy: Ballard, *In My Fashion*, 24.

Page 56: Geffroy's idiosyncratic patois . . . "complicated Proustian phrases": Ballard, *In My Fashion*, 24; "affected Antilles": Le-Tan, *Rencontres d'une vie*, 62; "drawn-out alembic phrases": Charles-Roux, *Théâtre de la Mode*, 22.

Page 56: Geffroy was given to chronic suffering: Ballard, *In My Fashion*, 24.

Page 56: A position at Jean Patou: Emmanuelle Polle, *Jean Patou: A Fashionable Life* (Paris: Flammarion, 2013), 185.

Page 56: Patou raised waistlines and dropped hemlines: Polle, *Jean Patou*, 216.

Page 56: Patou created the first suntan oil: Polle, *Jean Patou*, 124.

Page 56: Patou invented the tennis skirt: Polle, *Jean Patou*, 200.

Page 56: Knitted swimwear and the cardigan as a fashion item: Meredith Etherington-Smith, *Patou* (London: Hutchinson & Co., 1983), 61 and 68.

Page 56: Patou dressed Josephine Baker and Louise Brooks: Polle, *Jean Patou*, 42–43 and 44.

Page 56: The Crash had not been kind to Patou: Polle, *Jean Patou*, 72.

Page 56: He went so far as to dye his own yarn to attain perfect, saturated colors for his clothes: Caroline Rennolds Milbank, *Couture: The Great Designers* (New York: Stewart, Tabori & Chang, 1985), 141.

Page 56: Nearly a year before Geffroy's arrival, the company was in liquidation (Patou went into liquidation on July 12, 1935; Geffroy was hired at Patou on June 8, 1936): Polle, *Jean Patou*, 185 and 264.

Page 56: Under the direction of Patou's sister and muse (Patou's mother, Jeanne Grison, inherited the business, which she gave to her daughter, Madeleine Patou): Polle, *Jean Patou*, 260.

Page 56, caption: Patou handed out lipsticks in Cartier cases: *Fortune*, August 1932,76.

Page 56, caption: "He who thinks 'modern' is already outdated": *Connaissance des Arts*, no. 3, May 1952, 10–13.

Page 60: "To be truly soigné a man must have eighty suits": Polle, *Jean Patou*, 62.

Page 60: Rejecting dye lot after dye lot . . . and would start a project all over: Monsieur et Madame Antoine de Grandsaignes of Decour, interview with author, July 2015.

Page 60: Dressed in tawny suits, beautiful ties, and shirts the color of aged ivory: Jean-Marie Rossi of Aveline, interview with author, September 2015.

Page 60: Poised and chatting with Christian Bérard and Coco Chanel: *Vogue* (American), May 15, 1938.

Page 60: Geffroy coached Dior and introduced him to Robert Piguet: Dior, *Christian Dior et moi*, 204.

Page 60: Harcourt's hiring of Geffroy for the decoration of his eighteenth-century *hôtel particulier*: Duc d'Harcourt, *Regards sur un passé* (Paris: Editions R. Laffont, 1989), 111.

Page 60: The Duc d'Harcourt directed the decoration of his house . . . quickly learned he could count on Geffroy's subtle eye: Duc d'Harcourt, *Regards sur un passé*, 111 and 180.

Page 60: "Of which epoch?": Joseph de Cassagne, interview with author, November 2015.

Page 60: Geffroy, the only outsider at an intimate family wedding . . . resting on a skirted table in the duchesse's salon: Duchesse d'Harcourt interview, November 2015.

Page 60: Piguet hired Geffroy to design the private salon above his couture house: "À la recherche d'un climat," *Images de France*, April–May 1942, 12.

Page 62: Citing the input of two unknowns, Dior and Geffroy: *Vogue* (American), March 1940, 33; George le Cardonnel, "Courrier des Spectacles," *Le Journal de Paris*, February 17, 1940; *Paris Soir*, February 21, 1940.

Page 62: Recurrent psychotic episodes required isolation . . . demobilized after the Armistice of 1940: Georges Geffroy military record, Number 501, opened May 10, 1925.

Page 62: The "willow giraffe": Robert Saint-Jean, *Passé pas mort* (Paris: Grasset, 2012, e-book format), Chapter 6.

Page 62: Wisely, he respected the inherent character of the apartment: "Dans la mansarde d'un décorateur," Connaissance des Arts, November, 15, 1958, 116–20; "Rue de Rivoli," *Plaisir de France*, March 1950, 15–18.

Page 62: For overall coverage of Geffroy's apartment in its first iteration: "Rue de Rivoli," 15–18; *Vogue* (Paris), Winter 1945–46, 135-37. For the vestibule: "Le Vestibule doit jouer un role décoratif," *Connaissance des Arts*, May 15, 1953, 21. For updates to the apartment in the 1950s: "Dans la mansarde d'un décorateur," 116–20.

Page 62: Even the many flights of stairs . . . served a useful purpose: Rossi interview, September 2015.

Page 64: The impressive presence of an enormous, varnished tortoise shell: Petitjean interview, May 2017.

Page 65: Walls upholstered in a dark green satin-and-silk stripe and . . . leopard velvet throw pillows: "Rue de Rivoli," 15–18; "Dans la mansarde d'un décorateur, 116–20; "Choisir c'est de réfuser," *L'Estampille*, no. 26, November 1971, 51-55.

Page 65: Animal-print velvets [were] hand woven by Le Manach: Confirmed handwoven by Pierre Frey of Pierre Frey (now owner of Le Manach) in email of June 13, 2017.

Page 66: The mechanical mantel clock, emitting music and animation, a gift to Marie-Antoinette: *Collection Geffroy*, Ader, Picard, Tajan, Paris, December 2, 1971.

Page 66: The admiration of the young aesthete Philippe Jullian: Philippe Jullian, *Journal 1940-1950* (Paris: Grasset & Fasquelle, 2009), 62.

Page 67: Natalie Davenport of McMillen closely followed everything Geffroy created: Mario Buatta, interview with author, July 2016.

Page 67: These soirées were intimate . . . rarely more than eight: Guéranger interview, May 2017.

Page 67: Geffroy loved being both a host and the center of the attention: Grandsaignes interview, July 2015.

Page 67: A housekeeper who was said to be the daughter of Proust's maid: Duchesse d'Harcourt interview, November 2015.

Page 67: Chatting lightly about his projects, lunch dates, and Paris activities . . . casually rest a knee on an eighteenth-century chair: Guéranger interview, May 2017.

Page 67: Invitations printed by society stationer Cassegrain . . . florists would hang garlands: Details recorded in photographs found in the André Ostier archives.

Page 67: Everyone, including the Duchess of Windsor, would mount the six flights of stairs: Guéranger interview, May 2017.

Page 68: Robert Ricci, Pierre Le-Tan, society photographer André Ostier, decorator . . . Androuchka Braunecker, and a mix of patrons and pals: Guéranger interview, May 2017.

Page 68: Whisked him off immediately to see Baron de Redé's Hôtel Lambert: Thomas Michael Gunther, interview with author, November 2015.

Page 68: Arlette Ricci, a granddaughter of Nina Ricci and Geffroy's neighbor, would pop in: Guéranger interview, May 2017.

Page 68: Discreet, kindhearted, and even, perhaps, slightly sad: Duchesse d'Harcourt interview, November 2015.

Page 68: A fleeting expression of regret would register on his face . . . Geffroy would invariably scoop up the last stragglers and invite them to dinner: Guéranger interview, May 2017.

Page 68: Charles Soudant, a sculptor: Signed Art Deco hood mascots by Charles Soudant from the 1920s can be found on artnet.com, and in auction galleries.

Page 68: Commemorative stele to Resistance fighters in the Luxembourg Gardens: http://www.senat.fr/visite/jardin/statues.html.

Page 68: She died in Geffroy's apartment during the war: Jeanne Voelker, wife of the late Paul Geffroy, per death certificate on file in Paris, died at 248, rue de Rivoli on December 21, 1943; her funeral services took place at the Protestant Oratoire du Louvre on the rue Saint-Honoré and were announced in Paris Soir, December 24, 1943, 3E, by Geffroy and his three sisters and their spouses, Mme. Jean Cabon, M. et Mme. Charles Soudant, M. et Mme. J. W. Pruvost.

Page 68: Shady visits from powerful Germans: Jullian, Journal, 65; Patrick Buisson, 1940–1945: Années érotiques, vol. 2: De la Grande Prostituée à la revanche des mâles (Paris: Albin Michel, 2009), 299.

Page 68: The apartment sheltered Resistance leader Jean Desbordes: Ghislain de Diesbach interview with author, November 2015; according to Philippe Jullian, Desbordes and Geffroy had a complicated history. For further details, see Jullian, Journal, 55.

Page 68: Desbordes tortured to death: Jean Galtier-Boissière, Mon journal pendant l'Occupation (Paris: La Jeune Parque, 1944), 30.

Page 69: They turned to an old friend, the aesthete Charles de Beistegui, for advice: https://roomfordiplomacy.com/paris-3-residence-1940-2014.

Page 69: Recommended an up-and-coming designer: Artemis Cooper, Salve Amice et Lege. Hail Friend and Read. Salut à toi ami et lis: The Duff Cooper Library, Paris (Paris: The British Council and The British Embassy, Paris, 1997), 15.

Page 69: She always considered her friend Beistegui, who lent a guiding eye to the project, its true creator: Cooper, Salve Amice et Lege, 15; Diana Cooper, Diana Cooper: Autobiography (London: Michael Russell, 1979), 723.

Page 69: Slim colonettes, recalling those at Malmaison but in fact inspired by a room Beistegui greatly admired, the Grand Ducal bedroom at Tsarskoe Selo: Dimitri Shvidkovsky, The Empress and the Architect: British Architecture and Grandeur at the Court of Catherine the Great (New Haven, CT: Yale University Press, 1996), 80, Plate 85, and 81, Plate 88.

Pages 69–72: Geffroy achieved grand effects using inexpensive materials and special-effects painting . . . bas-relief medallions of former owners of the Hôtel de Charost: Cooper, Salve Amice et Lege, 18.

Page 72: An ostentation that Beistegui despised: Connaissance des Arts, May 1952, 10–13.

Page 72: The gilded inscription commemorating Duff Cooper: Ad Francos Feliciter Legatus Tacitae Librorum amicitiae Hunc Locum Dedicavit Duff Cooper ut Lectores Inter Amicos Suos Numeraret. SALVE AMICE ET LEGE (Duff Cooper, fortunate Ambassador to France, dedicated this room to the silent friendship of books so that readers might be numbered among his friends. Hail, friend, and read).

Page 72: The inscription was added in 1958: https://roomfordiplomacy.com/paris-3-residence-1940-2014.

Page 72: Beistegui selected the font: Cooper, Salve Amice et Lege, 36.

Page 72: A rug with the monogram of Elizabeth II . . . appeared in 1960: Maison et Jardin, February 1961, 78.

Page 72: Attracting the likes of Gaston Palewski, Louise de Vilmorin, Noël Coward, Jean Cocteau, Georges Auric, and Cecil Beaton: Cooper, Salve Amice et Lege, 19.

Page 72: Marcel Rochas, the premier couturier of the 1940s, and his new wife, Hélène, commissioned him to design their flat: "Chez M. et Mme. Marcel Rochas," Plaisir de France, November 1948, 45-48.

Page 72: Though hired in 1944: Sophie Rochas, Marcel Rochas: audace et élégance (Paris: Flammarion, 2015), 244.

Page 72: Empire-style gueridons: Collection Hélène Rochas, Christie's Paris, September 27, 2012, Lot 107.

Page 72: Geffroy placed two terra-cotta busts by Carpeaux on their original pedestals to either side of a divan. . . . The dining room was controlled and elegant with English mahogany furniture and plain eighteenth-century silver: "Chez M. et Mme. Marcel Rochas," 45.

Page 72: Geffroy was observed wearing makeup: Jullian, Journal, 359.

Page 72, caption: Geffroy invented the Louis XVII style: Jean-Pierre Gredy, Tous ces visages (Paris: Grasset, 2007), 285.

Page 73: Of note was the similarity of the desk . . . to one at Beistegui's Château de Groussay: Collection Hélène Rochas, Lot 86, note in description.

Page 76: The avid demand for eighteenth-century furniture after the war: Alexandre Pradère, interview with author, May 2017.

Page 76: Geffroy met Baron Alexis de Redé . . . in the entourage of Arturo and Patricia López-Willshaw: Hugo Vickers, ed., Alexis: The Memoirs of the Baron de Redé (Wimborne Minster, Dorset, U.K.: Dovecote Press, 2005), 10–12.

AN AESTHETIC ODYSSEY

Page 79: Per birth certificate on file, Henri Grandpierre was born March 27, 1856, to Emile Nicholas Grandpierre, a menuisier (joiner).

Page 79: He first practiced an earnest form of architecture . . . publishing tracts on housing reform: Henri Grandpierre, Assainissement de Paris: la réforme des logements ouvriers (Paris: E. Verneau, 1894); Henri Grandpierre, Les logements à bon marché: études sur les discussions du conseil municipal: projet de propositions (manuscript in the Bibliothèque Nationale, Paris).

Page 79: Inexpensive houses in Auteuil that earned him the accolade "architect of the future": Gil Blas, January 24, 1891.

Page 80: Neoclassical commissions . . . farther afield in Berlin: Le Figaro, May 15, 1896.

Page 80: Projects for such artists as Caran d'Ache and Henri Gervex: Gil Blas, March 17, 1898.

Page 80: Grandpierre would point out the house whenever he passed its limestone façade: Marie-Christine de Sayn-Wittgenstein, interview with author, November 2015.

Page 80: Henri Grandpierre's architectural practice was located in his townhouse on the rue Offremont: Rue Offremont is now rue Henri-Rochefort.

Page 80: The aristocratic Cercle d'Omnium, described as the Jockey Club of the cycling set: Le Figaro, June 18, 1895, 3, notes the Comte de Breteuil, the Comte de Luynes, and Portuguese royalty among the members of the Cercle d'Omnium.

Page 80: On Valentine's Day 1906, Le Figaro noted the wedding in Cannes of "the distinguished Parisian architect": Le Figaro, February 17, 1906.

Page 80: When signing the wedding register . . . Henri's best man was René Gilbert, portraitist of Paul Verlaine: Marriage certificate of Floarea Suditu and Henri Grandpierre dated February 14, 1906, on file in the municipal archives in Cannes.

Page 80: Death of Henri Grandpierre: His death certificate was filed April 18, 1906; mentioned in Le Temps, April 21, 1906; Chronique des arts et de la curiosité, April 28, 1906.

Page 83: Addresses, occupation, and details of military record found in Victor Grandpierre's military file, recruitment number 4663.

Page 83: He was living in the faubourg Saint-Germain on the rue de Bellechasse with Daisy Fellowes's daughter Emmeline de Broglie . . . and her newlywed husband, the Comte de Castéja: Victor Grandpierre supplied the Castéja address as his own in the 1933 update of his military file. The Broglie-Castéja wedding took place November 9, 1932 (http://www.europeana.eu/portal/en/record/2024904/photography_ProvidedCHO_TopFoto_co_uk_EU031375.html).

Page 84: Victor Grandpierre went off to India to interview Edwin Bourbon: Le Jour, February 23, 1935. For further information on Bourbons in India: https://groups.google.com/forum/#!topic/alt.talk.royalty/lnTBS2SVZDw.

Page 84: A last-gasp-of-the-Raj tiger hunt for *Vogue:* Victor H. Grandpierre, "An Indian Tale," *Vogue* (American), May 15, 1935, 52, 53, and 116.

Page 84: Attended a party given by Daisy Fellowes where Christian Bérard, Coco Chanel, Cecil Beaton, and Misia Sert smoked nargilehs and applauded legendary cabaret entertainer Bricktop: *Marianne,* June 26, 1935, 9.

Page 85: An extra man at dinner parties given by the Prince and Princesse de Faucigny-Lucinge and at the Sporting Club in Monte Carlo: *Paris Soir*, January 14, 1936, 6; *Le Figaro*, August 25, 1935, 2.

Page 85: The press mentioned him with Lady Mendl, Lady Cunard, Barbara Hutton: *Le Temps* (Paris), August 25, 1936, 4.

Page 85: The Pol Rogers, Baron Nicolas "Niki" de Gunzburg, and Lord Cholmondeley: *Le Figaro*, August 21, 1936, 2.

Page 85: He also rubbed shoulders, however gently, with Édouard Bourdet . . . writer-diplomat Paul Morand, and art patron Charles de Noailles: *Paris Soir*, January 14, 1936, 6.

Page 85: He and surrealist poet René Crevel were fellow houseguests of the Comte and Comtesse Jean de Polignac: Jean-Louis Gaillemin, interview with author, June 2017.

Page 85: Grandpierre whipped off a series of portraits and profiles of socialites for Lucien Vogel's *Le Jardin des modes: Le Jardin des modes*, December 1936 and May 1937. Thank you to Pierre Arizzoli-Clémentel for sharing this information.

Page 85: Daisy Fellowes on her boat, crisp in a simple shipmate's hat: *Vogue*, May 15, 1936, 52.

Page 85: Documented the season in Venice for *Vogue: Vogue*, November 1, 1935, 118.

Page 89: His inclusion in a photography exhibit alongside Jacques-Henri Lartigue, Hubert de Segonzac, and André Ostier: *Chasseurs d'Images* at the Carlton Hotel in Cannes, January (year not specified–1941?). Per Parisian photo curator Thomas Michael Gunther, this information was included in the catalogue of the exhibition on André Ostier at the Pierre Bergé-Yves Saint-Laurent Foundation: The newspaper clipping announced an *"exposition de groupe"* at the Hôtel Carlton in Cannes, entitled *Chasseurs d'Images*, a name commonly used at the time to designate photographers. The exhibitors were Georgette Chadourne, Docteur Boucard, Jacnar, V.-H. Grandpierre, H. de Segonzac, André Ostier, J.-H. Lartigue, and Bachelard.

Page 90: Teaming up with actor, director, and impresario Marc Doelnitz: Marc Doelnitz would resuscitate the nightclub Le Boeuf sur le toit after the war with an unknown *chanteuse*, Juliette Greco, who, in turn, would change her wardrobe from boatneck sweaters and ballerina flats to Christian Dior couture. Beevor and Cooper, *Paris after the Liberation*, Chapter 27.

Page 90 :Grandpierre and Dior's paths naturally crossed . . . Grandpierre mentioned his emerging interest in interior design to Dior: Dior, *Christian Dior et moi*, 27.

Page 91: Other forms of drama surfaced . . . triggering a minor *cause célèbre:* http://catalog.lib.kyushu-u.ac.jp/handle/2324/19165/yoshii1.pdf. (This link is no longer active.)

Page 91: Capri was mounting a revue . . . She cast Grandpierre in a piece by Jean Anouilh and in his own cameo, "Victor Makes Postcards": Program for the Agnès Capri revue, found in the Boris Kochno archives (item 1310), Bibliothèque Nationale, Paris Opera Museum branch.

Page 91: Like Dior, he connected with the neo-humanism in the paintings of Christian Bérard: Dior, *Christian Dior et moi*, 196.

Page 91: He wrote of paintings . . . but Bérard, evidently, was not much of a letter writer: Letters written by Victor Grandpierre to Christian Bérard and Boris Kochno, Boris Kochno archives (item 1424), Bibliothèque Nationale, Paris Opera Museum branch.

Page 92: He contacted her in hopes of getting updates from Bucharest: Letter written to Marthe Bibesco by Victor Grandpierre, dated September 21, year not specified, Princesse Marthe Bibesco Archives, Harry Ransom Center, University of Texas, Austin.

Page 92: Grandpierre could be found lunching at the British Embassy with Diana and Duff Cooper . . . as well as at the ambassador's country house in Chantilly: Olivier Muth (editor and compiler), Louise de Vilmorin, Duff Cooper, Viscount Norwich, and Diana Cooper, *Correspondance à trois (1944-1953)* (Paris: Gallimard, 2008), letter 45-38 and letter 45-149.

Page 92: Louise [de Vilmorin], famous for her charm and originality: Ballard, *In My Fashion*, 41.

Page 92: Renovation of the theater La Cigale . . . included a state-of-the-art hydraulic lift: *Architectural Record*, vol. 8, 1898-99.

Page 92: He wrote and photographed a story for *Vogue* on Nohant, the country house of George Sand: *Vogue* (Paris)*,* Winter 1946.

Page 92: He profiled the Saint-Tropez fisherman's house designed by Philippe Tallien: *Vogue* (Paris), March-April 1947, 70-73.

Page 92, caption: "Grandpierre absolutely must show you and Diana this project": Muth, *Correspondance à trois*, Letter 46-44.

Page 93: The art of interiors lies halfway between architecture and fashion: Alain (Émile-Auguste Chartier, 1868-1951). Thierry Coudert, *Café Society: Socialites, Patrons, and Artists 1920-1960* (Paris: Flammarion, 2010), 186.

A VISION BECOMES A STYLE

Page 99: Dior understood that he was living at the dawn of a new era: Dior, *Christian Dior et moi*, 12.

Page 100: Goya pump: Benaïm, *Dior: The New Look Revolution*, 19. Author note: The Goya pump, with its low vamp and high heel, was a significant departure from the heavy-soled utilitarian shoes worn by women during World War II. Dior showed it in his first New Look collection, accompanying the famous "Bar" suit and other models. Over the years, the typical pump at Dior became slightly more pointed.

Page 100: Uphold centuries-old French techniques of beading, embroidery, fine textiles, floral arts, and savoir faire: Palmer, *Dior: A New Look*, 22.

Page 100: It had been built in 1865-68 for the widow of Alexandre Colonna-Walewski: The House of Dior believes 30, avenue Montaigne was built for Alexandre Colonna-Walewski; https://fr.wikipedia.org/wiki/Avenue_Montaigne claims the house was built for Colonna-Walewski's widow.

Page 100: The last nail was hammered as the first guest arrived: Dior, *Christian Dior et Moi*, 27-31.

Page 100: It added to the buzz in Paris that Dior was breaking with the past, up to something daring and new: Dior, *Christian Dior et moi*, 24.

Page 100, caption: Bérard sketched the façade of 30, avenue Montaigne as a gift: Dior, *Christian Dior et moi*, 38.

Page 102: The couture house of Lucien Lelong . . . with sleek interiors by Jean-Michel Frank: Joanna Banham, ed., *Encyclopedia of Interior Design.* volume 1. (London and Chicago: Fitzroy Dearborn Publishers, 1997), 460.

Page 102: Schiaparelli's couture house was also designed by Frank and had catchy window displays by Salvador Dalí: "A Peek Inside the Extraordinary Life of Couturière Elsa Schiaparelli," *Architectural Digest* (online), December 31, 2014.

Page 102: Piguet, that master of sedate, understated clothes, had . . . neo-baroque furniture by Jansen and a ceiling painted by Drian: Pastori, *Robert Piguet*, 46-47.

Page 102: Dior admired the airy salons of Chéruit on the place Vendôme: Dior, *Christian Dior et moi*, 26.

Page 102: In the tradition of the house of Worth circa 1910 . . . whose regal showroom of white paneling trimmed with gold, fitted carpeting, and the occasional Louis XIII chair: "Créations Ephemères," *L'Oeil,* March 1959, 61. Article includes a photo of the Worth salon with a Louis XIII *Os de mouton*-style chair.

Page 102: Edward Molyneux, the couturier Dior most admired, opened a salon on the rue Royale: In 1925 Molyneux's salon moved from 14, rue Royale to 5, rue Royale, Paris.

Page 102: Edward Molyneux . . . that featured Trianon gray woodwork, Louis XVI bergères, Directoire side chairs, and even a sales staff dressed in gray: "La rue de la Paix, la place Vendôme, la rue de Castiglione," *La Renaissance de l'Art Français et des Industries* / Dir. Henry Lapauze, no. 6, July 1924; "Les Champs Elysées, la rue Royale, la rue de la Boétie, le Fbg St Honoré," *La Renaissance de l'Art Français et des Industries* / Dir. Henry Lapauze, no. 6, June 1924.

Page 103: Mitzah Bricard, the heavily jeweled and veiled former assistant of Edward Molyneux: Ballard*, In My Fashion*, 234.

Page 103: Dior's theme of highlighting light with dark in a collection: Dior, *Christian Dior et moi*, 96.

Page 106, caption: Workmen arrived before every collection to touch up walls and reinforce chairs: Dior, *Christian Dior et moi*, 110.

A PHILOSOPHY BEGETS A BRAND

Page 111: He wanted to slip on her shoes . . . and tuck a gift for her accommodating husband in her hand: Dior, *Christian Dior et moi*, 171.

Page 111: A small boutique modeled along the lines of an eighteenth-century luxury vendor: Dior, *Christian Dior et moi*, 27.

Page 111: Nearly all couture houses had small shops stocked with accessories, perfume, and novelties: Palmer, *Dior: A New Look*, 62.

Page 112: Whose profit on couture was, at best, slim: As early as the 1920s, the typical profit margin on Parisian couture was a scant 10 percent. Palmer, *Dior: A New Look*, 76.

Page 112: The initial ground-floor boutique . . . tucked into one side of the entrance hall: Pochna, *Dior*, 130.

Page 112: Expanded under the stairs: Palmer, *Dior: A New Look*, 62.

Page 112: Christian Bérard . . . came up with the notion of toile de Jouy: Dior, *Christian Dior et moi*, 27.

Page 112: Sepia toile de Jouy was duly sourced: "La Boutique Christian Dior," Christian Dior press release, undated; Pierre Frey, of Pierre Frey-Boussac, confirmed in an email dated September 8, 2017, that Boussac was the supplier of the toile de Jouy for the boutique.

Page 112: Robert Piguet restocked and restyled his boutique seasonally: Palmer, *Dior: A New Look*, 62. Though boutiques at couture houses were a given, Robert Piguet is credited with being the first couturier to restyle his boutique seasonally to entice return visits.

Page 112: Piles of boxes . . . scattered throughout the boutique were another Bérard suggestion: Dior, *Christian Dior et moi*, 27.

Page 112: The boutique served as good-will ambassador: Palmer, *Dior: A New Look*, 68.

Page 112: Exclusive silk scarves commissioned by artists Henry Moore and Graham Sutherland: Nigel Cawthorne, *The New Look: The Dior Revolution* (Edison, NJ: Wellfleet Press, 1996), 133.

Page 112: Beginning in 1948, the boutique offered a few simplified versions of the prevailing couture collection: "La Boutique Christian Dior," Christian Dior press release, undated.

Page 112: Whether beaded by Rébé, covered in feathers, or tipped with a satin rosette: Musée Christian Dior, *Christian Dior: Man of the Century*, 111.

Page 114, caption: Vivier, a former sculptor: Laurence Benaïm, *Yves Saint Laurent* (Paris: Grasset, 2002), 98.

Page 114, caption: Dior gray was a strictly guarded secret: Email correspondence from Elisabeth de Rothschild, dated October 5, 2017. Ms. de Rothschild relayed that only one painting company, Fasani, which worked with Grandpierre, was allowed to paint the Dior gray interiors of Christian Dior premises. As it was an era when paint colors were mixed with powders by hand, and Fasani held the exact recipe for the color, a company trademark, this gray was a closely guarded secret. According to Ms. de Rothschild, Christian Dior had expressly written a letter decreeing that only Fasani could paint the company interiors.

Page 116: Vivier insisted on calling his shoes "slippers": Katell Le Bourhis, interview with author, January 2016.

Page 116: In New York . . . there was an increased demand for cocktail dresses: Dior, *Christian Dior et moi*, 180.

Page 116: A Christian Dior suite styled by Victor Grandpierre: Palmer, *Dior: A New Look*, 103. Also confirmed in an email from Katelyn Rice, archivist for the Plaza, a Fairmont Managed Hotel, September 5, 2017.

Page 117: Young matrons who had grown up in their mothers' Poiret-inflected drawing rooms now placed inherited furniture in gray-and-white Grandpierre-style environments . . . not forgetting to add . . . white pompons to gray curtains: Le Bourhis interview, January 2016.

Page 117: Coats, knit suits, cashmere sweaters, and ski wear were now available . . . and Dior handbags, fine jewelry, and umbrellas: "La Boutique Christian Dior," Christian Dior press release, undated.

Page 118: Lamps, silver, crystal ornaments and other gifts, tableware, and even the occasional antique were among the offerings: Palmer, *Dior: A New Look*, 159–60; "La Boutique Christian Dior," Christian Dior press release, undated.

Page 118: Versailles had a fresh new roof: Andre Malraux, "The Face of France," *Realités*, October 1954, 17.

Page 118: Dior interiors supplied by Maison Tréherne: The working drawings for the corner boutique and later Dior specialty shops are now in the possession of Féau & Cie, Paris.

Page 118: The introduction of Dior lipstick: Palmer, *Dior: A New Look*, 91.

Page 118: The nineteen-year-old window designer was Jean-François Daigre, who later teamed with Valerian Rybar: Obituary of Jean-François Daigre, *New York Times*, April 2, 1992.

Page 118: The wares and gifts Frère commissioned were coveted . . . the Duchess of Windsor purchased a dessert service of faux-bois Limoges porcelain: Le Bourhis interview, January 2016; A set of these faux-bois porcelain plates appeared in the Duke and Duchess of Windsor sale at Sotheby's, New York, September 11–19, 1996, Lot 1063.

Page 118: Frère received help at night from Dior's twenty-year-old assistant Yves Saint Laurent: Laurence Benaïm, *Yves Saint Laurent* (Paris: Grasset, 2002, e-book format).

Page 118: At Christian Dior, Grandpierre was the decorator without whom nothing could happen: "Miss Dior prêt-à-porter Christian Dior," Christian Dior press release, undated. The boutique opened on September 11, 1967.

Pages 118–22: Grandpierre's personal friendship with Dior and his long history with the couture house gave him a unique link to the vision of the founder: Sayn-Wittgenstein interview, November 2015.

Page 122: Princess Grace of Monaco cut the white satin ribbon for the 1967 opening: "Baby Dior est né," Christian Dior press release, November 7, 1967.

Page 122: Grandpierre jazzed up the classic gray and white with stainless steel, laminate, and recessed lighting: *L'Officiel de la mode*, no. 547, 1967, 176.

Pages 122–25: Mahogany molding on gray walls, glass cases banded in stainless steel and mahogany, leather and metal club chairs: "Boutique 'Monsieur' Printemps/Été 1970," Christian Dior press release, April 14, 1970.

Page 125: His first contribution, in 1947, the addition of ringed handles to the amphora: Dario Cimorelli, ed., *Christian Dior: Esprit de parfums* (Milan: Silvana Editoriale, 2017), 45.

Page 125: When Grandpierre appropriated houndstooth: Pochna, *Dior*, 134.

Page 128: The black-and-white check had appeared repeatedly in the first New Look collection: Per Perrine Scherrer of Dior (July 17, 2017), the first Dior collection included four models with houndstooth: "Rien," "Oxford," "Montmartre," and "Promenade."

Page 129: A leather-bound book in his own library inspired Grandpierre's mottled-brown box: Sayn-Wittgenstein interview, November 2015.

Page 129: In a split second he could spot what was wrong, identify false notes . . . and suggest the perfect refinement: Sayn-Wittgenstein interview, November 2015.

Page 129: The design process for the container of a new cream: Sayn-Wittgenstein interview, November 2015.

Page 129: Grandpierre, whose first duty was to be faithful to the spirit of Dior, would calmly stand his ground: Sayn-Wittgenstein interview, November 2015.

THE NEW LOOK IN RESIDENCE

Page 133: A Matisse drawing hung next to a Gothic tapestry: Dior, *Christian Dior et moi*, 214.

Page 133: Florists in felt slippers noiselessly updated flower arrangements: Georgina Howell, "Fashion Legends: Christian Dior—The New Look Creator near Milly-la-Forêt," *Architectural Digest*, October 1994, 156.

Page 134: A French interior disdained comfort . . . now American and British notions of comfort insinuated their presence: Le Bourhis interview, January 2016.

Page 134: As the preeminent couturier in the world, Dior needed a dignified background: *Maison et Jardin*, October–November 1953, 42.

Page 134: After looking in the desirable faubourg Saint-Germain and concluding that only Americans could find houses there: Dior, *Christian Dior et moi*, 212.

Page 134: He had spent hours gazing at the villa's colonnaded façade and contemplating its mysterious actress occupant: Dior, *Christian Dior et moi*, 213.

Page 134: Few townhouses had been lavishly decorated from top to bottom since the war: Thomas Kernan, *Les réussites de la décoration française: 1950-1960* (Paris: Éditions du Pont Royal, 1960), 81.

Page 134: Common among the fashionable to divvy up design of private and public spaces: Marie-France Pochna, interview with author, January 2016.

Page 134: A chilly relationship at best: Jean-Louis Gaillemin, "Georges Geffroy, Victor Grandpierre, du Club 7 à la Motte-Tilly, quelques souvenirs . . ." (http://philocalies.blogspot.com/2017/06).

Page 134: Among the many documents on Shah Pahlavi's extravagant celebration of the Persian Empire: http://www.nytimes.com/2001/09/07/world/persepolis-journal-shah-s-tent-city-fit-for-kings-may-lodge-tourists.html.

Page 134: Delbée in charge of continuity: "Christian Dior's Paris House," *Vogue* (American), November 15, 1953, 92–93.

Page 134: An Aubusson rug, etc: "À Paris, l'hôtel du boulevard Jules-Sandeau," *Maison et Jardin*, February 1958, 67–70.

Page 134, caption: "If I *had* to name my favorite style for a house, I would choose Louis XVI, but it would be a resolutely 1956 Louis XVI": Dior, *Christian Dior et moi*, 214.

Page 136: Commanding Egyptian funerary figures: "Christian Dior's Paris House," *Vogue* (American), November 15, 1953, 92–93.

Page 136: Three shades of white: "Christian Dior's Paris House," 1953, 92–93.

Page 136: Candlesticks and Porcelaine de Paris: *Collection Catherine Dior*, Daguerre, Hôtel Drouot, Paris, March 26, 2012, Lots 47 and 48.

Page 136: Pyramids of Paule Dedeban: Howell, "Fashion Legends: Christian Dior," 156.

Page 136: In the tradition of the haute bourgeoisie: Natasha Fraser-Cavassoni, *Monsieur Dior: Once upon a Time* (New York: Pointed Leaf Press, 2014), 115.

Page 136: Table service of simple design but excellent quality: Pochna, *Christian Dior*, 215.

Page 136: Chef and sous-chef: Giroud, *Christian Dior 1905–1957*, 239; Howell, "Fashion Legends: Christian Dior," 156.

Page 137: *Maison et Jardin* lauded the mix: "La Rentrée: occasion de signaler des retours d'un autre ordre," *Maison et Jardin*, October–November 1953, 42–43.

Page 137: Red–the lucky color of the superstitious Dior: Giroud, *Christian Dior 1905–1957*, 73. In fact, every collection had to have one red dress: Cawthorne, *The New Look: The Dior Revolution*, 149.

Page 139: Flower bed plantings in Milly: Ballard, *In My Fashion*, 239-40.

Page 139: Empire chair with eagle: "À Paris, l'hôtel du boulevard Jules-Sandeau," 68.

Page 139: Bath inspired by Emilio Terry: Pochna, *Christian Dior*, 286.

Page 139: Elsie de Wolfe's bath on the avenue d'Iéna: Penny Sparke, *Elsie de Wolfe: The Birth of Modern Interior Design* (New York: Acanthus Press), 2005, 258–59.

Page 139: Long window curtains . . . upgraded bath into a boudoir: "À Paris, l'hôtel du boulevard Jules-Sandeau," 69.

Page 141: Grandpierre's whip-smart study: "Christian Dior's Paris House," 92–93.

Page 141: Paintings by Cocteau, Bérard, Dalí, and Derain, and a Flemish tapestry: Ballard, *In My Fashion*, 239; "À Paris, l'hôtel du boulevard Jules-Sandeau," 70.

Page 141: Tiers of shelves held sets of leather-bound volumes: Karnow, *Paris in the Fifties,* 389.

Page 141: "Very red and very velvet": Fraser-Cavassoni, *Monsieur Dior*, 115.

Page 141: Bettina Ballard described as one of the happiest rooms she had known: Ballard, *In My Fashion*, 239.

Page 141: Dior did not acquire antiques to form a collection but to re-create a manner of living: Alexis Kugel, interview with author, September 2015.

Page 141: Dior acquired what spoke to his eye rather than his reason: Olivier Kraemer, interview with author, October 2015.

Page 141: The long tradition of elegant austerity in French design: Pradère interview, January 2016.

MEASURED ELEGANCE

Page 145: "Exquis, *exquis*, EXQUIS!": Geraldine Forrester (daughter of the Vicomtesse de Bonchamps), interview with author, December 2015.

Page 145: Discourses on French furniture that could set a dinner party yawning: Duchesse d'Harcourt interview, November 2015.

Page 146: The Duc du Mouchy counseled a well-received young American: Alsop, *To Marietta from Paris*, letter dated February 23, 1947, 93-94.

Page 146: Accent of Marie-Laure de Noailles: Jullian, *Journal*, 238.

Page 146: English-accented French, the kind one heard in Switzerland: Diesbach interview, November 2015.

Page 146: Beistegui's dress requirements kept couturiers like Antonio Castillo afloat during the lean years: Ballard, *In My Fashion*, 201.

Page 146: "For the first . . . time, I see a work of quality that surpasses a decorative object": "Le lettre d'information de Francis Spar [editor in chief]," *Connaissance des Arts*, no. 17, July 15, 1953, 3.

Page 146: Mixing Balthus and bergères: "Une des maisons-clés pour l'histoire du goût au XXème siècle," *Connaissance des Arts*, October 1964, 68-91.

Page 148: A young Palladio who introduced a new classic order: Waldemar-George, *Moustache: Portraits d'homme du XVIème siècle à nos jours* (Paris: privately published by Marcel Rochas for the benefit of the Figaro Fund for Student Scholarship, 1949), 28.

Page 148: If you were an international sophisticate, you wanted Geffroy: James H. Douglas, interview with author, January 2015.

Page 148: In such a climate, a room of boiserie could be built . . . and then wholly rebuilt: Alain Demachy, interview with author, October 2015.

Page 149: Geffroy wrote the most deeply touching letter of hundreds: Duchesse d'Harcourt interview, November 2015.

Page 149: Jean-Marie Rossi on tea with Geffroy: Rossi interview, September 2015.

Page 149: Dolores Guinness's wedding dress: Email dated November 18, 2016, from Gaspard de Masse, archivist at Balenciaga, notes that *Vogue* (Paris), December 1955, wrote that the dress would be designed by Balenciaga. Balenciaga, however, has no further records about this dress.

Page 149: Listened attentively to the Vicomtesse de Bonchamps's adolescent daughter: Forrester interview, December 2015.

Page 149: Reminiscences of Geffroy as a godfather: Petitjean interview, May 2017.

Page 149: Running in rough company: Rossi interview, September 2015.

Page 149: Details on Tréherne: Alan de Lavalade, interview with author, November 2015.

Page 149: Jean Roche oversaw architectural renovations in the 1950s: Pierre Arizzoli-Clémentel, *Georges Geffroy* (Paris: Gourcuff Gradenigo, 2016), 129 and 225.

Page 151: Geffroy reviewed drawings with Tréherne three times a week: François Catroux, interview with author, September 2015.

Page 151: *Le Tour Geffroy:* Grandsaignes interview, July 2015.

Page 151: For background on the Hôtel Lambert: Laure Murat, *The Splendor of France: Great Châteaux, Mansions, and Country Houses* (New York: Rizzoli, 1991), 300; Philippe Jullian, "L'Ultime commande d'Arturo López," *Connaissance des Arts*, April 1959, 98 ff.

Page 151: Redé swapped his pied-à-terre at the Meurice for . . . the Hôtel Lambert: Vickers, *Alexis*, 47.

Page 151: Sovereign who dreamed of being a philosopher: Voltaire in a letter to the Prince of Prussia, April 15, 1739.

Page 151: A medal from the French government: Vickers, *Alexis*, 164.

Page 154: Spritzing flowers to simulate dew: Vickers, *Alexis*, 157.

Page 154: By 1954, Geffroy had fully rebuilt the pediment: This transformation is evident by comparing artist Alexandre Serebriakoff's 1949 rendering of the room (*Collection du Baron de Redé provenant du l'Hôtel Lambert*, Sotheby's Paris, March 16, 2005, vol. 2, Lot 682) and the subsequent photograph of the room (believed 1954) by artist Jean Vincent (*Collection du Baron de Redé*, vol. 1, Lot 296).

Page 154: Cecil Beaton suggested blue: Vickers, *Alexis*, 53.

Page 154: Alexandre Serebriakoff's rendering of the library at the Hôtel Lambert: *Collection du Baron de Redé*, vol. 2, Lot 682.

Page 154: Photograph of room near the end of Redé's life taken by Elizabeth Vickers: Vickers, *Alexis*, 52.

Page 154: Small brass tables by Lucien Toulouse: *Collection du Baron de Redé*, vol. 1, Lot 112, vol. 2, Lots 711 and 712.

Page 154: Redé hid telephone in an ottoman: Joseph de Cassagne, interview with author, November 2015.

Page 156: Chandeliers smothered in passementerie: *Vogue* (Paris), April 1950, 121. The source of the passementerie was G. Sailly.

Page 156: Lina Zervudaki had provided mannequins for Dior: *Le Jardin des modes*, vol. 347, 1950.

Page 156: Tufted velvet slipper chairs, ferns, and ruched awnings: *Art et Industrie*, vol. 19.

Page 156: As at Dior, the effect was luminous and airy: *Vogue* (Paris), April 1950, 120.

Pages 156-59: 250th anniversary of the place Vendôme: *Vogue* (Paris), July 1950, 56; *Plaisir de France*, July–August 1950, 60-61.

Page 159: Arturo López-Willshaw resembled Louis XIV: Cassagne interview, November 2015.

Page 159: Served guests on royal eighteenth-century silver: Douglas Cooper, ed., *Great Private Collections* (New York: Macmillan, 1963), 131.

Page 159: Nights spent at the Hôtel Lambert: Gredy, *Tous ces visages*, 332.

Page 159: Women forbidden to wear trousers on *La Gaviota IV*: Gredy, *Tous ces visages*, 317.

Page 159: A ratio of twenty-six crew to nine passengers: Vickers, *Alexis*, 90.

Page 159: López-Willshaw wanted to sail to Venice and Biarritz: Vickers, *Alexis*, 90.

Page 159: Madame López-Willshaw's Louis Vuitton trunks: Vickers, *Alexis*, 112.

Page 159: Gilt-wood armchairs . . . bronzier Lucien Toulouse . . . quality of workmanship–finer than that found in many a good house: *Connaissance des Arts*, October 15, 1952, 52-55; *Vogue* (Paris), July 1953, 21-24.

Page 159: López-Willshaw had a lifelong fascination with China: *Connaissance des Arts*, October 15, 1952, 52.

Page 159: Chinese paintings acquired from Princess Marina of Greece: Gredy, *Tous ces visages*, 278.

Page 162: Margarita Classen-Smith meticulously appliquéd ribbon on yellow felt–following Bérard's design for trompe l'oeil panels–for the Institut Guerlain on the Champs-Élysées: https://guerlainperfumes.blogspot.com/p/history.html.

Page 162: Tub chairs with flagrantly faux animal motifs: *Vogue* (Paris), July 1953, 21-24.

Page 162: Geffroy created a similarly exotic room in Neuilly: *Maison et Jardin*, November 1960, 92.

Page 162: Chairs copied from a pair Hagnauer had sold to Jean Marais: https://bofferdingnewyork.com/2012/06/05/past-window-displays/.

Page 162: Willow chairs and wicker tables: *Connaissance des Arts*, October 15, 1952, 52.

Page 162: For his new theater at Groussay, Beistegui cast aside the eighteenth century: "Premier lever de rideau sur le théâtre de Groussay," *Connaissance des Arts*, January 1957, 20-23.

Page 162: Beistegui commissioned a play to mark the opening: *L'Officiel de la mode*, no. 421-22, 1957, 200-201.

Page 162: Though decades later his grandniece would host school plays in the theater: Marie Malle, interview with author, October 2016.

Page 162: Like all great master builders, he grew bored: Vickers, *Alexis*, 72.

Page 162: A palazzo filled with frescoes by Tiepolo, Raphael, and Reni, some were original, some acquired: "Le Palais Labia à Venise," *Connaissance des Arts*, no. 34, December 1954, 86-91.

Page 162: Boris Kochno, Serge Diaghilev's former assistant, rehearsed and directed the entrances of the guests at Beistegui's ball: Vickers, *Alexis*, 73.

Page 162: López-Willshaw had costumes designed by Geffroy and sewn in the workrooms of Nina Ricci: Vickers, *Alexis*, 78.

Page 165: Geffroy's costumes were purportedly copied from a Beauvais tapestry: Vickers, *Alexis*, 78. There is, however, no discernible similarity between the costumes and the actual tapestries, *The Voyage of the Emperor,* from the series *The History of the Emperor of China*. To view the actual tapestries, see Edith A. Standen, "The Story of the Emperor of China: A Beauvais Tapestry Series," *The Metropolitan Museum of Art Journal,* vol. 11, 1976.

Page 165: Redé admired Daisy Fellowes's innate style: Vickers, *Alexis*, 77.

Page 165: For background on Daisy Fellowes, including her jewelry: Beaton, *The Glass of Fashion*, 174; Ballard, *In My Fashion*, 73-74.

Page 165: Her eighteenth-century house in Neuilly . . . done up for her by the architect Louis Süe: Annette Tapert and Diana Edkins, *The Power of Style* (New York: Watson-Guptill, 1994), 87.

Page 165: She amused herself by hosting dinners for guests who despised one another and flustering young brides: Tapert and Edkins, *The Power of Style*, 75.

Page 165: The story recounted by Philippe Jullian . . . has a ring of plausibility: Jullian, *Journal*, 360, entry dated May 24, 1950. (Then again, Jullian was a close friend of Daisy's estranged daughter, Isabelle de Moussaye, so the story might also be discounted.)

Page 165: Description of Fellowes's house in 1952: *Maison et Jardin*, October-November 1952, 16-19.

Page 168: Later description of Fellowes's house: "Dernier regard sur l'hôtel de Mrs. Reginald Fellowes," *Connaissance des Arts*, no. 302, April 1977, 86-93.

Page 168: Seventeen-carat Potemkin pink diamond: Tapert and Edkins, *The Power of Style*, 83.

Page 168: The rest of the house became rich and exotic: "Dernier regard sur l'hôtel de Mrs. Reginald Fellowes," 86–93; Tapert and Edkins, *The Power of Style*, 82.

Page 168: Description of Gloria Guinness: Ballard, *In My Fashion*, 211.

Page 168: Tufted sofa and two chairs from Decour: Pradère interview, May 2017. Per written comments from Pradère, these models of tufted chair and sofa were later copied by Decour in red damask for Élie de Rothschild.

Page 172: Sobriety and drama joined forces in the double-height living room . . . sleek as a Jaguar XK: "Voici un appartement exceptionnel: Un maison sur le toit," *Maison et Jardin*, March 1957, 93-97.

Page 172: A fur rug warmed the floor: Tapert and Edkins, *The Power of Style*, 178.

Page 172: The Vicomte de Bonchamps, . . . an old-school aristocrat. . . hired the fashionable decorator: Barnaby Conrad (great-nephew of the Vicomtesse de Bonchamps), interview with author, December 2015.

Page 172: For more on Givenchy's "Les Muguets" dress for the Vicomtesse de Bonchamps: http://collections.vam.ac.uk/item/O110813/les-muguets-lilies-of-the-dress/.

Page 175: Nearly two hundred could be seated for dinner: Forrester interview, December 2015.

Page 175: Separated from the gallery by white Ionic columns . . . silk stripe on the settee: "Rhythmes purs, nudité des surfaces," *Maison et Jardin*, no. 80, September-October 1961, 80-81.

Page 175: From Prelle in Lyon: Arizolli-Clémentel, *Georges Geffroy, 1905-1971*, 102.

Page 175: East Turkestan rug: Hubert de Givenchy acquired this rug for his residence on the rue des Saints-Pères. It was later sold as Lot 62, *The Collection of M. Hubert de Givenchy*, Christie's Monaco, December 4, 1993. Thank you to James A. Ffrench of Beauvais Carpet, New York, for showing me this rug and providing further scholarship. The Vicomtesse de Bonchamps was so protective of this rug that she made any guest in high heels walk around the outside of it, on the parquet floor: Forrester interview, December 2015.

Page 175: The tawny velvet sofa . . . that Hubert de Givenchy hoped to acquire . . . the dogs eventually got the better of them: Forrester interview, December 2015.

Page 175: Electric light was supplied only by torchères: Forrester interview, December 2015.

Page 176: Tabletops should be garnished with evidence of pastimes . . . marble and semiprecious stone would do: Philippe Jullian, *Les styles* (Paris: Gallimard, 1992; first published 1961 by Librairie Plon), 112.

Page 176: Seventeenth-century Chinese export wallpaper . . . in the inventory of Brighton Pavilion. This wallpaper was acquired by Mr. and Mrs. Charles Wrightsman and later sold at Sotheby's: Forrester interview, December 2015.

Page 176: Maison Fontaine, Geffroy's preferred locksmith-metalworker: Christian Magot-Curvu, interview with author, June 2017. For more on the metalworker Maison Fontaine, founded in 1740: http://www.artisans-patrimoine.fr/serrurerie-dart-fontaine-s-2293.html.

Page 176: In the blue, white, and blonde dining room . . . the blue-and-white Portuguese tile . . . for the vicomtesse's bath: "L'essence d'une grande époque," *Maison et Jardin*, no. 80, November 1961, 111.

Page 176: Large crystal galleon chandelier . . . much admired by Hubert de Givenchy: Forrester interview, December 2015.

Page 176: Rose silk on the Pluvinet benches (later these benches would be covered in yellow silk): "La Collection Geffroy," *L'Estampille*, no. 26, November 1971, 51-55.

Page 176: By 1958 . . . tiger . . . on the seat cushions: "Dans la mansarde d'un décorateur," 116-20.

Page 176: Riesener desk . . . Jacob lyre-back . . . gueridon by Charles Topino: "La collection Geffroy," 51-55; "Dans la mansarde d'un décorateur," 116-20.

Pages 176-80: More furniture had accumulated . . . pleasure in the events unfolding before him: "Dans la mansarde d'un décorateur," 116-20.

Page 180: Though he added a few spectacular touches . . . for the Duc d'Harcourt's sister: Ernest de Ganay, "Daubeuf: pur château de famille," *Connaissance des Arts*, month unknown, 1958, 91. (Thank you to Alexandre Pradère for supplying these tearsheets.)

Page 180: Renovation for Georges Litman: "Comment décore-t-on à Paris?" *Maison et Jardin*, no. 40, January 1957, 130-35.

Pages 180-83: The finished reception rooms . . . shimmer of ormolu: "Climat d'une tapisserie et rigueur alentour," *Maison et Jardin*, November 1963, 104-7.

Page 183: Elizhinia Moreira Salles . . . bejeweled by Schlumberger: "Venue de Brésil . . . ," *Vogue* (Paris), December 1962, 76-79.

Page 183: Bedroom upholstered in sumptuous hand-embroidered yellow silk: Laurence Mouillefarine, "Georges Geffroy: Reinterpreting Past Eras for the Upper Echelons of Paris Society," *Architectural Digest*, January 2000, 180.

Page 183: Recalled Geffroy's unfailing eye . . . the only decorator who mattered: Douglas interview, January 2015.

Page 184: Writing table . . . attributed to Garnier: This desk was later purchased by Galerie Kugel.

Page 185: With a vanishing-point perspective . . . over the mantel: "Un Maître de la décoration révise la tradition," *Maison et Jardin*, November 1969, 144-49.

Page 185: Curtains . . . lined in suede: Magot-Curvu interview, June 2017.

Page 187: Editors . . . praised his designs: *Plaisir de France*, January 1969, 48-49.

Page 187: Geffroy also aligned with the antiques dealer Jacques Kugel: Kugel interview, September 2015.

Page 187: Double flying staircase . . . executed by ironmaster Raymond Subes: "Un Magasin insolite," *L'Amateur d'art*, May 1971.

Page 187: An elegant spiral, enclosed in ingenious trompe l'oeil coffering: Seen at 4, square des Écrivains-combattants-morts-pour-la-France, visit kindly arranged by architect Christian Magot-Curvu, June 2017.

Page 187: A circular staircase . . . in the townhouse of the actor Alain Delon: Mouillefarine, "Georges Geffroy: Reinterpreting Past Eras for the Upper Echelons of Paris Society," 180.

Page 187: Tortoiseshell and ormolu Boulle cabinets: *The Patiño Collection*, Sotheby's New York, November 1, 1986, Lot 103.

Page 187: A Louis XV parquetry commode with black Chinese lacquer: *The Patiño Collection*, Lot 96.

Page 187: Writing table with sumptuous mounts by Dubois: *The Patiño Collection*, Lot 114.

Page 187: Cabinets signed BVRB with Japanese lacquer panels: *The Patiño Collection*, Lots 83 and 84.

Page 187: Bergères signed by Tilliard: *The Patiño Collection*, Lot 89.

Page 188: *Vogue* had noted . . . his . . . quest for perfection: *Vogue* (Paris), June 1949, 58.

Page 188: When visiting Lady Kenmare and Rory Cameron at La Fiorentina: Le-Tan, *Rencontres d'une vie*, 62.

Page 188: The ultimate synthesis of wit, aesthete, and dandy . . . bitter at the passing of time: Michael Wishart, *High Diver* (London: Quartet Books, 1978), 47–48.

Page 188: Geffroy coughed between sentences: Guéranger interview, May 2017.

Page 188: Mention of several strokes: Wishart, *High Diver*, 48.

Page 188: Whisky had hastened his demise: Le-Tan, *Rencontres d'une vie*, 63.

Page 188: After his demise . . . portrait dubiously attributed to Cecil Beaton: Rossi interview, September 2015.

Page 188: An obituary ran in *Le Monde*, impressive but inaccurate: Obituary of Georges Geffroy, *Le Monde*, May 4, 1971, 28.

LUXE, CALME, ET VOLUPTÉ

Page 191: The subtlest designer of his era: *Collection Maître et Madame Michard-Pellissier*, Christie's Paris, June 27, 2007 (Foreword by François de Ricqlès), 9.

Page 192: Leather doors in the Saint Laurent-Bergé apartment: Catroux interview, September 2015.

Page 192: Rouaults or Rembrandts for Liliane de Rothschild: Cooper, ed., *Great Private Collections*, 178.

Page 192: Introduced a small dining table into a private sitting room: Suzy, *Chicago Tribune*, December 17, 1968, A8.

Page 192: The Belle Époque restaurant of the . . . Hôtel Saint-Jacques: Suzy, *Chicago Tribune*, February 27, 1972, section 5, page 11.

Page 192: Cécile de Rothschild: Gaillemin, http://philocalies.blogspot.com/2017/06.

Page 195: A home renovation with the bathroom *farther* from the bedrooms: *Plaisir de France*, March 1947, 42.

Page 195: When Princesse Laure de Beauvau-Craon . . . dined at the Windsors': Pradère interview, January 2016. Pradère recounted this story, told to him by the late Princesse de Beauvau-Craon.

Page 195: A René Prou apartment on the Quai d'Orsay: *Plaisir de France*, July 1944.

Page 196: A rare seventeenth-century Isfahan carpet: Author gratefully acknowledges James A. Ffrench of Beauvais Carpets for identifying this rug.

Page 196: A home in which to raise two sons: Sayn-Wittgenstein interview, November 2015.

Page 196: Comparison of Victor Grandpierre and Mario Praz: Pierre Bergé, interview with author, February 2016.

Page 197: Grandpierre understood how his clients lived: Sayn-Wittgenstein interview, November 2015.

Page 199: For more on Roger Imbert: http://files.shareholder.com/downloads/BID/0x0x103704/24c436c3-9ff1-4a8a-bd3b-a694cd898207/20011129-65912.pdf.

Page 199: He routinely thickened postwar walls to establish a sense of solidity . . . and oversaw architectural details down to the last window pull: "Une vraie maison du XVIIIème siècle avenue Foch," *Connaissance des Arts*, no. 118, December 1961, 116–23.

Page 200: In the Meudon manor house of collectors Monsieur and Madame Claude Hersent: "La Tour Villebon," *Vogue* (Paris), October 1951.

Page 200: Bohemian kitchen dinners when the chef was away: Laurence Benaïm, *Marie Laure de Noailles: La vicomtesse du bizarre* (Paris: Bernard Grasset, 2001, e-book format), Chapter 12: "La Café Society Queen (1945–1956)."

Page 200: Romanticism held sway in Patricia López-Willshaw's sitting room: *House and Garden*, October 1949, 32.

Page 200: A living room for the Marquise de La Falaise: "Le Gris avec les ors," *Maison et Jardin*, October–November 1951, 57.

Page 200: A shell-pink . . . Venetian bedroom: *Connaissance des Arts*, January 15, 1954, 38.

Page 200: Transforming the Cirque Fanni into a fairy realm . . . for Prince Sturdza's ball: *Vogue* (Paris), September 1951, 80.

Pages 200–202: An early commission . . . or a suite at the George V: Princesse Eugénie de Brancovan, interview with author, January 2016.

Page 203: The smoking room, tented . . . and hung with landscapes and miniature paintings: "Une décoration bouleverse l'ordonnance," *Connaissance des Arts*, February 15, 1954, 30–35.

Page 203: *Maison et Jardin* commented that Delacroix would have loved being in this room: "L'appartement du Prince Matei de Brancovan," *Maison et Jardin*, April–May 1952, 88–92.

Page 203: Arturo López-Willshaw summoned . . . Gredy: Gredy, *Tous ces visages*, 277.

Page 203: The Princesse de Brancovan wore Schiaparelli before the war, Dior after the war: Princesse Eugénie de Brancovan interview, January 2016.

Page 204: The prince retreated to a room . . . worthy of a grand field marshal: "L'appartement du Prince Matei de Brancovan," *Maison et Jardin*, April–May 1952, 90.

Page 204: Similar soldierly bedroom for couturier Jean Dessès: *Maison et Jardin*, February 1952, 45; Kernan, *Les réussites de la décoration française*, 226.

Page 204: For the Marquis de La Falaise: "Rencontre du classicism et d'un charme nouveau," *Maison et Jardin*, February 1965, 104.

Page 204: For Eugène Weinreb . . . a Percier and Fontaine Empire bed . . . and ruby petit point Charles X rug: "Renouveau de la sensibilité sur les données XVIIIème," *Maison et Jardin*, May 1956, 108.

Page 205: Grandpierre and Geffroy . . . tolerating (and carefully avoiding) each other: Gaillemin, http://philocalies.blogspot.com/2017/06.

Page 205: Redé referenced both decorators . . . particularly the upstairs rooms: Vickers, *Alexis*, 59.

Page 206: Working around tricky beams . . . to the dense interiors of the nineteenth century: "Le Baron de Redé reconstitue dans l'Hôtel Lambert la chambre à coucher du Comte d'Artois à Bagatelle," *Connaissance des Arts*, April 15, 1954, 67.

Page 206: Fortunately for the room . . . sold off in the Redé auction: *Collection du Baron de Redé*, vol. 2, Sotheby's Paris, March 16 and 17, 2006, Lots 671, 672, and 673.

Pages 207–8: The Baronne de Rothschild was fond of the refined Grandpierre: Sayn-Wittgenstein interview, November 2015.

Page 208: The Baron Élie de Rothschild had custom-made white canvas redingotes to don . . . after polo: Cassagne interview, November 2015.

Page 208: Grandpierre put a dining table in the study of Élie de Rothschild, who loved it: Suzy, *Chicago Tribune*, December 17, 1968, A8.

Page 208: He described the Dior-gray-and-white palette as the interaction of shadow and light: *Maison et Jardin*, October–November 1951, 56.

Page 208: For Lilia Ralli's salon, he combined gray velvet walls with cerise and leopard: *Maison et Jardin*, March–April 1956, 94.

Page 208: Princess Sofia . . . asked Dessès to design her wedding gown: *L'Art et la mode*, no. 3 1961, 138–39.

Page 208: In 1958 he mixed, copper, emerald, periwinkle, rose, Chinese red, maize, and leopard . . . salon overlooking the Bois de Boulogne: "Décor à l'Ancienne," *Maison et Jardin*, December, 1958, 89–90.

Pages 208–12: A warm setting of light oak paneling . . . one of the prettiest rooms in Paris: *Connaissance des Arts*, December 1961, 123.

Page 212: Pale blue walls . . . in Saint Laurent's living room: *Maison et Jardin*, September–October 1962, 80.

Page 212: In the home of Yves Lanvin . . . chairs signed Lelarge and Tilliard: *Maison et Jardin*, November 1965, 152.

Page 212: Grandpierre combined shell-pink walls, moss curtains, lettuce-green silk faille undercurtains . . . for fresh, surprising, and intelligent design: "Splendeurs et cadre en harmonie," *Maison et Jardin*, March, 1966, 108–13.

Page 212: Ralli . . . a fixture on the López-Willshaws' cruises: Vickers, *Alexis*, 92.

Page 212: Her distinctive style, delineated by Cecil Beaton: Beaton, *The Glass of Fashion*, 178.

Page 212: When socialite and confidant of royals Lilia Ralli moved . . . made the room a magnet to anyone seeking a drink and the news of Paris: "Escalier et arbustes en font une vraie maison," *Maison et Jardin*, no. 108, November 1964, 114–19.

Page 212: Madame Ralli had a "day" for receiving, when everyone passed through: Ariel de Ravenel, interview with author, January 2016.

Page 212: Lemaire, to this day provider of trellises for Versailles: For more on Lemaire (now Lemaire-Tricotel): http://www.leparisien.fr/espace-premium/seine-et-marne-77/le-specialiste-du-treillage-et-de-la-cloture-marie-art-et-securite-04-04-2016-5683893.php.

Page 212: The amateur landscaper Charles de Noailles . . . created a textured green garden, relieved only in spring by a few flowering white dog roses: "Escalier et arbustes en font une vraie maison," 114–19.

Pages 212–16: Noailles also introduced a novelty: avant-garde green plastic grass, of which both landscaper and client were . . . inordinately proud: Ravenel interview, January 2016.

Page 216: Arturo López-Willshaw's *cabinet des gemmes*: Philippe Jullian, *14, rue du Centre* (Monaco: privately published, 1961), 77.

Page 216: This life-size jewel box . . . was reinstalled at the López-Willshaws' Hôtel Rodocanachi in Neuilly: Philippe Jullian, "Le Dernier roi mage," *Connaissance des Arts*, December 1960, 42–47; "Collections . . . et collections," *Plaisir de France*, April 1956, 41.

Page 216: Joël le Moal remembers when . . . he first saw Grandpierre's apartment: "Objects of His Affection," *World of Interiors*, February 2009, 84–91.

Page 216: "Very grand, very *français* apartment": Nicky Haslam, note to author, July 1, 2015.

Page 221: An apartment full of masculine, neoclassical furniture, in particular a robust Empire settee: Gaillemin interview, June 2017.

Page 221: Grandpierre . . . refrained from speaking of . . . his accomplishments: Gaillemin, http://philocalies.blogspot.com/2017/06.

Page 221: Attended Redé's first dinner in the Galerie d'Hercule: *Collection du Baron de Redé*, vol. 2, Lot 834, shows seating chart for the dinner, indicating Grandpierre's place.

Page 221: Alongside Dior and Madame Jean Larivière, at a ball given by Étienne de Beaumont: *Vogue* (Paris), September 1950, 76.

Page 221: At the Bal des Oiseaux with Christian Bérard and Patricia López-Willshaw: *Vogue* (Paris), February 1949, 74.

Page 221: Lunching with Ned Rorem and painters one day: Ned Rorem, *Paris Diary, New York Diary 1951–1961* (Open Road Media, 2013, e-book format; first published 1966 by George Braziller).

Page 221: Lunching with . . . Dior, Boris Kochno, and the old crowd the next: Pochna, *Christian Dior*, 279.

Page 221: He stopped in almost nightly at Fabrice Emaer's Club 7: Gaillemin, http://philocalies.blogspot.com/2017/06.

Page 221: An aquamarine signet ring that matched . . . his eyes: Sayn-Wittgenstein interview, November 2015.

Page 221: Including a luxurious household linen boutique for Christian Dior: Solène Auréal at Dior, email dated October 9, 2017.

Page 222: Callas purchased an apartment in 1966 at 36, avenue Georges-Mandel: Bertrand Meyer-Stabley, *La Veritable Maria Callas* (Paris: Éditions Pygmalion, 2007, e-book format).

Page 222: Jean-Paul Faye, Grandpierre's assistant, recalls that the decorator also worked for Onassis: Gaillemin, http://philocalies.blogspot.com/2017/06.

Page 222: Her former home in Milan . . . influenced by the director Luchino Visconti: Arianna Huffington, *Maria Callas: The Woman Behind the Legend* (New York: Simon & Schuster, 1981), 139.

Page 222: The salon, accessed via a pair of Venetian lacquered doors . . . music stand held operatic scores: C. Boisgirard, A. de Heeckeren, Hervé Chayette, *Succession Maria Callas*, Hôtel George V, Paris, June 14, 1978, Lots 105, 121, 131, and 139, among others.

Page 222: As in Dior's Empire boudoir-bath . . . like a glamorous Violetta: Huffington, *Maria Callas*, 279 and 345.

Page 222: A friendship developed between Grandpierre and his client: Sayn-Wittgenstein interview, November 2015.

Page 222: One did not tamper with a château: Cassagne interview, November 2015.

Page 230: Grandpierre knew Comtesse Claire-Clémence de Maillé in Paris: Aymeric Peniguet de Stoutz, director of the Château de la Motte-Tilly, interview with author, September 2015.

Page 230: Claire-Clémence de Maillé was a favorite of Arturo López-Willshaw: Vickers, *Alexis*, 90.

Page 230: Grandpierre shepherded a Louis XV monument into the mid-1960s: Renovation of the Château de la Motte-Tilly began after the death of the Duc de Rohan-Chabot in 1964.

Page 230: Underscoring his connection to Christian Dior, Saint Laurent called on Grandpierre: Bergé interview, February 2016.

Page 233: Full of portières and palms, velvet and tassels, Napoleon III furniture and tapestries: "Yves Saint Laurent' s Château Gabriel: A Passion for Style," *Vogue*, December 1, 1983.

Page 233: The luminous winter garden of the Princesse Mathilde Bonaparte: Carolle Thibaut-Pomerantz, *Wallpaper: A History of Style and Trends* (Paris: Flammarion, 2009), 123; "Le Décor de la vie sous Napoléon III," *Connaissance des Arts*, no. 32, October 1954, 39.

Page 233: Grandpierre introduced Charles Sevigny to Christian Dior: related by Thomas Michael Gunther in a study of Charles Sevigny for Dior Parfums.

Page 233: Grandpierre brought Jean-Claude Donati to Dior's apartment: Jean-Claude Donati in discussion with Marie France Pochna, 1990. Interview with Donati on file in Dior archives.

Pages 233–36: Information on Jean-Paul Faye: Laurent de Commines, interview with author, October 2015; Diesbach interview, November 2015; Sayn-Wittgenstein interview, November 2015; Gaillemin interview, June 2017.

Page 236: Calm, philosophical, and inclined to see humor: Sayn-Wittgenstein interview, November 2015.

Page 236: What appears to have been a stroke in the mid-1970s: Bergé interview, February 2016.

Page 236: Two new Dior boutiques in Paris; openings presided over by Princess Caroline of Monaco: *L'Officiel de la mode*, no. 655, 1979, 118.

Page 236: Grandpierre dark and forbidding: Pradère interview, January 2016.

Page 236: Grandpierre sat next to Margaux Hemingway: *L'Officiel de la mode*, no. 680, 1982, 162–63.

APPENDIX

Page 241: Dior sketched his New Look collection in a rented cottage in Fleury-en-Bière: Vincent Leret, "La petite maison de Fleury-en-Bière," Dior Mag: http://dior.com/diormag/fr.fr/dior-parchristiandior-1947-1957 (no longer active).

Page 241: "A ruin in a swamp": Dior, *Christian Dior et moi*, 211.

Page 242: Close friends would come on Sundays: Le-Tan, *Rencontres d'une vie*, 73.

Page 242: Denise, the Martiniquan cook with a wardrobe by Christian Dior . . . the couturier distilled his own *framboise* liqueur: Ballard, *In My Fashion*, 239.

Page 242: Geffroy Schaison, architect for Le Moulin du Coudret: "La Campagne de M. Dior," *Maison et Jardin*, Spring 1951, 42–47.

Page 242: Dior added multiple bathrooms: Ballard, *In My Fashion*, 239.

Page 242: House believed to have been professionally decorated: Pierre Barillet, interview with author, January 2015.

Page 242: It is possible that Victor Grandpierre decorated Le Moulin du Coudret: Barillet, interview, January 2015; Le Bourhis interview, January 2016.

Page 242: A country house designed by Grandpierre: "La Tour de Villebon," *Vogue* (Paris), October 1951, 104.

Page 242, caption: "The peace and quiet calm of the country are essential to me": Dior, *Christian Dior et moi*, 28.

Page 242, caption: Simplicity was "indispensable to the standard of good taste of old France": Dior, *Christian Dior et moi*, 212.

Page 247: Dior made a soutane for Curé Letellier: http://salon-parfum-milly.blogspot.com/2010/02/christian-dior-le-moulin-du-coudret.html.

Page 247: "Palais de Glace": Spring-Summer 1957 "Libre" collection.

Page 248: Dior grew flowers solely for the pleasure of their scent: Ballard, *In My Fashion*, 240.

Page 248: Chair by Sené: *Collection Catherine Dior*, Daguerre, Hôtel Drouot, Paris, March 26, 2012, Lot 98.

Page 248: Biedermeier chair: *Collection Catherine Dior*, Daguerre, Hôtel Drouot, Paris, March 26, 2012, Lot 187.

Page 248: Saul Steinberg drawing: *Collection Catherine Dior*, Daguerre, Hôtel Drouot, Paris, March 26, 2012, Lot 201.

Page 248: Paintings by Leonid Berman: *Collection Catherine Dior*, Daguerre, Hôtel Drouot, Paris, March 26, 2012, Lots 117 and 118.

Page 251: Plastic tablecloth: *Maison et Jardin*, no. 31, September-October 1955, 29.

Page 251: Grace Kelly photographed for *Vogue*: *Vogue* (Paris), March 1956, 152.

Page 254: Interiors and clothes that were in sync with the time were . . . without gimmick or artifice: Dior, *Christian Dior et moi*, 215.

Page 254, caption: "I think of my work as ephemeral architecture": Dior, *Christian Dior et moi*, 210.

BIBLIOGRAPHY

Alsop, Susan Mary. *To Marietta from Paris, 1945–1960*. New York: Doubleday & Company, 1975.

Arizzoli-Clémentel, Pierre. *Emilio Terry: Architecte et décorateur*. Paris: Gourcuf Gradenigo, 2013.

——. *Georges Geffroy, 1905–1971: Une légende du grand décor français*. Paris: Gourcuf Gradenigo, 2016.

Bachelard, Gaston. *The Poetics of Space*. New York: Orion Press, 1964.

Ballard, Bettina. *In My Fashion*. New York: David McKay Company, 1960.

Banham, Joanna, ed. *Encyclopedia of Interior Design*. 2 vols. London and Chicago: Fitzroy Dearborn Publishers, 1997.

Barillet, Pierre. *À la ville comme à la scène*. Paris: Éditions de Fallois, 2004.

Beaton, Cecil. *The Glass of Fashion*. New York: Rizzoli, 2014. First published 1954 by Doubleday.

Beevor, Antony, and Artemis Cooper. *Paris after the Liberation 1944–1949*. Rev. ed. New York: Penguin Books, 2007.

Benaïm, Laurence. *Marie-Laure de Noailles: La vicomtesse du bizarre*. Paris: Bernard Grasset, 2001 (e-book format).

——. *Yves Saint Laurent: Biographie*. Paris: Bernard Grasset, 2002.

——. *Dior: The New Look Revolution*. New York, Rizzoli, 2015.

Bothorel, Jean. *Louise, ou la vie de Louise de Vilmorin*. Paris: Grasset & Fasquelle, 1993.

Buisson, Patrick. *1940–1945: Années érotiques*. Vol. 2: *De la grande prostituée à la revanche des mâles*. Paris: Albin Michel, 2009.

Cawthorne, Nigel. *The New Look: The Dior Revolution*. Edison, NJ: Wellfleet Press, 1996.

Charles-Roux, Edmonde, Herbert Lottman, Stanley Garfinkel, and Nadine Gasc. *Théâtre de la Mode Fashion Dolls: The Survival of Haute Couture*. Rev. ed. Portland, OR: Palmer/Pletsch Publishing, 2002.

Cimorelli, Davio, ed. *Christian Dior: Esprit de parfums*. Milan: Silvana Editoriale, 2017.

Commines, Laurent de. *Caprices du Siècle: Esthètes et décorateurs du XXᵉ siècle*. Paris: Gourcuff Gradenigo, 2011.

Cooper, Artemis. *Salve Amice et Lege. Hail Friend and Read. Salut à toi ami et lis: The Duff Cooper Library, Paris*. Paris: The British Council and The British Embassy, Paris, 1997.

Cooper, Diana. *Diana Cooper: Autobiography*. London: Michael Russell, 1979.

Cooper, Douglas, ed. *Great Private Collections*. New York: Macmillan, 1963.

Coudert, Thierry. *Cafe Society: Socialites, Patrons, and Artists 1920–1960*. Paris: Flammarion, 2010.

"Dictator by Demand." *Time*, March 4, 1957, 32–40.

Diesbach, Ghislain de. *Nouveau savoir-vivre: Éloge de la bonne éducation*. Paris: Perrin, 2014.

——. *Un esthète aux enfers: Philippe Jullian*. Paris: Plon, 1993.

Dior, Christian. *Je suis couturier*. A compilation of eight articles for *Elle* magazine, 1951. Bound and published 1952.

——. *Talking about Fashion to Elie Rabourdin and Alice Chavane*. London: Hutchinson & Co., 1954.

——. *Christian Dior et moi*. Paris: Vuibert, 2011.

"Dior Celebrates a Decade at the Very Top." *Life*, March 4, 1957.

"Dressmakers of France." *Fortune*, August 1932.

Etherington-Smith, Meredith. *Patou*. London: Hutchinson & Co., 1983.

Faucigny-Lucinge, Jean-Louis, prince de. *Un gentilhomme cosmopolite: Mémoires*. Paris: Perrin, 1990.

Fraser-Cavassoni, Natasha. *Monsieur Dior: Once upon a Time*. New York: Pointed Leaf Press, 2014.

Galtier-Boissière, Jean. *Mon journal pendant l'Occupation*. Paris: La Jeune Parque, 1944.

Giroud, Françoise. *Christian Dior 1905–1957*. Paris: Éditions du Regard, 1987.

Gredy, Jean-Pierre. *Tous ces visages*. Paris: Grasset, 2007.

Harcourt, François, duc de. *Regards sur un passé*. Paris: Éditions Robert Laffont, 1989.

Hayward, Helena. *World Furniture*. London: Hamlyn Publishing Group, 1965.

Hillairet, Jacques. *Connaissance du vieux Paris*. Paris: Editions Princesse, 1956.

Huffington, Arianna. *Maria Callas: The Woman Behind the Legend*. New York: Simon & Schuster, 1981.

Jullian, Philippe. *Les styles*. Paris: Gallimard, 1992. First published 1961 by Librairie Plon.

——. *Journal 1940–1950*. Paris: Grasset & Fasquelle, 2009.

Karnow, Stanley. *Paris in the Fifties*. New York: Times Books, 1997. Reprint, New York: Broadway Books, 1999.

Kernan, Thomas. *Les réussites de la décoration française: 1950–1960*. Paris: Éditions du Pont Royal, 1960.

——. *Nouvelles réussites de la décoration française: 1960–1966*. Paris: Éditions Robert Laffont, 1966.

Kochno, Boris. *Christian Bérard*. London: Thames & Hudson, 1988.

Koda, Harold, and Richard Martin. *Christian Dior*. New York: The Metropolitan Museum of Art, 1996.

Ladd, Mary-Sargent. *The French Woman's Bedroom*. New York: Doubleday, 1991.

Le-Tan, Pierre, *Rencontres d'une vie 1945–1984*. Paris: Aubier, 1986.

Loukomski, Georges. *Charles Cameron: Architect*. London: Nicholson & Watson, 1943.

McAuliffe, Mary. *Dawn of the Belle Epoque*. Lanham, MD: Rowman & Littlefield, 2011.

——. *Twilight of the Belle Epoque: The Paris of Monet, Zola, Bernhardt, Eiffel, Debussy, Clemenceau, and Their Friends*. Lanham, MD: Rowman & Littlefield, 2014.

Milbank, Caroline Rennolds. *Couture: The Great Designers*. New York: Stewart, Tabori & Chang, 1985.

Minnaert, Jean-Baptiste. *Pierre Barbe: architectures*. Liège, Belgium: Mardaga, 1991.

Murat, Laure. *The Splendor of France: Great Châteaux, Mansions, and Country Houses.* New York: Universe, 1991. Reprint, New York: Rizzoli, 2004.

Murphy, Robert. *Les paradis secrets d'Yves Saint Laurent et de Pierre Bergé.* Paris: Albin Michel, 2009.

Muller, Florence. *Dior Impressions: The Inspiration and Influence of Impressionism at the House of Dior.* New York: Rizzoli, 2013.

Musée Christian Dior. *Christian Dior: Man of the Century.* Paris: Editions Artlys, 2011.

Muth, Olivier (editor and compiler), Louise de Vilmorin, Duff Cooper, Viscount Norwich, and Diana Cooper. *Correspondance à trois (1944–1953).* Paris: Gallimard, 2008.

Nicolay-Mazery, Christiane de. *The Finest Houses of Paris.* New York: Vendome Press, 2000.

Palmer, Alexandra. *The Transatlantic Fashion Trade in the 1950s.* Vancouver, BC: UBC Press, 2001.

———. *Dior: A New Look, a New Enterprise (1947–1957).* London: V&A Publishing, 2009.

Pastori, Jean Pierre. *Robert Piguet: Un prince de la mode.* Lausanne: La Bibliothèque des Arts, 2015.

Perkins, Jeanne. "Dior." *Life*, March 1, 1948.

Pochna, Marie-France. *Christian Dior: The Biography.* London: Duckworth Press, 2008.

Polle, Emmanuelle. *Jean Patou: A Fashionable Life.* Paris: Flammarion, 2013.

Praz, Mario. *An Illustrated History of Interior Decoration: from Pompeii to Art Nouveau.* London and New York: Thames & Hudson, 1981. First published 1964 by George Braziller.

Prevost-Marchilhacy, Pauline. *Les Rothschilds: une dynastie de mécènes en France.* Vol. 3. Paris: Somogy, 2016.

Rae, Isobel. *Charles Cameron: Architect to the Court of Russia.* London: Elek Books, 1971.

Ray, Cyril. *Lafite: The Story of Château Lafite-Rothschild.* 3rd ed. London: Christie's Wine Publications, 1985.

Réthy, Esmeralda de, and Jean-Louis Perreau. *Monsieur Dior et nous: 1947–1957.* Paris: Anthèse, 1999.

Rochas, Sophie. *Marcel Rochas: audace et élégance.* Paris: Flammarion, 2015.

Sargentson, Carolyn. *Merchants and Luxury Markets: The Marchands Merciers of Eighteenth-Century Paris.* London: Victoria & Albert Museum, in association with the J. Paul Getty Museum, Malibu, California, 1996.

Shvidkovsy, Dimitri. *The Empress and the Architect: British Architecture and Gardens at the Court of Catherine the Great.* New Haven, CT: Yale University Press, 1996.

Smith, Sally Bedell. *Reflected Glory: The Life of Pamela Churchill Harriman.* New York: Simon & Schuster, 1996.

Tarica, Sami. *Comment je suis devenu marchand de tableaux.* Paris: L'Échoppe, 2003.

Thibaut-Pomerantz, Carolle. *Wallpaper: A History of Style and Trends.* Paris: Flammarion, 2009.

Vickers, Hugo, ed. *Alexis: The Memoirs of the Baron de Redé.* Wimborne Minster, Dorset, U.K.: Dovecote Press, 2005.

Wilcox, Claire. *The Golden Age of Couture: Paris and London 1947–1957.* London: V&A Publishing, 2007.

Wishart, Michael. *High Diver.* London: Quartet Books, 1978.

AUCTION CATALOGUES

Collection Catherine Dior, March 26, 2012. Daguerre, Salle Drouot, Paris.

Collection du Baron de Redé provenant du l'Hôtel Lambert, 2 volumes, March 16 and 17, 2005. Sotheby's Paris.

Collection Geffroy, December 2, 1971. Ader-Picard-Tajan, Paris.

Collection Hélène Rochas, September 27, 2012. Christie's Paris.

Collection Maître et Madame Michard-Pellissier, June 27, 2007. Christie's Paris.

The Patiño Collection, November 1, 1986. Sotheby's New York.

Succession Maria Callas, June 14, 1978. C. Boisgirard, A. de Heeckeren, Hervé Chayette. Hôtel George V, Paris.

MAGAZINE COLUMNS

Flanner, Janet. "Letter from Paris," *The New Yorker*.

Lane, Lois. "On and Off the Avenue," *The New Yorker*.

ACKNOWLEDGMENTS

Like the New Look itself, *Dior and His Decorators* springs from a convergence of constellations on either side of the Atlantic.

Though the story begins in Paris, the book has its roots in New York. I am forever grateful to Mark Magowan and the extended family at Vendome Press: James Spivey, Nina Magowan, Meghan Phillips, Dana Cole, and particularly my editor, Jacqueline Decter, for providing the project with an infallible compass. Simultaneously, Beatrice Vincenzini and David Shannon of Vendome London brilliantly charted its overseas course. Crossing the Atlantic, I thank Geneviève Rudolf, Editorial Director, Gwenaël Ben Aissa, editorial assistant, and Matthieu de Waresquiel, General Director, of Citadelles & Mazenod: *vive l'édition française*! Two in particular helped shape an idea into substance: graphic designer Susi Oberhelman spread her stardust on every page, and Cécile Niesseron in Paris conjured photos seemingly out of thin air. Jennifer Ash Rudick is this book's guardian angel. Hamish Bowles burnished all with his stylish foreword.

So many contributed to creating a portrait of three gifted men and the golden moment when haute couture accorded with high design. Some of my sources were as gracious as Christian Dior, others were as thoughtful as Victor Grandpierre, and a few—lucky me—were as colorful as Georges Geffroy. With their tales, experiences, knowledge, suggestions, nuances, and introductions, all added immeasurably to my body of knowledge.

Invaluable for reflections, insights, memories, and knowledge that opened up the story and infused it with particular vitality were Pierre Arizzoli-Clementel; Pierre Barillet; the late Pierre Bergé; Princesse Eugénie Brancovan; Pierre Cardin; Joseph de Cassagne; François Catroux; Laurent de Commines; Barnaby Conrad III; Thierry Coudert; Alain Demachy; Ghislain de Diesbach; Guillaume Féau; Geraldine Forrester; James A. Ffrench; Jean-Louis Gaillemin; Antoine and Renate de Grandsaignes; Michel Guéranger; Julia Guillon, former archivist at Marcel Rochas and Givenchy; Thomas Michael Gunther; the Duchesse d'Harcourt; Olivier Kraemer; Alexis Kugel; Alain de Lavalade; Katell Le Bourhis; the highly generous Christian Magot Cuvru; Thierry Millerand; Dominique Paulvé; Aymeric Peniguet de Stoutz, director of the Château de la Motte-Tilly; Nicolas Petitjean; Marie-France Pochna; Madame Jacques Politis; Alexandre Pradère; Serge Proutchenko; Ariel de Ravenel; Jean-Marie Rossi; and Marie-Christine Sayn-Wittgenstein. Further, David Sprouls, Philippe Le Moult of Dior, Alexandre Pradère, Maggie Lidz, and Charlotte Moss brought their expertise to reading and commenting on the text.

Chez Dior, Olivier Bialobos, Jérôme Pulis, Jérôme Gautier, and Frédéric Bourdelier supported the project from its inception. With consistent politesse and charm, Perrine Scherrer of the Dior archives graciously retrieved photos, records, drawings, and interviews. Brigitte Richart and Ophélie Verstavel of the Musée Dior in Granville cordially received me at the cradle of Christian Dior. Philippe le Moult accompanied me on a wonderful, hot August day to Le Moulin du Coudret and the pastoral environs of Milly. Another glorious day at La Colle Noire—lunch *en plein air* included—was arranged by Guillaume Garcia-Moreau, curator of Dior's house in Provence, and Frédéric Bourdelier. The erudite Vincent Leret of Dior Parfums flattered me with his presence at the Sorbonne symposium, where I spoke about the preservation of craftsmanship in the work of Dior, Geffroy, and Grandpierre. I also sincerely thank Soizic Pfaff, Sandrine Damay, Solène Auréal, and Pierre Sarraute for their knowledge and precision.

I express my profound gratitude to four special professionals: agent *extraordinaire* Rob McQuilkin, translators Jean-François Cornu and Jean-François Allain, and publicist Ron Longe; each added his own special savvy to the project. Others whose contributions have become part of the fabric of this book include: Mario Buatta; Vincent Bastien; Minnie de Beauvau-Craon; Diane de Beauvau-Craon; Vanessa Bernard of Condé Nast Paris; Sarah Burningham; Natasha Fraser-Cavassoni; Patricia Clément, director of the Fondation Singer-Polignac; Madison Cox; Anne-Sophie Chevalier; Étienne Coffinier; Laurent Cotta; Marie-Françoise Dhoutaut; Arthur Dreyfus; Emily Eerdmans; Gretchen Fenston, formerly of the Condé Nast archives in New York; Patrick Frey; Pierre Frey; Wendy Goodman; Laure Harivel, archivist at Lanvin; Nicholas Haslam; Frédéric Malle; Peter Marino; Mitchell Owens; Pierre Passebon; Jacques Perrin; Morgan Rémond, Pierre Bourriaud, Joëlle Racary, and Eric Ehlers of the 17th arrondissement city hall, who helped clarify details on the Grandpierre family; Dominique Revellino, librarian of the Musée Galliera; Jane Roberts of Jane Roberts Gallery; Maître Guillaume Roehrig; Élisabeth de Rothschild; Nathaniel de Rothschild; Sophie Rouart; Pascal Sittler of the Pierre Bergé-Yves Saint Laurent Foundation; Suzanne Slesin; Carolle Thibaut-Pomerantz; Guillaume Verzier of Maison Prelle; Hugo Vickers; Carol Vogel; Deborah Webster; and John Yunis.

My first, and last, thanks, as always, go to Thong Nguyen, who has accompanied me on the journey of *Dior and His Decorators*, from its origins in my decorative arts studies at the École du Louvre many years ago, to its final chapter. I look forward to our next adventure, wherever the North Star leads.

PHOTOGRAPHY CREDITS

adoc-photos/Getty Images: p. 180

© Laure Albin-Guillot/Roger-Viollet: p. 102

Alinari Archives/Getty Images: p. 54

Photo courtesy of the Art Institute of Chicago/Art Resource, NY; © 2018 ADAGP, Paris/Avec l'aimable autorisation de M. Pierre Bergé, président du Comité Jean Cocteau: p. 68

© 2018 Artists Rights Society (ARS), New York/ADAGP, Paris: pp. 19, 152–53, 156, 197, 220

SERGE BALKIN/Condé Nast Archive: p. 10

Cecil Beaton © The Cecil Beaton Studio Archive at Sotheby's: p. 164; Getty Images: p. 166

© Christian Bérard: p. 98

© Pierre Berdoy: pp. 184, 185

© Roger Berson/Roger-Viollet: p. 50

© Philippe Berthé/Centre des monuments nationaux: p. 224

© Bibliothèque Marguerite-Durand/Roger-Viollet: p. 77

© David Bordes/Centre des monuments nationaux: pp. 226–27, 2 28

Jacques Boucher/© Condé Nast Paris: pp. 174, 175, 177, 178, 179, 215, 217

René Bouët-Willaumez/Getty Images: p. 59

© Pierre Boulat/Cosmos/Redux: p. 211 right

© Celette/CC by SA 4.0: p. 81

Henry Clarke/Getty Images: pp. 134, 173

© Robert Alan Clayton: p. 231

© Condé Nast Paris: pp. 160 (top), 186, 194, 221

© Connaissance des Arts: pp. 22 right, 65, 160 bottom, 161, 169, 199, 202, 204, 206, 211 left, 218, 219

Bruce Dale/Getty Images: p. 155

© 2018 Salvador Dalí, Fundació Gala-Salvador Dalí, Artists Rights Society: p. 39 left

© Raphaël Dautigny: p. 29

DEA/G. DAGLI ORTI/Getty Images: p. 220

Loomis Dean/Getty Images: pp. 106, 140

© Anthony Denney: pp. 2, 136, 137 right, 138, 139, 182, 183, 193, 194, 201, 203, 205, 209, 210, 213

© Raymond Depardon/Magnum photos: p. 123

DEUTSCH Jean-Claude/Getty Images: p. 163

Courtesy of the Dior archives: pp. 26, 34, 39 right, 42, 44, 47, 78, 114, 116, 117, 120, 122, 125, 128, 190

Courtesy of the Christian Dior Parfums collection: pp. 121, 126, 131

Collection Musée Christian Dior, Granville: pp. 30, 51

© Robert Doisneau/Gamma-Rapho: pp. 52, 158; © Condé Nast Paris: 167, 200; Getty Images: 147

Courtesy of the Embassy of the United Kingdom, Paris: pp. 23, 70–71, 81

Photo by Pat English: p. 100

© 2018 Estate of Pablo Picasso/Artists Rights Society (ARS), New York: p. 77

© Miguel Flores-Vianna: p. 251 left

© Archives Jean-Louis Gaillemin: p. 78

© Galliera/Roger-Viollet: p. 36

Victor H. Grandpierre/Vogue © Condé Nast: pp. 84–85, 88; © Condé Nast Paris: p. 89

Jorg Greuel/Getty Images: p. 63

René Gruau/www.gruaucollection.com: pp. 24, 96, 110, 142

© Roger Guillemot/Connaissance des Arts akg-images: pp. 16, 144, 170–71

© Jacqueline Guillot/Connaissance des Arts: 22 left, 190, 196

© Laziz Hamani: pp. 124, 246

Horst P. Horst/Vogue © Condé Nast: pp. 132, 234–35, 237; Getty Images: 137 left

George Hoyningen-Huene/Getty Images: p. 58

Hulton Deutsch/Getty Images: p. 57

Kertész André (told), Kertész Andor (1894–1985) © RMN-Grand Palais - Gestion droit d'auteur/Localisation: Charenton-le-Pont, Médiathèque de l'Architecture et du Patrimoine/Photo © Ministère de la Culture - Médiathèque du Patrimoine, Dist. RMN-Grand Palais/André Kertész: 74–75, 198

Keystone-France/Getty Images: p. 46, 49, 101

Kitrosser/Vogue © Condé Nast: p. 82

LE TELLIER Philippe/Getty Images: p. 223

© Alain Lonchampt/Centre des monuments nationaux: p. 229

© Association Willy Maywald: pp. 4, 10, 40, 104, 113, 216, 243, 244, 245

© The Metropolitan Museum of Art. Image Source: Art Resource, NY: pp. 12–13

© Jean Mounicq/Roger-Viollet: p. 15

C. Neubert-Horak/© Condé Nast Paris: p. 157

© Janine Niépce/Roger-Viollet: p. 151

Courtesy of l'Office du tourisme Aube-Champagne: p. 225.

© Claus Ohm: p. 232

PAGÈS François/Getty Images: p. 150

© Georges Pallot/Connaissance des Arts: 181

Norman Parkinson Archive/Getty Images: p. 21

© Plaisir de France: pp. 64, 66, 67| Private Collection, photo © Christie's Images/Bridgeman Images: p. 33 both

Private collection, Paris: p. 197

Karen Radkai/Getty Images: p. 239

Willy Rizzo/Getty Images: p. 105

© Roger-Viollet: pp. 14, 37, 86–87, 240

© Collection Roger-Viollet/Roger-Viollet: p. 119

Photo Roger Schall © Collection Schall: p. 48

Frank Scherschel/Getty Images: p. 43

© Philippe Schlienger: pp. 25, 97, 127, 130, 143

© Mark Shaw/MPTV Images: front cover, pp. 9, 108–9, 248

Courtesy of Sotheby's London: pp. 19, 207

Photo by Bruno Suet: p. 254

© André Svetchine/Collection Luc Svetchine: pp. 249, 250, 252, 253

ullstein bild Dtl./Getty Images: p. 103

© Sabine Weiss: p. 115

Best efforts were made to verify all photo credits. Any oversight was unintentional and should be brought to the publisher's attention so that it can be corrected in a future printing.

INDEX

Dior and His Decorators: Victor Grandpierre, Georges Geffroy, and the New Look
First published in 2018 by The Vendome Press
Vendome is a registered trademark of The Vendome Press, LLC

NEW YORK
Suite 2043
244 Fifth Avenue
New York, NY 10001
www.vendomepress.com

LONDON
63 Edith Grove
London,
UK, SW10 0LB
www.vendomepress.co.uk

Distributed in North America by Abrams Books
Distributed in the United Kingdom, and the rest of the world, by Thames & Hudson

ISBN 978-0-86565-353-5

Publishers: Beatrice Vincenzini, Mark Magowan, and Francesco Venturi
Editor: Jacqueline Decter
Production Director: Jim Spivey
Production Color Manager: Dana Cole
Designer: Susi Oberhelman

Library of Congress Cataloging-in-Publication Data
available upon request

Printed in China by 1010 Printing International Ltd.
First printing

PAGE 2: Dior's drawing room, designed by Georges Geffroy. PAGES 4-5: Modeling Dior's 1951 ball gown "Tableau Final" on the landing of the Christian Dior couture house, designed by Victor Grandpierre. PAGE 9: Ruches and flounces in a ball gown modeled by Sophie Litvak mirror Victor Grandpierre's dressmaker details in Dior's winter garden. The dress is from Dior's Autumn-Winter 1953 couture collection. PAGE 239: Gray walls, limestone floor, and discreet Louis XVI furniture channel Victor Grandpierre's interiors for the house of Dior to provide an elegant backdrop for Dior's pink satin coat. Vogue, July 1955.